JAZZ ON RECORD
A History

Brian Priestley

BILLBOARD BOOKS
An imprint of Watson-Guptill Publications/New York

This edition published 1991 by Billboard Books, an imprint of Watson-Guptill Publications, a division of BPI Communications, Inc. 1515 Broadway, New York, NY 10036.

First published in Great Britain in 1988 by Hamish Hamilton

Library of Congress Cataloging-In-Publication-Data

Priestley, Brian, 1946–
    Jazz on record: a history / Brian Priestley.
       p.   cm.
    "First published in Great Britain in 1988 by Elm Tree Books"—T.p. verso.
    Includes bibliographical references and index.
    ISBN 0-8230-7562-1
    1. Jazz—History and criticism. 2. Jazz—discography.
I. Title.
ML3506.P74   1991
781.65′026′6—dc20   90-20187
                                           CIP
                                           MN

Manufactured in the United States of America
First printing, 1991

1 2 3 4 5 6 7 8 9 / 96 95 94 93 92 91

This book is dedicated to the late Albert McCarthy, whose writing first interested me in the workings of the record industry

The author and the publisher would like to thank the following for permission to use copyright photographs in this book:

Duncan P. Schiedt Collection: 1, 2, 3, 4, 6, 7, 8, 10, 11, 27
Max Jones Collection: 5, 9
Jazz Music Books: 12
Flying Dutchman Records: 14
Verve Records: 23, 31
Frank Driggs Collection: 24 (photo: "Popsie" Randolph)
Columbia Phonograph Company: 15
Commodore Music Shop: 16
Jazz Selection: 17
Tempo Records: 18
Ace Records: 19
Antilles Records: 20
EMI Ltd.: 21
Denon: 22
Institute of Jazz Studies: 13 (photo: Zinn Arthur), 25, 26, 28 (courtesy of Sy Johnson), 29, 30, 32, 33, 34, 35, 36

ACKNOWLEDGMENTS

◆

I am deeply indebted to Joan for giving me the space and the incentive to complete this project, and to Richard James for his crucial encouragement.

For various information and other kindnesses, I am also grateful to Hugh Attwooll, Art Blakey, Ian Carr, John Chilton, Billy Cobham, Michael Cuscuna, Digby Fairweather, Ole Vestergaard Jensen, Max Jones, Herbie Mann, Albert McCarthy, Tony Middleton, Alun Morgan, Dan Morgenstern, Sy Oliver, Evan Parker, Sigrun Parsiegla, Brian Peerless, Sonny Rollins, Christine Rozier, Duncan Schiedt, Miroslav Vitous and Dick Wellstood. None of them are to be blamed for the opinions expressed herein, some or other of which are bound to annoy each one of the above.

I have drawn on many printed sources, most of them listed in the bibliography, but also including periodicals such as *downbeat*, *Jazz Times*, *Jazz Hot*, *Crescendo*, *Jazz Express*, *Jazz Monthly* and *Wire*, plus, of course, record liner notes. The quotations from Evan Parker and Derek Bailey are from my interviews for the National Sound Archive, to whom I extend my thanks.

Finally, I must acknowledge the assistance of Andrew Reid, whose love of the subject matter complemented his secretarial abilities; Caroline Taggart, who commissioned this book and oversaw its writing, and Linda Longmore, who trimmed my text so expertly, both at Elm Tree; and Fred Weiler at Billboard Books.

CONTENTS

◆

INTRODUCTION

◆

There have been numerous surveys of jazz published, starting as long ago as the 1930s. Of course, the history of the music was rather shorter then, and if anything has made it less fashionable in recent times to attempt such a project, it is the sheer volume of sounds and styles covered by the word "jazz." There has been a welcome proliferation of books dealing with particular areas of jazz and individual biographies, as well as reference works containing separate articles on jazz musicians. But it seems that about once a decade, somebody realizes that there has been no general historical survey written for quite a while; even if a writer is out of sympathy with the latest developments (as has sometimes been the case), he still has a revised perspective on earlier styles simply because of those later developments.

I think it's also true to say that there has never been a history of jazz like this one. The original idea as proposed to me was for a guide to specific recommended records but, if the book was going to be a manageable length, this presented considerable problems. Saying even as much as a decent-sized review about each record would have restricted the choice to about 100 albums from the entire spectrum of the music; this has actually been attempted by one writer in the past. Expanding the number of choices to even 300, which still feels dangerously small, would have made the text about each item so short as to be meaningless. Compromising at 200 records would have fallen between all possible stools. So writing a historical survey of the development of jazz that would discuss the key recordings appeared to get everyone off the hook. It did, though, make me wonder how different such a book could be from any of the previous historical works.

In the past, most authors ostensibly treating the history of jazz wrote instead about their favorite records. All well and good, perhaps, if their favorites coincided with generally accepted opinions as to what the most important jazz records are—rather confusing for all concerned if they didn't. But what is especially confusing is that such writers did not admit to themselves or to their readers that they were only writing about what had been *recorded*, implying that this was the only jazz worth writing about.

At least two further misconceptions arise from such an approach, both more insidious than the original error. One is the convenient, but unhistorical, journalistic assumption that as soon as X made his first record, the world of jazz took immediate note and amended its musical habits accordingly. Occasionally, this has actually happened. Yet there have been instances where, for example, a musician is taken as having made an impact in the 1920s whose early records in fact sank without trace, but who was rediscovered and justly acclaimed in the 1940s. Even worse is the belief that the process of recording, whether it produces a masterpiece or not, is somehow comparable to the way a European composer painstakingly works out music on paper. The fallacy of such published commentaries is perhaps not so different from the attitude of the fans they influence. Almost without realizing it, these fans memorize improvised solos and then credit them with an inevitability that the performer may have been far from feeling at the moment of creation.

If jazz musicians say during interviews (as they do all the time) that they cannot bear to listen to their own records, it *may* be because some contemporary recording procedures require a lot of preparation and considerably more in the way of post-production work, to borrow a term from the film world. As a result, by the time the record is finished, those involved are thoroughly sated with the project. But it is equally likely to be the case that insufficient time was allowed for preparation, that they were not allowed to participate in any post-production, so that the musicians feel inadequately represented by the finished record.

My own experience of interviewing performers and of hanging around recording studios (the latter sometimes in order to do the former) has led me to look closely at the circumstances under which jazz has been created and preserved, and to understand the pressures which have been endured and overcome. When you hear a famous veteran musician say of a record producer, "He reminds me of Y [another producer], I used to call him Motor-mouth"—and when you later meet Y and see exactly what the musician meant—you wonder how these two could ever have worked together satisfactorily. Of course, anyone who succeeds in the professional music world, jazz or not, tends to develop a hard exterior, performers and producers alike. Anyone who doesn't suffers accordingly from the recording process, and his reputation among fellow musicians might end up somewhat higher than his reputation with the jazz public. Recording has also enabled some with hard exteriors and softer talents to benefit from an inflated public image which becomes the envy of their more creative colleagues. Add to this the difficulties of even trying to capture such a volatile improvisatory music for posterity—difficulties that affect both the producers and the musicians—and it is clear that the history of jazz on record is far from being the same thing as the history of jazz. It represents only a minuscule proportion (0.00001 percent?) of the music that has been played, and it is not even properly representative.

Despite all this, the records are what survive. They preserve a likeness of the music in live performance which record collectors, if they have sufficient experience of hearing music live, can re-create in their mind's ear. Listening to music on records is not even the same kind of experience as listening to a live performance; even hearing a recording of the live performance you have attended merely underlines how much the listener is in a totally different physical relationship to the music. Yet records, unlike photographs of musicians and press reports of their activities, at least tell us what the music sounds like. Despite the deliberate unreality of their sound picture (even with today's technology, no one wants a recording to sound the way music does in a concert-hall or even a nightclub) and despite the more subtle distortions of the recording situation and its philosophy, records are an invaluable source of pleasure. They are also an inexhaustible subject for study and, unlike music heard live, they can be repeated. Separate extracts or individual features of the recorded performance can be isolated and put under the aural microscope, either to illuminate the piece in question or to draw wider conclusions about entire bodies of work.

Records are the audible documentation for a history of jazz. Since this is the only time I shall write such a full, chronological survey, I have not resisted the temptation to discuss the stylistic changes in the music and in the way it has been put together. I especially treat the area which jazz collectors and jazz educators conspire in ignoring—that of rhythm. I have also knowingly fallen into the trap of selecting a small number of performers who did amend others' musical habits, focusing on an even smaller number of significant items from this tiny percentage of music which has been stored for our benefit.

We are fortunate indeed that so much of recorded jazz is currently available in the marketplace. It used to be that most of the historically important records were not to be heard except by recourse to the larger lending libraries or by making a pilgrimage to listen on site at the National Sound Archive. Like book publishers, record companies tended to keep in print only the most popular artists who could be relied on to sell, year in and year out. This limited selection included few jazz figures, and even then much of their work was allowed to disappear—except when some record-company employee had a bright idea about a series of repackages.

Now that the first two decades of jazz recording are no longer subject to copyright restrictions, and anyone is free to reissue such material, the coverage is much more homogeneous. Why this should be such an important factor will doubtless emerge from the following pages, and may disillusion those who dislike thinking about the motivations of the music business. But whether great jazz records happen only because of the record company's profit motive—or in spite of it—we would all be spiritually poorer without them.

· 1 ·

THE BEGINNINGS

———————◆———————

I t is now close to three-quarters of a century since the making of the first acknowledged jazz records. That the music was thought worthy of preservation confirms the impact of jazz on popular taste. The fact of being published and marketed on those fragile but (to us) weighty 78 RPM discs magnified its impact, and accelerated its dissemination, more than could possibly have been imagined at the time. It also began the frequently charged interaction between jazz and what later came to be called the music industry.

The five young white musicians from New Orleans calling themselves the Original Dixieland Jazz Band were riding the crest of a wave that had been building for some time. Like the 1970s phenomenon of the Sex Pistols, they were the most outrageous and newsworthy group around. Both the enthusiasm of their young white audience, and the hostility of parents and other guardians of morality, were inflamed by the wind-up gramophone (or phonograph) and the acoustic amplification of its "sound horn." The record business was in its infancy, commercially speaking, but it was already showing its customary ambivalence towards new trends. Of the two larger companies in existence, Columbia (ancestor of today's multinational CBS) was first to record the Original Dixieland Jazz Band four days after the group arrived in New York in January 1917. But, allegedly because of the misgivings of their sound engineers, Columbia failed to move fast enough in releasing their disc. Consequently, their major rivals Victor (later RCA) took the band into their own studios just four weeks later, and, a mere seven days after that, the ODJB's first issued single was on sale for 75 cents a copy.

In the publicity jargon of the day, they "caused a sensation"—not only in the eyes of the fans who had heard them live and wanted to re-create this invigorating experience at home, but also with listeners elsewhere across the country (and eventually those abroad) who had no immediate expectation of seeing the ODJB in the flesh. Of course, "Livery Stable Blues" and "Dixie Jazz Band One Step" also caused a sensation in the shops where records were sold. It would be several decades before there were stores in which records were the only, or even the main, goods on sale. In the 1910s and during the fashion-conscious 1920s, records were found in general stores. They were also sold in furniture shops, as an adjunct to phonographs. The phonograph, after all, was considered an item of furniture, like the piano before it (although more people eventually came to play the phonograph because it was easier). And two record companies that helped to document the jazz boom of the 1920s—Gennett and Paramount—

were subsidiary ventures of, respectively, the Starr Piano Company and the Wisconsin Chair Company.

Gennett indirectly did the most to fuel the expansion of the record industry by being, in 1918, the first label to break the monopoly of Victor and Columbia over the production of discs with the standard-cut grooves, the record format still familiar in the 1980s (as opposed to the Edison-style cylinders). Since Victor and Columbia were also the chief manufacturers of phonographs, then selling for around $50, they had hoped to remain the sole suppliers of records to play on them. But when they were defeated in court, the way was open for dozens of smaller companies to start up and seek their share of the growing record market. Gradually, the sale of phonograph records was reluctantly admitted to the musical-instrument stores, which also sold the printed sheet music considered indispensable for performing "real music." In those days, printed copies of the latest songs sold in vast quantities; only after the mass media took hold on people's lives from the 1930s onwards did the sale of hit records overtake the sale of sheet music.

It was crucial that jazz should be preserved by sound recording and not merely in printed sketches. Most of the composed and even the folk music that preceded it—everything from Victorian ballads to early Tin Pan Alley products, from spirituals to fiddle-and-banjo dance music—consisted of a melody with an accompaniment. This could be written down for others to play or sing and, even if originally played with folky fluctuations of pitch or irregular timing, could be ironed out on the page to a standardized version. However, jazz as it developed during the first two decades of the century—more or less throughout the South but with the greatest clarity of conception in New Orleans—was hardly printable at all. In this way, jazz was markedly different from that other early 20th century style, ragtime.

Often considered the most direct predecessor of jazz, ragtime also had folk roots but came to fruition in written compositions for piano, published by people like Scott Joplin from the late 1890s onwards. Simultaneously, and long before it became an important influence on the commercial dance music and popular song of the 1910s, ragtime had been adapted by brass bands in their own arrangements. Both the large touring concert ensembles led by John Philip Sousa (and subsequently by others, including his trombonist/composer Arthur Pryor) and the small untutored community bands, black and white, performed it. The small bands played an important part in the social life of a multi-cultured city as New Orleans. As in other Southern towns, ragtime infiltrated the repertoire of marching music, sharing similar compositional characteristics, and the ragtime feel dominated even the work of jazz-inclined musicians into the 1920s.

Certainly Jim Europe (one of the many figures in this book who died prematurely) maintained a strict ragtime beat in the music he created for Irene and Vernon Castle, the purveyors of the prurient foxtrot. Indeed, in 1912, when Europe created New York's Clef Club Orchestra, he became the first black musician to form a big-band to play rags. "Novelty" clarinetist Wilbur Sweatman, whose "Down Home Rag" was recorded by Europe in 1913, hardly varied this approach in his own popular discs of the late 1910s and early 1920s. Ragtime also figured in the music of black New Orleans cornetist Freddie Keppard. (Keppard worked in Los Angeles in 1914 with the Original Creole Band, which hit Chicago and New York in 1915 before the ODJB.) Most of his few records were made in 1924–26, but rhythmically, the brass work wears a ragtime badge. Incidentally, Keppard's status as a jazzer illustrates the minefield of popular music terminology. The first generation of what we now think of as jazz players usually described their style as "ragtime," equating the term with improvisation, i.e.

not sticking to a written arrangement. In this book, however, the word is used in the technical sense, to refer to a timing based on eight equally short notes per bar.

Keppard and the Creole Band were not only touring up North before the Original Dixieland Band, but there is a widespread rumor that they were invited to make records first. Like the legend that New Orleans's earliest trumpet king, Buddy Bolden, recorded before his terminal confinement to a mental hospital, the Keppard story has yet to be substantiated. (It may have been inspired by the documented fact that a group called the Creole Jazz Band made a test record, now lost, two years after the studio debut of the ODJB.) By far the most persistent anecdote about Keppard was that he turned down the initial offer to appear on disc, fearing that many other musicians would hear and copy his style, yet such a justifiable fear had apparently been overcome by the mid-1920s. It seems reasonable to assume that, if his 1916 playing had been preserved, it would have had the same rhythmic approach as his famous 1926 Chicago recording of "Stock Yards Strut." Indeed, in most respects, he sounds simply like an improved version of ODJB cornetist Nick LaRocca. Keppard seems to play more emphatically and dynamically than LaRocca, partly because recording techniques were already improving. His tone is more varied, and frequently more coarse; his accentuation of single notes points to black vocal styles of blues and gospel.

To a musically trained Italian-American boy like LaRocca, Keppard's technique would not have been an improvement—indeed, by the time of the Keppard disc, LaRocca had disbanded the Dixielanders because their initial success had turned sour in 1925. However, the Original Dixieland Jazz Band's trail-blazing inroads into the consciousness of white Americans were crucial. That first single for Victor sold one million copies in a year (though Victor had not secured their services and the band recorded frequently that year for a smaller label with less effective distribution, before signing an exclusive Victor contract in 1918). The ODJB followed this up with a few years of excellent discs and spent 15 months in 1919–20 making headlines in England. The British were exposed to what they thought was a new white-originated style, just as France was being turned on first by Jim Europe and then by black ex-Europe sidemen like drummer Louis Mitchell and trumpeter Crickett Smith.

As to the Original Dixieland Band's own complicity in spreading the preposterous idea that black musicians might have imitated *them*, it was only really during their brief 1936 "comeback" that they became embroiled in claiming precedence in their music as well as in the studio. Ironically, the 1936 records not only have greatly superior sound to their earlier material, but also swing in a more relaxed manner, thanks to slightly slower performance speeds. Even if LaRocca's cornet lead is a bit stiff and strict, trombonist Eddie Edwards (later Emil Christian) and especially clarinetist Larry Shields still sound lively today, thanks to their varied rhythm and articulation. More importantly, these three players, not to mention their rhythm section of piano and drums, each gave the impression of doing his own thing, but together; they demonstrated to the white world that instrumental interplay (or counterpoint, as it was called in certain European music) was going to be the distinctive feature of the group style that became known as jazz.

Unlike the written compositions played by the brass bands, or the arranged ragtime associated with Jim Europe and others, jazz was destined to become known as music with a lot of different things happening simultaneously, especially rhythmically. The knowledge we now have of a wide variety of Afro-American musics means that we can be far more confident than were novice listeners in the 1910s of the African derivation of this rhythmic complexity. But one dramatic demonstration, which was available even then, of the true nature of this embryonic music, lies in the work of the soloists who cut piano rolls for the mechanical player-piano. By strict mechanical definition, this was not "recording" at all, and indeed one of the standard reference works for jazz records omits such material—rather like a history of European painting which mentions Durer but excludes any reference to his engravings or woodcuts. Given the slender quantity of jazz-related music on disc in the 1910s, it is of considerable importance that these piano rolls exist. Many have since been transferred onto albums, particularly those originally issued by QRS (an acronym never deciphered, according to another standard reference book, although it actually stands for "Quality Reigns Supreme").

The Harlem-based "stride pianists" whose playing was recorded at this period were a competitive but homogeneous bunch. The best-known these days is undoubtedly Eubie Blake, partly because of his unusual feat of living to see his 100th birthday. Blake was a fine player and composer in the post-ragtime "stride" style, as shown by the 1917 piano roll of "Charleston Rag" (retitled "Sounds Of Africa" in the more roots-conscious days of 1921, when he made a disc version). He was also an extremely successful songwriter whose royalties enabled him to retire from performing at least twice before being rediscovered in the ragtime revivals of the 1940s and the 1970s. This songwriting success was something Blake shared with both Luckey Roberts and the great James P. Johnson. Both of these gentlemen (like Scott Joplin) also had a strong ambition to write extended compositions using rag and folk material in works of symphonic proportions. Unfortunately, it was too early for the music world to accept such aspirations from black writers—nothing was recorded apart from a solo rendition of Johnson's "Yamekraw—A Negro Rhapsody" done in the mid-1940s, some 20 years after it was written.

However, James P. (or "Black James," as he was called by
Eubie Blake) provided the clearest example of stylistic changes
in the 1910s with his stride showpiece "Carolina Shout," first
issued as a piano roll early in 1918. The four left-hand beats per
bar had been even and restrained in classic ragtime, and had
usually occupied a small span of keyboard. With stride piano,
the left-hand beats became a dynamic rhythm section, not least
because of the energy involved in moving the hand two octaves
or more between each beat and the next (hence the term
"stride"). This left-hand rhythm section worked both together
with and in counterpoint to right-hand melodies which, compared to the very simple syncopations of ragtime, were now
being accented much more freely and unpredictably. The eight
notes per bar of the right hand, even where they were not
accented, were beginning to switch from the strictly equal timing still heard in the ODJB's work.* This 2:1 division between
successive right-hand notes sounds rather stiff and jerky in
1918 compared to later versions of "Carolina Shout," yet there
is already an interesting interplay and tension with the left-
hand rhythm section. "Carolina Shout" not only shows how a
solo performer could get a convincing rhythmic counterpoint
from just two hands, but it points to developments usually
associated with the 1920s.

"Carolina Shout" also anticipates the use, at several
points, of the pianistic equivalent of "blue notes." The vocal
effect of deliberately slurred notes which were not to be found
in the European major and minor scales was not yet present on

---

* The even-eighths-notes timing was possibly influenced by the New Orleans
accent of spoken French and other Latin languages, as in the even syllables of
"Fre-re Jac-ques . . . Son-nez les ma-tines." The music of marches and certain dance forms, however, reflected the alternating 2:1 ratio of the more
clipped Anglo-Saxon speech, as in the English music-hall ditty "Oh I *dooo* like
to be be-side the *sea*-side." These are not suggested as in any way jazz-related
songs, but merely as examples of timing.

any vocal records, although blue notes were already known to several generations of black instrumentalists. In James P.'s generation, however, were the first trained musicians (at least in the northern U.S.) to employ such sounds as a conscious instrumental "effect." On the piano, you couldn't roughen up your tone like Freddie Keppard, or play notes of indeterminate pitch, but you could play two notes simultaneously of nearly the same pitch (such as the minor third and the major third) just to get a buzz from it—literally, because of the overlapping vibrations of similar but differing frequencies. The only reason this was documented first in the North is that the North was already the entertainment mecca. Johnson himself as a teenager observed the contribution of incoming pianists: "These fellows brought all the latest styles of playing from the cabarets and sporting houses of the south and west to Jersey City, and that's where I heard them."

James P.'s first printed song hit was "Mama's Blues," which he cut for four different piano-roll companies in 1917, the year of its publication. "Mama's Blues," a fully-fledged blues piece in which a 16-bar verse alternates with the standard 12-bar sequence, shows what musicians of the day called "uneven" phrasing at its most relaxed and natural, especially in the Universal piano-roll version. Most interestingly, the only one of the ODJB's early sides which approaches this relaxed phrasing is another 12-bar in B-flat recorded mid-1918. "Bluin' The Blues" was written by and featured ODJB pianist Henry Ragas. In some choruses, Ragas fills out the 2:1 division of each beat into three equal triplets—just as Johnson does at the end of the first chorus of the Universal "Mama's Blues."

Clearly this timing was already seen as typical of the blues, for another stride pianist, Willie "The Lion" Smith, is just about audible doing the same thing behind the first recorded vocal 12-bar blues, Mamie Smith's "Crazy Blues" in 1920. Although blues music has its own ongoing tradition, and researchers to go with it, it is interwoven with jazz in a number of ways. Johnson's "Mama's Blues" was an example of his songwriting work but was never recorded by a singer. Yet according to Johnson, the historically significant vocal recording of "Crazy Blues" based its verse on the same folk melody which he had borrowed for "Mama's Blues." And, while the popularity of blues had a vital influence on subsequent jazz, it was the initial popularity of jazz which had made possible the recording of blues in the first place, and thus made possible the absorption of blues into both jazz as well as the mainstream of pop music.

Instrumental blues had been published since 1912 and recorded at least since 1913, and was usually arranged in a straight (i.e. not uneven) ragtime style. (Revealingly, W.C. Handy's "Memphis Blues" was published as "A Southern Rag," not only because of the musicians' loose use of the term "ragtime," but also because the standard performance style in the 1910s—except among obscure, unrecorded folk musicians—was still that of ragtime.) By this point, some 15 years after the first examples appeared in print, ragtime had become a craze run into the ground by the Tin Pan Alley sheet-music industry. Like the minstrel-show music before it, ragtime was becoming outmoded. Similarly, jazz as performed by the Original Dixieland Jazz Band enjoyed huge popularity and widespread imitation almost immediately, thanks to the impact of sound recording, then went out of fashion (or, rather, became absorbed and diluted into more popular forms) by the early 1920s. But jazz—and blues, after its initial recorded success in the 1920s—was able to renew itself internally, particularly in terms of rhythmic development, in a way that ragtime never did.

It was a major step when General Phonograph Corp recorded a vocal blues on its OKeh label; the World War I slang name of the series title proclaimed an intention to issue some with-it sounds, but not necessarily or exclusively black music.

James P. Johnson had done an unissued test record for OKeh in 1917, and later opined that the record companies of that day had been decidedly cautious about using black musicians; a few had been recorded but, apart from Wilbur Sweatman and W.C. Handy, hardly any on a regular basis. And, because jazz was as yet barely distinguishable from ragtime and was being popularized by whites, who was to know that Sweatman and Handy were black? Little about their records would give it away, while the different mechanical process of piano rolls was by definition colorless. Even fewer records by black vocalists had been produced, except by comedian Bert Williams, perhaps for the very reason that the racial origin and distinctive styles of the performers would be fairly unmistakable, and it was said that retailers in the South had threatened to boycott companies recording black music. Nonetheless, OKeh, who had taken a tentative interest in jazz at the end of 1918 by marketing an ODJB clone called the Original New Orleans Jazz Band (led by pianist and later star comedian Jimmy Durante), was ready to take a chance on the blues.

OKeh's acceptance of Mamie Smith was based on the knowledge that she had already gained a reputation in prominent Harlem clubs; the label's interest may also have been fueled by learning that Victor Records had just turned Mamie down. Her first issued single with an all-white or mixed band got around Harlem more or less by word of mouth. The follow-up, "Crazy Blues," featured an all-black quintet including Willie the Lion Smith and cornetist Johnny Dunn. "Crazy Blues" opened the floodgates: 75,000 sold in four weeks, one million within six months, three million in total—the figures may perhaps be exaggerated, but the message is clear. There was a substantial audience for records of this music, since the black population across the U.S. now numbered 12 million. The relative prosperity of the 1920s would at least allow them to buy a phonograph, and much more readily if they could also buy records of black music. It's true that some middle-class blacks of this and subsequent generations, especially the staunch Christians, were horrified by this development. But there was also a growing minority of white intellectuals who were becoming genuinely interested in the unfettered self-expression of the minority race.*

The year 1921 saw record industry sales exceed 100,000,000 units for the first time, and it also saw the birth of the marketing concept of "race records." The idea was that "the race" would buy certain records provided they were targeted and advertised accordingly—and some of the advertising was extremely crude. Each of the existing companies had a list of such records, usually distinguished by a separate catalogue number series for the ease of record company employees. Nearly all the recordings of black musicians until the 1940s came under the designation of "race records." There was even a black-owned record company founded in 1921 (and sold to Paramount in 1924): the Pace Phonograph Company of New York, run by Harry Pace. The Pace-Handy Music Company had published not only W.C. Handy but "Crazy Blues"; their Black Swan label earned $100,000 in its first year. Alberta Hunter, one of the first artists signed to a year's contract with Black Swan, and Edith Wilson were among the most successful Mamie Smith imitators (both Hunter and Wilson were still around to be rediscovered and re-recorded in the 1970s). And then, beginning in 1923, blues mistresses Bessie Smith and Ma Rainey, respectively the "Empress" and the "Mother of the Blues," began their prolific recording careers.

---

* This small group was merely the advance guard of the white Broadway audience who, in the 1920s, feted the performers of several highly successful all-black musicals with scores by such as Eubie Blake and James P. As a result, the same white middlemen who oiled the wheels on Broadway also helped the sheet-music industry to colonize the blues songs, which became a craze in their own right by the mid-1920s.

Both Bessie and Ma made a couple of studio dates with country-blues accompaniments, the promising nature of which led to the equally prolific recording of folk artists like Blind Lemon Jefferson and of many early gospel singers. Rainey and Hunter were polished performers, spiritually close to the jazz idiom of the time. They each appeared in vaudeville, often headlining their own package tours and always with the rhythmic counterpoint of their own jazz instrumentalists in attendance. Alberta Hunter recorded with Eubie Blake and with the important female pianist-bandleader Lovie Austin, among others; at different times Hunter, Rainey and Smith all worked in the studio with groups led by Fletcher Henderson.

Johnny Dunn, who played first for Mamie Smith and then Edith Wilson, became a star in his own right specifically through his work on their records. He made three totally instrumental singles for OKeh in 1921 as "Mamie Smith's Jazz Hounds," then left her to form his own "Original Jazz Hounds" and tour with Edith Wilson. At the same time, Dunn signed a separate contract in his own right with Columbia, Edith Wilson's label. Though a little rhythmically unsteady on his earliest sides, by 1922 Dunn had firm command of both the triplets and the "even" timings. In addition, his varied expressive devices made him the first important cornet soloist. To quote Gunther Schuller, "He brought blues trumpet playing, particularly King Oliver's wah-wah technique, to New York."

The playing of Joe Oliver is one of the delights of early jazz, and his records will ensure that its appeal never dies. The one piece of good timing in a career not noted for fortunate accidents was Oliver's becoming the top jazz bandleader of Chicago by the time recording studios there were multiplying. He had been slow to get established in his native New Orleans, waiting until the younger Freddie Keppard had made his name and moved on. Oliver was in New Orleans long enough, though, to be an influence on other departing trumpeters such as Mutt Carey (when Oliver spent ten months in Los Angeles during 1921–22, he was accused of copying Carey, instead of the other way round!).

Mutt Carey's 1922 recording with Kid Ory's Band, the first of the very few jazz sessions cut in LA in the 1920s and a year before Oliver's first discs, shows an impressive player, a rather untogether group and a terrible singer. This studio date also allows fleetingly for direct comparison with Oliver on "Krooked Blues" and an early version of what turned into "Someday Sweetheart" ("Maybe Someday"). The importance of records or the lack of them—not only for the historian, but in making reputations at the time—is such that Carey's band, when he inherited leadership from Kid Ory in 1925, is a completely unknown quantity, because it remained in Los Angeles, unrecorded.

The great strength of King Oliver's style lies in its subtlety, and he is really the first jazz player of whom this can be said. He places his notes forcefully enough to provide a strong lead for the ensemble but, especially in short solos, he often sounds restrained and thoughtful. Whether using his favorite mutes or not, he touched the emotional core of black music in a manner that is worlds away from the jolly Original Dixielanders, and at least several steps ahead of Freddie Keppard or Johnny Dunn. On slower tempos, he injects a feeling of cautious optimism or uplifting determination, while with faster pieces—almost despite himself—he exudes sober realism and melancholy self-control. Oliver achieves this emotional ambiguity, which is the hallmark of the profoundest jazz, through perfectly manipulated combinations of tone and timing. It is not only in emotional terms that the influences of blues and ragtime are finally blended: the bluesy "uneven" quality is added to ragtime tempos such as "Weather Bird Rag" and the famous "Dipper Mouth Blues," while the slow blues numbers like "Jazzin' Babies Blues" (also recorded four months later in a version by Johnny Dunn) are played with a joyous ragtime lilt.

Oliver's own playing also set the seal on his whole band, and indeed, it is as the leader of his 1923 band that posterity has honored him most. This band contained the burgeoning solo talents of Johnny Dodds and young Louis Armstrong on second cornet, and they spent a lot of their time concentrating on ensemble work. Sometimes it was an Oliver lead with harmonized backing, often it was collectively improvised around a chordal sequence. Throughout, Oliver's timing pervaded the continuing counterpoint between the "horns" (as wind instruments were generally known) as well as the simultaneous counterpoint between horns and rhythm section. It is important to remember that unlike most of the white small groups recorded to date, Oliver's band performed principally for dancing. The former were perceived more as visual attractions, and played up this aspect with slightly hysterical consequences. Oliver's Chicago audiences, however, required a steady and relaxed rhythm against which their own movements could form yet another simultaneous counterpoint.

It is unfortunate that 1923 recording techniques were not quite up to the complexity of Oliver's music. Specifically, drummer Baby Dodds (like all other drummers of the period) was obliged to use a severely depleted kit to avoid overloading the recording equipment. The string bass could not be picked up at all, so Bill Johnson—the former leader of the Original Creole Band, who did quite prolific studio work later in the decade with Johnny Dodds and Jimmy Blythe—did not record on bass with Oliver. The eight-piece line-up was maintained, though, by the use of a bass saxophone on the last few sessions of this band.

One other way in which the fact of making records affected their content relates to the famous harmonized two-cornet breaks created by Oliver and Armstrong on numbers

such as "Snake Rag." Musicians who witnessed their live performances noted how the leader would play a fill-in phrase in
Louis's ear at the end of an ensemble chorus so that, by the
middle of the next chorus, the rest of the band could stop
while the two cornets startled the populace with an apparently
spontaneous fit of telepathy. On the records, however, there is
no sign of such last-minute collusion and, therefore, they must
have played safe and decided which break to use before commencing the number.*

The two-cornet breaks by Oliver and Armstrong are interesting for another, directly musical reason. On the OKeh
version of "Snake Rag," the next to last break (i.e. following
the one taken by the clarinet) enshrines a rhythmic feature that
pervades jazz, blues, ragtime and other Afro-American music.
The repetition of a three-note phrase during bars of eight notes
per bar—often described as "secondary ragtime," and apparent, for example, in "Maple Leaf Rag" and "Down Home Rag"
—is here spaced out over two bars, with the timing of the
notes unequal. Nevertheless, every third note is accented in a
manner that sets up an unmistakable cross-rhythm to the basic
meter of four notes per bar. (This is by no means the first
occurrence of this technique on record: James P. Johnson had
already used it to break up his left-hand stride patterns.) The
longer-term cross-accenting is especially clear here and became
a basic resource of jazz arranging and improvising.

---

* This is especially likely to be the case because the first company to record
them (Gennett) found Armstrong's bright tone much more penetrating than
Oliver's mellow sound, and placed Louis ten feet or more further away from
the recording horn. Interestingly, the longer cornet duet on "Mabel's
Dream," done at two different sessions in June and December, shows that
Paramount's engineers took this precaution to absurd lengths and rendered
Louis's part almost inaudible. The OKeh company, on the other hand, had a
justified faith in the fidelity of their system and did not try to rig the balance;
as a result, Armstrong stands out very well on their recordings, and nowhere
more so than on "Mabel's Dream."

In retrospect, it seems a little surprising that Oliver worked for four different labels in nine months (the fourth was Columbia). While few jazz and ragtime artists had yet been signed to exclusive contracts, at least the ODJB, Jim Europe, Wilbur Sweatman, W.C. Handy and all the successful blues singers gave their services to a specific company over a defined period. But they were based, like most of the companies, in New York, whereas Oliver was in Chicago, which was still almost virgin territory for recording. There, Oliver's relative fame brought him enough studio opportunities to ensure him eventual immortality. In the short run, however, the competing labels courted the risk of exhausting the market for King Oliver discs. Such a fear may explain why the OKeh issues were spread over two years and, of the planned second batch of Gennett singles, one was withdrawn immediately after issue and two others were never issued, even their test pressings being lost and therefore presumably destroyed.

Whether this overexposure in itself was sufficient to delay the continuation of King Oliver's recording career, or whether he found himself on some informal blacklist, is idle speculation on my part. The record companies (and those who later took them over) have been repaid more than amply over the ensuing decades. Oliver's band was not recorded again until the spring of 1926, and then as part of a new "race list" for Vocalion. Soon afterward, he cut "Someday Sweetheart" featuring Johnny Dodds, which became by far his best-selling single, but which three years earlier had been one of the unissued Gennett discs. In 1927, Oliver moved to New York, attempting with only mixed success to follow up his hit. His lack of career development from then on may, ironically, be the indirect result of making too many wonderful records in 1923.

·2·

THE PROSPEROUS TWENTIES AND THE FIRST STARS

---◆---

I n the early days, the payment of musicians for making records was far from standardized. Usually insufficient to be very exciting in itself, such payment was only a significant source of income if recording was a frequent activity. James P. Johnson made relatively few discs under his own name and was estimated to have been paid as little as $30 per record, whereas he received more than $100 for each piano roll he cut. That first Columbia session by the ODJB earned them $50 a man for two tracks. Duke Ellington's first big-band session in 1926 was apparently undertaken for a total fee of $125, but Ellington agreed to the paltry sum for the privilege of using an enlarged group in the studio. The players who backed

Mamie Smith, on the other hand, were each paid $50 for every tune recorded; however, this was because she was a big star and her records were selling in unprecedented quantities. Smith was one of a few leading performers to be paid royalties based on sales figures, rather than a flat fee, and as early as 1913 Jim Europe was offered a royalty of one percent per copy. He was quoted as saying that a white bandleader would have earned more, but naturally, he accepted what was offered.

Historically, because of the primacy of printed music, publishers and composers of the music used on records were in a much stronger position than the performers. The need to collect royalties had already led in 1914 to the formation of the American Society of Composers, Authors and Publishers (ASCAP). Although the membership was initially exclusively white, and also very elitist, the existence of ASCAP reinforced the clout of even non-members whose efforts had resulted in words and music enshrined on paper, as opposed to mere players or improvisers. W.C. Handy earned peanuts from his own few records, but rather more from other people performing (and recording) his songs. A successful 1919 Victor recording of "Yellow Dog Blues" by the society orchestra of violinist Joseph C. Smith, for instance, brought Handy a check for $7,000 early in the following year. Since such payments came out of their sales, the record companies were not above trying to save the odd penny. For example, Perry Bradford, author of "Crazy Blues" (Mamie Smith's version of which earned him two cents per copy), was propositioned by Columbia Records in the following terms: "I'm going to make the 'Crazy Blues' a big hit for you, if you'll waive your royalties."

Often, of course, the composer and the performer (or, at least, the bandleader) were one and the same. That is to say, even though individual improvisation and ensemble interplay were an important part of the performance, the tune on which these elements were based was sometimes originated by the musicians themselves. The creators of such "original material" seldom had need for written publication of their own individual repertoire, nor did they often have access to the purveyors of sheet music—not until the appearance of their records constituted a first publication of the material, and created a consequent need for copyright protection. In such cases, actual registration for copyright was often left to the staff of the record company and, even if (a big "if") they correctly credited the composer, the situation was a prolific source of problems. King Oliver, trying to take legal action against the incorporation of his "Camp Meeting Blues" into Duke Ellington's "Creole Love Call," discovered that his tune had been incorrectly registered.

Problems arose especially because, where jazz was concerned, even the composition of new material was often the collective activity of several members of a group, and usually drew on folk sources or on melodies that were "in the public domain." The main section of the ODJB's "Livery Stable Blues" apparently came into being as an improvisation on the 19th-century religious ballad "The Holy City" (in this instance, the derivation is obscured but the same song is quoted openly in King Oliver's "Chimes Blues" and in Duke Ellington's "Black And Tan Fantasy"). There were no difficulties with "The Holy City," by then old enough to be out of copyright. But because Victor Records had only registered "Livery Stable" under its alternative title of "Barnyard Blues," the ODJB's former clarinetist went to court for recognition as the originator of "Livery Stable"'s most distinctive features. He won, and the recognition was financially very considerable.

The few musicians who benefited from the existence of publication rights were, not surprisingly, those (like W.C. Handy) who formed their own publishing companies. This meant competing with the major Tin Pan Alley firms to influence recording directors to use their material with artists who were under contract, and encouraging lesser-known performers hoping to get themselves on record to become identified with particular tunes. Thus, composers would often make themselves artists' managers, sometimes unofficially, with this role overlapping that of the company's recording director.

A notable example was pianist Clarence Williams, who had moved from New Orleans to New York on the strength of the royalties from one of his compositions, and ran a successful publishing house there for 25 years. He managed to get Bessie Smith recorded in 1923 by OKeh, singing his number "Sister Kate" (which some have claimed was actually written by Louis Armstrong and sold outright to Williams). When Bessie's record was turned down, he promptly took her to Columbia, who offered her a contract which Williams signed for her. They imposed a different choice of material and, commencing an extremely successful musical and sales relationship, she received from Columbia a flat fee of $62.50 for each tune released.

A few months later, Bessie discovered her "manager," Williams, was receiving $125 for each of these recordings. Out of his share he paid himself as pianist and a couple of other accompanists, but his work as middleman was already well rewarded by publishing royalties when his material was used. Bessie, in contrast, never earned any artist royalties, only income from actual record sessions (royalties from sales of her 1970s reissue albums were paid to the executive producer of the *reissue* series). Yet when Clarence Williams retired in 1943 and his publishing catalogue was sold to Leeds Music (now part of MCA Music), it was worth $50,000.

Williams' position made him, at the very least, a good talent-spotter. Playing the soprano saxophone on Bessie's unissued OKeh test session was the first of a new generation of jazz soloists, Sidney Bechet, who made his recording debut on a Williams date six months later. Among Clarence's noteworthy productions were a handful of tracks pairing Bechet with his great contemporary Louis Armstrong, whose impact is discussed later.

However, most of the full-time company-appointed talent-spotters acted more like asset-strippers. The company's sales figures were the most pressing consideration and, after that, a personal profit never came amiss; the frequent need for record companies to register copyrights of original material often meant that it was "simpler" for the producer to form his own publishing company to handle these formalities. Paramount's black producer J. Mayo Williams (no relation to Clarence) was known in the business as "Ink" Williams, because of his fondness for artists' signatures finding their way onto little bits of paper that just happened to be contractually-binding documents naming him as publisher. It was said of him that he eventually owned the rights to "a catalogue of thousands of tunes, *one* of which he composed."

Ironically, perhaps, the white jazz musicians of the period were a little less likely to be exploited for their lack of commercial acumen, but their musical ideals were often easier to pervert, possibly because of their wider potential market. For instance, the New Orleans Rhythm Kings made their best records in 1923 as a quintet with the same instrumentation as the ODJB, after an initial session covering some of the ODJB repertoire. The NORK may have been overpraised, in fact, because unlike the ODJB, they made friendly noises about black bands such as King Oliver and were influenced by him. Indeed, clarinetist Leon Roppolo was the jazz world's first Great White Hope—the fact that he was soon confined to a mental home, the standard treatment in those days of a marijuana addict, also contributed to the band's posthumous appeal. On the whole, the New Orleans Rhythm Kings were clearly serious in their pursuit of the depth and the swing of the best jazz. However, whether or not the Gennett recording director Fred Wiggins played a determining role, their third and final session fatally weakened their punch by adding as many as three would-be jazz saxophonists (only two of the alleged three seem to be audible, but two is more than enough despite the use of some arrangements by Jelly Roll Morton).

It was a saxophone which brought about the greatest success (and thus sealed the fate) of the ODJB. Many recording directors, from about the start of the 1920s boom onwards, had absolute control over the repertoire used by performers and believed in the infallibility of their own musical instincts. On the ODJB's return to New York from England in 1920, Victor Records producer Eddie King insisted upon the addition of the newly popular saxophone to the front line, and steered the band toward pop songs instead of New Orleans-style jazz. Their first new release, a medley of "Margie" and "Singin' The Blues," was a far bigger hit than their previous efforts and, from then on, there was no looking back until their eventual break-up. This confirmed that, in terms of sales, King had been right.

King's commercial instincts were also on target with Paul Whiteman, whom he signed to Victor in 1920. Whiteman was one of a growing breed of popular orchestra leaders who diluted and deodorized their source music. He obviously believed that his saxophone section and string-dominated orchestrations were a distinct advance on the crude, emotive, potentially disruptive sounds originally associated with the word "jazz." Indeed, Whiteman's famous Aeolian Hall concert of 1924 included a parody of "Livery Stable Blues," before introducing Gershwin's "Rhapsody In Blue" to show just how things had "improved." The fact that people are still learning to play the early repertoire of the ODJB (and the NORK) to this day, whereas few have even tried to re-create Whiteman's pompous pretensions, says most of what needs to be said about Paul White-person.

Perhaps the great American public believed in Whiteman because they had always been sold on the idea of "progress."

Indeed, not only the public, but the majority of the white musicians believed in him, apart from a few recalcitrants who were
hooked on the improvised feel and the interplay of small-group
jazz. Even black instrumentalists tended to look up to
Whiteman because of the almost military precision and the mu-
sicianship that went into his moribund performances; this is
certainly true of Fletcher Henderson, the pianist who began his
recording career in 1921 as the accompanist of singers such as
Ethel Waters. (Dissatisfied with Henderson's abilities, Waters
ordered him to listen to and learn from the discs of James P.
Johnson—the earliest documented example of studying records
in order to make more records.)

Fletcher Henderson may have been a so-so pianist but, as
the first black big-band leader of consequence, he aspired to
have an organization of all-round versatility, like Whiteman
had. But since recording directors (and he worked with several
for different companies) could only see a black band as a jazz
band, this aspect of Henderson's repertoire is preserved for
posterity; Henderson himself was disappointed that the waltz
medleys he featured for dancers at the Roseland Ballroom were
not deemed suitable in the studio. Fortunately, he, too, was
a great talent-spotter, featuring soloists such as Coleman
Hawkins (from 1923 to 1934), Louis Armstrong (for just over a
year from late 1924) and many other leading players of the
1920s and 1930s.

More importantly, the strength of Henderson's soloists
was matched by the arrangers he employed, Don Redman and
later Benny Carter, who each subsequently led their own
bands. With their work for Henderson, Redman and Carter
showed how to counterpoint solo improvisation with ensemble playing, and how ensemble playing (even by saxophonists
like themselves) could be made to swing. In other words, the
written figures arranged for whole sections of trumpets or
saxes could have the correctly ambivalent relationship to the

rhythm section, provided the writing was firmly based on the way that improvising soloists worked.

In this discovery, Henderson's band members were greatly aided, to say the least, by having Louis Armstrong in their midst. As Don Redman explained, "Louis, his style and his feeling, changed our whole idea about the band musically." Very soon, Armstrong came to have a decisive influence not only on arrangers but on the players of all manner of instruments, beginning with Coleman Hawkins. What is immediately noticeable about Armstrong's early solos with the Henderson band (and his occasional emergence within the King Oliver group) is the imperious authority of his sound. Even though it's obvious that the indifferent recording of the period would be as unfavorable and unfaithful to his actual tone as to any of the other players, it feels as if he is communicating without the need for a recording-horn (or, from the mid-1920s onwards, a microphone) and speaking directly to the heart of the listener. This is an illusion, of course, caused by his superb control of the cornet and, later, the trumpet.

Because he had been put into care by the city of New Orleans as a teenager, Armstrong had received better training than most of the black brassmen of Oliver's generation. Still, what he did with what he learned was created by his ears and his soul. He didn't retain the legitimate tone he had been taught to use, but he built upon the power that that tone had put at his disposal, and varied it with all the consummate skill of the very best blues singers. His talent lay not so much in muting and distorting his tone like Oliver, Keppard or his contemporary (and initial rival) Johnny Dunn—although Louis had imbibed this ability, too—but in giving light and shade to each note within each phrase.

Naturally, Armstrong's timing and articulation were of crucial importance in making his work sound as effortless as it did. The mixture of the "even" ragtime phrasing with that bluesy triplet feel, which Dunn had struggled to master while the old players never did, permeated Louis's whole approach. What seems to be merely an extremely flexible and expressive approach to timing is, on closer inspection, a continual to-and-fro of slight anticipations and delays in the solo line compared to the underlying beat. For example, "Cornet Chop Suey," with its introduction based on "High Society," confirms that Louis's subtle phrasing is all based on the division of four beats per bar into twelve triplets, continually juggled at a speed which would be impossible if done with conscious deliberation.

There were two consequences following Armstrong's rhythmic expertise from 1925 onwards. The first was the immediate decrease in counterpoint between the melody instruments; even if all the other performers were equally expert, such counterpoint became more unwieldy to attempt, and harder to listen to unless one "horn" played a clear leading role and others were subordinate. The other consequence was the automatic *increase* in counterpoint between the solo or lead line and the work of the rhythm section. This development also helped to consolidate and underline a change in the rhythm-section work, which had been started by the stride pianists in their movement away from ragtime. Instead of the two strong beats with two weak beats, alternating in each bar as in ragtime piano or in the ragtime-based New Orleans generation, there were now four equal beats, each capable of pushing a performer or a performance along. Armstrong's playing needed this sort of backing. According to drummer Baby Dodds, who recorded with Louis in both the Hot Seven and (earlier) the Oliver band: "With Louis, I don't care how fast you played it, Louis wanted four . . . King Oliver wanted two. His mind didn't develop that fast."

The fact that expanded technical virtuosity went hand in hand with a broader range of expression became evident to a wide public as soon as Louis returned to Chicago in late 1925. There he began to make hugely popular records under his own name for OKeh, with his all-star group the Hot Five (briefly becoming a Hot Seven), his Savoy Ballroom Five and eventually his own big band. For the initial small-group records, the uncredited musical director was his wife Lil (who had been with the Oliver band at the time he himself was); studio supervision was by pianist-songwriter Richard M. Jones (whose sideman Oliver had originally been, and who was now the Chicago representative of Clarence Williams' firm).

With the encouragement of Richard Jones, Louis began a series of increasingly amazing trumpet features leading up to such profound works as "Potato Head Blues" and "Tight Like That." He also started doing the vocals which laid the foundation for his eventual worldwide fame as an entertainer. Jones, for instance, saw to it that Louis soon recorded the first extended scat singing (creating rhythmic nonsense syllables in a way that helped listeners to feel the stylistic connection between his singing and his playing). Jones also spread the story that Louis had accidentally dropped the songsheet of "Heebie Jeebies," in order to convince everyone (starting with the OKeh front office) that Louis's anarchic and apparently African-sounding vocal was fit to print and to be enjoyed. It was probably Jones who persuaded OKeh to promote Louis's early records by giving a free photo of the artist to each purchaser, very likely the first time such a gimmick had been used for a black performer.

By the time electrical recording (i.e. with microphones) became the norm in the late 1920s, Louis had his first white producer, Tommy Rockwell, and producers could play a more specific role in deciding how a record should sound. Louis was also working with pianist Earl Hines and drummer Zutty Singleton, who were even more alert than their predecessors to his complex rhythmic approach. The three proved so compatible, musically and personally, that they formed a co-operative group to run their own venue (this brief venture was unsuccessful). In the studio, they convinced Rockwell of the desirability of Singleton using brushes on his snare drum for the opening section of the classic "Muggles"; he not only agreed, but found a novel way of making this effect more audible, personally holding the drum above the microphone and in front of Singleton as he played.

Rockwell heard that Richard M. Jones had produced for the Vocalion label a group called "Lil's Hot Shots," led by Lillian Armstrong and featuring a trumpeter and singer who sounded remarkably like Louis, while the latter was under contract to OKeh. Louis's classic reply on being asked who this performer was? "I don't know, but I won't do it again."

OKeh was understandably anxious to protect their "property," for Armstrong continued to make salesworthy singles for them until 1931. The competition tried to sign up Armstrong imitators. Vocalion, for instance, had the adventurous Georgia-born trumpeter Jabbo Smith attempt a similar series of records in 1928-9, just as Victor did with Louis's younger New Orleans compatriot, Red Allen. But the grandeur, musical sophistication and down-home simplicity of Louis's playing—immortalized on the masterpiece called "West End Blues"—eluded those musicians asked to mimic him, as well as all the others who merely wanted to.

The OKeh company had converted to the electrical process only after being taken over by Columbia in 1926, although OKeh maintained the identity of a separate label more or less continuously till the end of the 1960s. This enabled them to continue, for at least the remainder of the 1920s, a policy started in 1923 by Ralph Peer (OKeh's recording manager, who had been an assistant at the time of "Crazy Blues," and who had tried to persuade Columbia to record some jazz back in 1918). From his office in New York, Peer sent out what was probably the first mobile recording unit on twice-yearly trips to capture both jazz, blues and country artists all over the South. This venture—and the espousal of the same idea by the few other labels interested, such as Columbia and eventually Vocalion and Victor—provides something like an in-depth picture of jazz activity across the country (except for the West Coast).

The fruits of Peer's forays tend to confirm that the outstanding musicians, with some notable exceptions, usually migrated to the main centers of the entertainment industry and were not content to remain with the so-called "territory bands," who stayed in the area where they had built up their local popularity. There are, therefore, some fairly indifferent performers heard in the recordings from these "field trips," and those who are more promising are often strongly influenced (even at this early stage) by records already released from New York and Chicago. It is extremely interesting to hear, for instance, the first OKeh sessions of Kansas City's Bennie Moten (done in St. Louis); St. Louis's own Charlie Creath band (with its New Orleansian rhythm section of Pops Foster and Zutty Singleton); and the many New Orleans natives, black and white, who had not moved north, such as Papa Celestin, Wingy Manone, and Tony Parenti.

The merging of OKeh with Columbia led to the amalgamation of their field trips, and threatened to make Ralph Peer's services redundant. He immediately moved to the previously reluctant Victor and started their "race series," signing Bennie Moten, Mamie Smith and others to exclusive contracts and initiating field trips to record artists on a one-off basis. Perhaps to protect his employment prospects in the future, he also became the publisher of much of the material he was responsible for recording, founding the empire of Southern Music and later Peer International.

It was inevitable that listening to jazz records became, very early on, the chief method for aspiring musicians to learn to play themselves. Whether they were already professional players before turning on to jazz, or younger but old enough to hear jazz in the flesh, the live experience often had a greater impact; but records were always around to be heard again and again in a way that live performers seldom were. So, when Leon Roppolo repeated Larry Shields' ensemble parts (not his improvised breaks) on the NORK version of "Livery Stable Blues," it was because he had consciously or unconsciously memorized every note of the original ODJB record. (This is not a particularly surprising feat, for even non-musicians have been known to be able to do the same thing, especially with records first heard and loved during their impressionable teenage years.) Soon, arrangers writing for bands were anthologizing the short phrases (or "licks") that improvisers used in building their solos; sometimes, they would even copy out whole solos which they had admired on record. Roppolo had his improvised solo on "Milenburg Joys" transcribed and harmonized by Don Redman as part of his 1928 arrangement for the Detroit band McKinney's Cotton Pickers. As early as 1924, Bix Beiderbecke's first recorded solo (from "Jazz Me Blues") had been copied out by an enterprising arranger named Eddie Kilfeather to be played by cornettist Red Nichols on an otherwise undistinguished dance-band record. In the same year, the incorporation of transcribed solo improvisations from records into published sheet-music arrangements began with "Copenhagen," one of the tunes written and recorded by the Wolverines, the band which first brought Beiderbecke to attention.

Although they are in some ways comparable, Bix Beiderbecke was what has come to be called a "musician's musician," whereas Red Nichols became almost a household name, like that of Paul Whiteman. Nichols began his recording career in 1924, the same year as Bix; he was soon featured with radio bands and quickly gained a reputation for musical dependability in the studio. Even before he formed his own popular recording group, the "Five Pennies" (a play on the word "nickel"), Red had established himself as one of the first jazz-inclined sessionmen. Rather like Dave Sanborn in more recent times, he captured the imagination of both colleagues and producers with a few well-chosen phrases during other people's performances. Nichols was, in fact, so successful at providing what was required that he was then entrusted with his own recordings, on which the expression of emotion is as carefully measured as the actual notes.

A tightly-knit association of like-minded players soon evolved which included Miff Mole and saxophonist/clarinetist Jimmy Dorsey (sometimes with the pioneer bass saxophonist Adrian Rollini). These musicians often played on each other's records, as well as working together for all the premier studio orchestra leaders. Nichols became a top conductor himself, assembling and directing the pit band for the Gershwin musical *Girl Crazy*, also doing hundreds of sessions under pseudonyms like "The Arkansas Travellers" or "The California Ramblers." Such dates were often for "dime-store" labels (like the Cameo group or Columbia's cheap series, Harmony Records) which had sprung up with the 1920s boom in record sales. One of his Red's band names for the Cameo group, "The Five Birmingham Babies," was probably intended (like the slightly earlier "Ladd's Black Aces" which sometimes included Miff Mole) to suggest that these white sessionmen were of another race.

In personality, Beiderbecke could not have been more different from Nichols. Bix had no idea what to do with a conductor's baton, any more than he knew how to solve his prematurely fatal drink problem. The contrast was all the more marked because (like Nichols himself, briefly) Bix worked for the Paul Whiteman orchestra, which he joined immediately after being in a similar Detroit-area outfit led by

Jean Goldkette. Some of the other players snapped up by
Whiteman from the Goldkette band—saxophonist Frankie
Trumbauer, guitarist Eddie Lang, and Joe Venuti, the first convincing jazz violinist—showed a distinct preference in their
later careers for fairly free-wheeling small-group jazz. They were
valued by leading black musicians, chiefly for technical profi-
ciency on the instrument of their choice, and for the idiomatic
feel of their solo work. But black players admired Bix most of
all. He was not setting any new technical standards—indeed, his
self-taught apprenticeship put him at a certain disadvantage
compared to, say, Armstrong. Nevertheless, Armstrong and
everyone else instantly recognized that, rather than playing *at*
jazz like many of his white contemporaries, Bix was playing the
only way he knew how. While many white musicians have been
strongly attracted to jazz but have still managed to "keep it in
perspective" (and pay the rent at the same time), Beiderbecke
was sufficiently alienated from mainstream society to be truly
happy *only* when he was playing jazz.

Like all great jazz soloists, Bix Beiderbecke found that jazz
provided a necessary emotional release, and his ambiguous attitude to life and society were writ large throughout his equally
ambiguous music. Armstrong's bright and edgy tone acknowledged adversity while proclaiming triumph over it, but Beiderbecke's velvety chimes (on the same instrument!) spoke of
over-optimistic attempts to cushion the adversity. This quality
emerged only gradually, for in his work with the Wolverines—
shortly before his 21st birthday and during the months following—Bix's sound is more open, with a suggestion of vibrato
not dissimilar to the ODJB's Nick LaRocca, whom he had
begun copying via record. And correspondingly, although his
lines have a pleasing melodic reticence, they are somewhat
dissatisfying due to his ragtime approach to phrasing.

A considerable change in Bix's playing is noticeable once
Beiderbecke heard Armstrong and learned how to relax, or

how to be himself, and the result sounds nothing like Armstrong. The delays which Armstrong used with some notes that seemed to fall on the beat (delays of one triplet's worth) became a constant in Beiderbecke's playing—to such an extent that there is a continuous tension between his notes and those of the rhythm section. On Bix's great OKeh recordings of three years later (despite some fussy and over-cute written arrangements influenced by Whiteman and Nichols), this tension not only makes the rhythm section play better than for other soloists, but also creates the illusion of Bix floating in a separate sphere—an achievement which produced some beautiful music, and also became widely influential later on. Even more immediately, his (and Frankie Trumbauer's) recorded improvisations on the ODJB tune "Singin' The Blues" were among the most widely-imitated music on disc, by white and black musicians alike. These improvisations were also the first to be re-recorded (by vocalist Marion Harris) with new lyrics specially written to fit the improvised melodic lines.

The conscious craftsmanship of adding words to jazz solos, which became a more popular exercise in the 1950s, was not very dissimilar to the jazz arranger laboring to organize notes on paper, in the hope that they might sound spontaneous when played. Both activities were deliberate, and pretty remote from the concerns of the great majority of 1920s jazzmen. After all, players like Louis Armstrong or Bix Beiderbecke remained unaware that their off-the-cuff improvisations would be captured and re-created this way. They enjoyed playing, they enjoyed challenging themselves, and they enjoyed the competition of their colleagues, but they didn't set out to prove anything. Even if there had been such a thing as a jazz critic in the 1920s to explain the profound changes they were bringing about, they would not have believed it. Only working in the studio—which required recording additional versions or "takes" of a piece (many of them irretrievably lost from the 1920s output of both Bix and Louis)—would eventually lead to self-conscious reflection about improvisation.

Other jazz innovators shared Louis's and Bix's spontaneity, people like Earl Hines, whose 1928 piano solos or his duo performance with Louis Armstrong on the King Oliver item "Weather Bird Rag" went far beyond the stride pianists in making the beat more fluid and right-hand melodies more adventurous. The important clarinetist Jimmie Noone (with whom Hines also worked) was technically impressive even to trained white musicians including French composer Maurice Ravel; he was content to remain in Chicago leading a small pre-Louis Jordan-style jump band, not much different in approach from the one led by the more obviously blues-influenced Johnny Dodds. For both of these New Orleans exiles, Chicago and its thriving illicit nightlife represented the height of their ambitions, so that as Chicago saw less jazz recording in the following decades, their careers (on record) faded prematurely.

The second half of the 1920s saw the blossoming of a few bandleaders with new musical ambitions, combining the talents of the pianist-composers of ragtime and stride with the skills of arrangers who incorporated improvising soloists. At that time, records not only captured existing performance styles, they also stimulated the thought processes of writers who might not have developed in the same way without records. It is hardly an exaggeration to say that for those musicians who thought hard about how to fill them, the grooves of a record became like the canvas to a painter or the stage to a playwright—the average time limit of three minutes (maximum three-and-a-half minutes) of the 10-inch 78 RPM disc was a fact of life, like the frame of the canvas or the proscenium arch. Because it existed, you created within it; and what now, looking back, may seem a limitation, was accepted as an unbridgeable boundary. To players who merely wished to preserve their current playing routines (and who, if like King Oliver they played for dancers, had to abbreviate their longer routines by 80 or even 90 percent), the idea of having to finish in time before the end of the side was just one more reason to be nervous in the recording studio. Born organizers who wanted to create a good impression, however, turned the limitations of this new medium into an advantage.

It is pointless to speculate how much Jelly Roll Morton had considered this aspect of recording by the time of his studio debut in 1923 (he had been performing by 1905, and claimed to have made some unissued pre-1923 sessions in California). While it took three years before his band records really hit their peak, his solo piano discs (in which the organizer and the performer were one and the same) seemed effortlessly worked out from the moment he set foot in the studio. Morton's piano-playing was also far more advanced, even avant-garde, than his rather unsuccessful early recorded attempts at bandleading. It conveyed a fluent post-ragtime style, with a New Orleans lilt that made it more dynamic and less stilted than stride piano—and, unlike that of northern-bred modernists beginning with Earl Hines, his approach included unmistakable references to blues piano stylists.

There were more of these itinerant or immigrant blues players in Chicago than in other northern centers. Yet at this stage, it was mainly the New Orleans exiles who managed to incorporate an idiomatic blues influence into jazz. To take just one notable example, Morton's "New Orleans Blues" (or "Joys") sounds far more earthy than James P. Johnson's or Hines's blues numbers; it included an eight-note left-hand solo figure (also used in Charles Davenport's "Cow Cow Blues" piano roll of two years later) which could just as easily be the work of a country blues guitarist. The other side of the coin is rhythmic innovation of a high order; Morton's left hand introduces the cross-rhythm that he termed "the Spanish tinge" (accenting the third eighth-note in an *accompaniment* was instinctively associated with Afro-Latin dances such as the tango and habanera). In one brief chorus, his right hand flies free of the continuing beat with a controlled burst of fireworks that anticipates Hines by five years.

There is no such complex interplay on Morton's earliest band records, whether with the New Orleans Rhythm Kings (the same session at which he did the solo "New Orleans Blues") or under his own name. These first sparse recording opportunities certainly set him thinking about effectively arranging for an ensemble his piano compositions, which in any case often sounded like imitations of a New Orleans band such as King Oliver's. Unlike Don Redman, however, Jelly Roll was not functioning as an outside contributor arranging someone else's songs for a big band in which he himself was only a "section man." He was often taking material he had already organized compositionally and, because of his organic use of improvisation and of the blues influence, he wanted his music performed with those values uppermost. In other words, he wanted to have improvisers but with one composer in charge, or a hydra-headed version of himself playing all the instruments.

Having worked through this ultimately insoluble problem, Morton was good and ready when Victor Records (at the time of Ralph Peer's arrival) agreed in 1926 to let Morton's white publisher, Walter Melrose, produce a series of sessions in Chicago by what he christened "Jelly Roll Morton and his Red Hot Peppers." The composer began by choosing seven-piece groups of standard New Orleans instrumentation, stocked them with mainly New Orleans-raised players such as Kid Ory, and rehearsed them before recording so that their best improvised ideas became thoroughly memorized while still sounding spontaneous. Doubtless this was assisted by Morton's good sense in paying the musicians for the rehearsals as well as the actual sessions. This practice must have left little out of his recording fees, but since he stood to earn composer royalties, it was money well spent.

Tracks such as "Black Bottom Stomp," "Grandpa's Spells" and "Dead Man Blues" succeed brilliantly as compositions of a complexity comparable to the best ragtime, but they also convey the energy and apparent spontaneity of an all-star get-together. Aside from Morton's key role in the proceedings, this music has impact to this day because the sound is so clear. Up to this point, one chief limitation of records (apart from their brief time-span) had been the hit-and-miss balance achieved with acoustic recording, and the fact that some individual instruments were far easier to pick up than others. Jelly Roll had taken part in an early experiment in electrical recording, in a 1924 duo session with King Oliver. But once the use of microphones became the norm, the Victor company matched the technical superiority which OKeh had mastered a few years earlier. Perhaps because Morton had learned about problems of balance in his initial band records, he knew how to have prominent solos accompanied in the way best suited to bringing them out (or not accompanied at all with the piano, which still posed engineering problems for decades to come). This makes for great variety of texture as well as thematic content, and a different kind of organization from the collective counterpoint of the Oliver band.

Morton followed Oliver to New York in pursuit of increased fame, ceased his association with Melrose and started being published by Ralph Peer's Southern Music. Not only is there less certainty of aim in his New York sessions, but even the recording is sometimes less focused, while his musical ambitions vacillate from the Don Redman style of section writing ("Burnin' The Iceberg") to the atmospheric Ellington-style simplicity of a string of solos ("Deep Creek"). As with Oliver, Jelly Roll was unable to take his best musicians with him to New York. By 1930, New Orleans clarinetists who had worked for him in Chicago, such as Barney Bigard and Albert Nicholas, were reluctant to leave the successful bands of Ellington and Luis Russell, respectively.

Neither Ellington nor Russell was in the same class at the keyboard as Morton. But as the 1920s drew to a close, Russell and Ellington each had one of the requirements for survival at this period: residency in a nightclub which, despite its inevitable criminal connections, didn't mysteriously close or change owners overnight. Russell's six-year stay at the Saratoga Club helped him to keep together a big band that grew out of King Oliver's 1926 unit (for which he had played and written arrangements) and that went on to be Louis Armstrong's backing group—in fact, an initial one-off recording with Louis in 1929 undoubtedly helped Russell's band to secure their OKeh contract.

Russell hardly ever featured himself on piano, but he had a fine collection of soloists, including New Orleanians Albert Nicholas and Red Allen. Russell also had, from the same city, probably the tightest rhythm section in New York at the time, with bassist Pops Foster and drummer Paul Barbarin. But the Russell band's routines lacked both the variety of Morton's and the finesse of Don Redman's arrangements for Fletcher Henderson. For example, the ensembles on "Saratoga Shout" and others offer the simplest kind of harmonization, with the saxophones duplicating the brass. The textural interest, on the other hand, comes from the wide-open tone of the soloists, who often seem in playful competition with the arranged section work. In other words, despite being recorded in the North, Russell's outfit sounds like the New Orleans equivalent of a "territory band," with all the rough edges and gutsy exuberance which the term implies.

In some ways, Duke Ellington was slow to realize that he had been born with a proverbial silver spoon in his mouth. From the viewpoint of 1929 and given the priorities of jazz so far, Luis Russell's might have been the superior band (indeed Duke's "Stompy Jones" seems directly inspired by the Russell version of "Panama"). But the ultimate doyen of the jazz aristocrats already had several advantages. For a start, like no other bandleader until then—but like the greatest soloists—he relied on his own instincts and his own taste, good and bad. While ready to listen to advice and take advantage of any and all opportunities, he went his own way musically and eventually developed a seemingly all-embracing taste in jazz and black music in general. His writing of the late 1920s sometimes seems like a cut-and-paste job combining bits of Jelly Roll Morton, bits of Don Redman, bits of Paul Whiteman and some more commercial but less suave bands, along with sounds from the crudest, funkiest bars "for blacks only." (Ironically, the Cotton Club, which served as Duke's working base, admitted only well-heeled white customers.) Perhaps sensing that this one-man anthology could be too amorphous, Ellington was equally open to the thoughts of the sidemen he chose, who began to supply some of the immediacy and the continuity that his written work alone might have lacked.

Even before Duke got inside a studio, his selection of co-workers showed an ear for quality and for questioning the norms of the day. For instance, there was the wild and sometimes surrealistic trumpeter Bubber Miley, who had replaced Johnny Dunn in Mamie Smith's group and who created the main themes of the early Ellington masterpieces "East St. Louis Toodle-oo" and "Creole Love Call." Miley, too, imported the "Holy City" quotation for the opening of Duke's "Black And Tan Fantasy," and the Chopin "Funeral March" quotation it ends with. There was also the great Sidney Bechet, whose live duets with Miley prompted Ellington to say later, "Oh, what a pity some of those things weren't recorded." After his studio career was under way, Duke chose replacements who were always superior to their predecessors: baritonist Harry Carney, trombonist Tricky Sam Nanton (the most moving muted-brass player of all), New Orleans bassist Wellman Braud, clarinetist Barney Bigard, altoist Johnny Hodges and—to replace the irrepressible Miley—the more controlled and more expansive Cootie Williams.

As well as his musical sensitivity, Ellington had by 1927 acquired one further advantage: a personal manager and agent named Irving Mills. Mills was undoubtedly "well-connected," which, at least until the end of Prohibition in 1933, usually meant staying on the right side of the criminal underworld; but his background was as a music publisher. The company founded by his brother, Jack Mills, had shown an early interest in popular blues at the start of the 1920s, and in the mid-1920s, Mills Music had bought up the catalogues from other publishers who lost interest when the blues "craze" was over.

Not only did Irving Mills encourage Ellington to write original material so that Mills Music could copyright it and collect the publishing royalties, but his personal membership in ASCAP as a lyric-writer overcame that organization's resistance to any but the most established composers. At this period, about the only black musicians who had been allowed to join ASCAP were the successful songwriters W.C. Handy, Eubie Blake, James P. Johnson and Clarence Williams. Duke did not acquire membership in his own right until 1953! In the meantime, Ellington could receive at least a proportion of the composer royalties of his works, provided Mills was listed as co-author.

Wearing the publisher's other hat as negotiator of recording deals, Mills worked wonders for Ellington (and thus for himself) in these early years. He arranged for the band to appear virtually simultaneously on several different record labels, often using the same material many times as a way of making it more popular (and, of course, persuading other bands to use Ellington tunes as well). Then, when the composer's name had become sufficiently known for an exclusive contract to be offered by Victor, Mills allowed the other labels which had also recorded Ellington to continue to do regular sessions with "The Jungle Band" (on Brunswick), "The Washingtonians" (on Cameo and its subsidiaries), "Joe Turner and his Memphis Men" (Columbia), "The Harlem Footwarmers" (OKeh) and a few other names, all of which turned out on inspection to be the Ellington band playing Ellington material. As a result, in the four years from 1927 through 1930, Duke recorded far more sides than any other black artist (two and a half times as many as Armstrong, three times as many as Henderson, Oliver or Bessie Smith). In addition, the choice of Victor, with its superior sound quality, as the "official" Ellington label stimulated the composer's search for new textures. It was once said that his first hit in the popular market, "Mood Indigo," was scored "for trumpet, trombone, clarinet and microphone."

Mills pulled off other coups as well. He made sure that his ensemble stayed at the Cotton Club, except during out-of-town tours to capitalize on their popularity, for the simple reason that this allowed Ellington's men to be the first black band to broadcast nightly on radio (the medium which had helped to spread Paul Whiteman's fame nationwide). They were first to have a short sound film built around them (called *Black and Tan Fantasy*) and first to appear in a black-oriented Hollywood feature film (*Check and Double Check*, with comedians Amos & Andy). And, while in Hollywood, they not only made records of the three tunes used in the film, but Mills managed to have Bing Crosby and the Rhythm Boys (vocal group of the Whiteman band) guesting on one track—surely the earliest example of big-name white performers lending their prestige to a black group.

One of Mills' recording ideas that didn't come off—or was not considered successful enough to be released—was a simulated live broadcast called "A Nite At The Cotton Club," intended to be spread over both sides of a single record. But already in early 1929, Mills had followed Paul Whiteman's example of Gershwin's "Rhapsody In Blue" by having Duke do a double-sided arrangement of the ODJB perennial "Tiger Rag." Even more far-sighted was Mills' encouragement of Ellington to become, as it were, Whiteman and Gershwin combined, and to write an original extended work for himself and his band called "Creole Rhapsody." Just as the record industry went into the doldrums in 1931, this was cut in two different versions: once under a new Brunswick contract by "Duke Ellington and his *Famous* Orchestra," on a double-sided standard-size disc, and once for Victor on the double-sided 12-inch records normally reserved for European "classical" music.

· 3 ·

DEPRESSION AND RECOVERY

◆

The Wall Street Crash and the subsequent Depression had a catastrophic effect on the record industry worldwide, even more than on some other aspects of the entertainment business. The very day that the bottom fell out of the stock market (October 29, 1929), an obscure jazz record entitled "Goin' Nuts" was cut; it was attributed to the "Six Jolly Jesters," actually an 11-piece group consisting largely of the Duke Ellington band. Perhaps even more appropriately, on that same day, the latest product of the popular-song industry, "Happy Days Are Here Again" (one of the earliest song hits to trade on the third-note accentuation), was first recorded at the debut session of an important 1930s band, the Casa Loma

Orchestra. The British release of the disc rechristened them the "Carolina Club Orchestra," a name apparently more marketable than the band's own chosen one.

Of course, records everywhere became less and less saleable. The standard retail price for popular music releases in the U.S. was still 75 cents, with only the dime-store labels (including some of the pseudonymous Ellington items) selling for 25 or 30 cents. Suddenly, money had to be economized, and eventually millions were thrown out of work, so it is hardly surprising that the record business nearly went under. Average annual sales had reached 150 million units by the end of the 1920s, but a couple of years later, the entire remaining industry sold 5,000,000 discs.

Particularly significant was the competition from commercial radio and from sound films, both developments of the 1920s which came into their own in the 1930s. As soon as the process of recording soundtracks was perfected, occasional individuals made moves to incorporate the work of jazz musicians (such as Dudley Murphy, who directed the 20-minute film featuring Ellington, *Black and Tan Fantasy*, and also built one around Bessie Smith). But this, too, was a sideline halted by the Depression. The big studio bosses sensed that cinema could be *the* mass medium, if its efforts were angled towards romantic stories and slushy music expressing the hopes and fears of the downtrodden populace. And so, for the price of a cheap-label record which lasted three minutes per side, you could spend a couple of hours being taken out of yourself and back into a comforting, darkened womb. Not many Americans, or Europeans, had so far learned to view music (and especially jazz music) in that way.

Radio was even stronger competition for records because it provided entertainment in the home. And even though the largest radio sets cost over $100, or more than a record-player (they still came separately in those days), once you had bought the radio, all the sounds on it were free. All the news and sports commentaries, all the early "soap operas" and a large amount of music were free—not only to the listeners, but also, in many cases, to radio station managers. Music was usually broadcast live from a venue which, once it had persuaded the radio station to put in a couple of microphones, was only too happy to have its address and its in-house entertainers publicized over the airwaves, without requesting further payment either to the owners of the venue or to the aforesaid entertainers. Jazz had already been promoted in this way as early as 1923 by Kid Ory in Los Angeles, by Jelly Roll Morton the following year, and by many others on the multitude of stations dotted through the land. This practice continued as fully as nightclub business would allow throughout the Depression. However, the only musicians who got paid in radio were the stations' own studio orchestras, which played for the programs with commercial sponsorship. Even they—including some of the jazz sessionmen previously mentioned—were expected to give back some of their payment from sponsors to the radio station, in recognition of their privileged status.

Small wonder that the record business was in some difficulty even before the Depression. Long before they took over OKeh, Columbia Records had been about to declare bankruptcy in 1923; after this was forestalled by the tremendous sales figures of Bessie Smith, the label had turned by financial maneuver into a subsidiary of the UK Columbia company.

Shortly after the first major network of radio stations was formed, the Radio Corporation of America in 1929 bought the successful Victor Records (henceforth RCA Victor) and set about influencing its musical policy. RCA Victor dropped most of their jazz acts like Jelly Roll Morton and Red Allen in 1930, for the general move towards sentimentality was propagated in popular music releases, too. Groups with longer contractual commitments (Bennie Moten, for instance) were given fewer and fewer chances to record. Any opportunities that did exist were much like that of McKinney's Cotton Pickers—the first black band allowed, in the words of pianist Todd Rhodes, "to record a waltz tune because of the splendid intonation of the band." Perhaps this was slightly better than having your contract picked up by some organization which would refuse to honor the commitment unless you had been a best-seller.

Both the Gennett and Paramount labels disappeared, in 1930 and 1932, respectively. Brunswick/Vocalion was much more fortunate in being taken over by Warner Bros. Pictures, in the same way that Consolidated Film Industries bought American Record Corporation (a group of small labels which had merged in 1929). Warners then leased Brunswick to ARC, which in 1934 also purchased Columbia/OKeh for about $250,000 and which was, in turn, acquired by CBS radio in 1938 for $750,000.

By then, of course, the economy in general was looking up again. Fortunately, one side effect of hard times in the record industry was the accidental creation of jazz's first independent producer. John Hammond, child of rich parents and then just out of college, was trying in 1932 to interest theater and record entrepreneurs in the idea of jazz, simply because of its artistic merit. He became a correspondent of the British pop-music periodical *Melody Maker*—and of the U.S. equivalent *downbeat*, founded in Chicago in 1934—to encourage their readers' enthusiasm. When the ailing Columbia company was made aware of a demand from the UK for some new jazz product, they turned to Hammond for advice.

Offering his production services for nothing, Hammond supervised a Fletcher Henderson session and, after the favorable response, he recorded Henderson again, brother Horace Henderson, Henderson's star saxophonist Coleman Hawkins with a smaller group, Benny Carter, Teddy Wilson and others.

Hammond also set up Bessie Smith's last studio date and the first relatively popular Benny Goodman discs, and on a couple of these, he persuaded Goodman to use his new "discovery," vocalist Billie Holiday. The band members on each of these occasions were paid according to the new minimum rate established by the union, the American Federation of Musicians. (Another beneficial side effect of the Depression was that the Chicago-based union gained enough muscle to fix separate specific scales for nightclub work, radio and recordings, the latter initially at $20 per musician per three-hour session.) However, in the case of Bassie Smith, Hammond had to chip in and beef up her payment.

In the meantime, some other jazz was being recorded. Activity at RCA Victor remained sporadic for several years but included a series by the Washboard Rhythm Kings, whose members' names were not noted because they were not union members and didn't have to be paid the proper rate. There was some recording with Louis Armstrong and an isolated date by the New Orleans Footwarmers, the first splendid small-group session led by Sidney Bechet. Late in 1933, bands associated with Irving Mills and the Cotton Club began appearing on RCA Victor. Also in 1933, Victor started its own 35-cent label, Bluebird, to reissue previously-released tracks, including material by the Washboardists and earlier items by such as Ellington and Henderson. Bluebird eventually cut new material and became increasingly important once the record business picked up.

The bands which were recording most regularly in the early 1930s were nearly all on Brunswick and/or the small labels that originally went to make up ARC. Most of them were managed by Irving Mills, sometimes in partnership with Tommy Rockwell. These were the outfits of flamboyant singer Cab Calloway, Duke Ellington, Don Redman and the Mills Blue Rhythm Band. Also on Brunswick were the white Casa Loma Orchestra and the Dorsey Brothers' Orchestra—at this stage, mainly a studio-based group which (like Goodman's so far) was inspired by the popularity of the Casa Lomans, especially with college kids.

With the slight improvement in the economy in 1934 came an increase in competition in the record field. When the Columbia label was sold to the operators of Brunswick, another interested purchaser had been the recently formed UK company, Decca; far from being outmaneuvered, its managing director persuaded the head of Brunswick, Jack Kapp, to leave and found the U.S. Decca outfit. Going about this in no uncertain fashion, Kapp announced that all his records would be sold at 35 cents. He brought with him Brunswick's best-selling popular artists, Bing Crosby and Guy Lombardo, plus the Casa Loma and the Dorsey Brothers, all of whom sold enough copies at the lower price so that no one was out of pocket. For good measure, Kapp signed Earl Hines's band, also from Brunswick; Fletcher Henderson; the popular Chick Webb, who was in residence at Harlem's Savoy Ballroom; and the new incumbents at the Cotton Club, the Jimmie Lunceford band. The financial rewards of the foregoing acts may have been more slender, which would explain why Kapp also brought in "Ink" Williams to produce some of his black artists.

Jimmie Lunceford might even have looked to Decca's business dealings and rationalized his own exploitation of his sidemen, for he remained with the label most of the time until his early death in 1947. Lunceford had the liveliest and most innovative big band of the mid-1930s, which subsequently became very influential. Often employing the massed weight of the whole ensemble rather than the sectional dialogues pioneered by Henderson and used to somewhat different ends by Ellington, Lunceford forged a stylistic unity and precision which was the envy of both black and white big bands. The showmanship that went with it was also expressed in touches like a Mills Brothers-type vocal group drawn from the ranks of the players, and the baton-twirling antics of the trumpeters with their horns; the musical equivalent was the screaming high-note solo trumpeter capping the ensemble on up-tempo numbers such as "Lunceford Special."

The level of ability needed to achieve this glittering spectacle was considerable, and Lunceford arrangers like Sy Oliver required not only virtuoso blended saxophone work (as on "Sleepy Time Gal") but strange Ellingtonian voicings used in a deliberately gimmicky manner ("Organ Grinder's Swing"). Most significant were the rhythmic changes which the band contributed in their occasional reversion to a 2/4 beat. As established by Louis Armstrong, the underlying 4/4 feel had become absolutely essential in the preceding ten years, the earlier style being gradually relegated to a "businessman's bounce." But with the Lunceford brass section charging ahead in 4/4 and the rhythm section loping along in 2/4, a delightful tension was set up that was to be perpetuated by Erroll Garner and by the Miles Davis group of the mid-1950s.

It was not the ill-managed, underpaid black bands like Lunceford's that earned the applause of young white college students and eventually of the entire nation. Nonetheless, the sudden success of Benny Goodman—the direct result, incidentally, of a 26-week NBC radio series—was helped considerably by his astute employment of Fletcher Henderson and other black writers. These black musicians included Chick Webb's Edgar Sampson (author of "Stompin' At The Savoy" and "Don't Be That Way," among Goodman hits) and Earl Hines's Jimmy Mundy (arranger of "Sing, Sing, Sing"). The common factor in all these pieces is that, like some of the white jazzmen of the 1920s, the black big bands that broke through in the 1930s were playing a fairly straightforward, optimistic, anti-Depression music. It was the more subtle and ambiguous Duke Ellington who popularized the use of the decade's key word with his song "It Don't Mean A Thing (If It Ain't Got That Swing)."

Naturally, Benny Goodman has often received the credit for popularizing the concept of swing. The basic ensemble style, with its emphasis on the power of large numbers of musicians pulling together through the hard times, was inspirational for the mass audience. It needed a visually acceptable, well-trained white performer to become its standard-bearer; then the media and the music business could do the job of creating the Swing Era. So Benny Goodman became the "King of Swing," in the same way that Paul Whiteman had been hyped as "King of Jazz" during the 1920s. Actually, Goodman was a far worthier incumbent than Whiteman, for his own Chicago-trained clarinet style was one of the band's strongest jazz voices, along with a succession of "hot" (i.e. Armstrong-influenced) trumpeters including Bunny Berigan and Harry James, the whole being driven by the great Chicago drummer, Gene Krupa.

The way in which this popular version of jazz caught on is illustrated by the amount of recording the top bands did. In the four years from signing an exclusive Victor contract in 1935 (during the course of the original radio series), Goodman cut about 20 percent more tracks than Ellington in 1927–30. Whereas Duke's were spread over a variety of record labels, Goodman's were all for a single company!* The big-band sound swept aside the sentimental outpourings of early 1930s pop, and became the music to identify with for those who saw themselves as surviving the Depression. This change of climate benefited the black bands as well (Ellington almost equaled Goodman's rate of recording if you take a four-year period beginning in early 1936, but he was

---

* Naturally, the musicians were paid "scale" for each of the 60 studio sessions that created the 224 sides in question. But when NBC radio archived the band for their own Thesaurus transcription library, they were renamed "The Rhythm Makers" and were asked to cut 51 pieces—over two hours' actual music—in the space of a three-hour session for a total payment of $51 per man.

constantly taken into the studio by Irving Mills in order to expand the catalogue of Mills Music and with a view to starting his own record label).

It's equally true that, being swallowed whole by the popular music industry, the big bands also had to swallow a lot in terms of third-rate songs in order to have work for their first-rate musicians—"Goody Goody" by Goodman, featuring Helen Ward, or the equally childish "A-Tisket A-Tasket," which spotlighted young Ella Fitzgerald at the expense of Chick Webb, will suffice as examples. So it cannot be assumed that even the majority of records cut by the top bands were hardcore jazz or that they stand up to scrutiny today.

Most of the bandleaders were not looking to posterity, anyway. They were set on immediate fame and fortune, and therefore eagerly embraced the idea of a package show in which the band would back up singers, comedians, tapdancers, amateurs from the audience, and so on, while shining on its featured instrumentals. No one was happier or more successful in this respect than Tommy Dorsey. After leaving the Dorsey Brothers band to Jimmy, Tommy, in his first four years with his own outfit, recorded nearly 50 percent more material than Goodman—and all for Victor, Goodman's label. Dorsey stayed with Victor for 15 years, a record unbeaten by any jazz-associated artist until Stan Kenton's 25 years with one label, which began in 1943.

In addition to the wide acceptance of a form of jazz (acceptable, provided it was referred to as "swing"), the early 1930s saw the emergence of a dedicated interest in earlier forms preserved on record. Although many of the classics of the 1920s had sold thousands of copies, only a tiny minority of these had found their way into white households, and an even smaller minority of whites who heard them realized their musical value and started to build a collection of "hot" records. Collectors who had become hooked by the time the poorer households were having to pawn things like record-players (and the sounds that went with them) learned the art of junk-shopping for old discs, since there were so few new releases of value to them. This activity was fermented by excitable correspondence between collectors in different towns, some of the most articulate correspondents eventually founding "jazz appreciation societies" and little private magazines, in order to discuss whether Louis Armstrong or Johnny Dodds might be on a record newly discovered. In these matters, collectors had little to go on except each other's opinions.

By the mid-1930s, there was even the first of the specialty retailers, in the shape of the Commodore Music Shop in New York. Commodore sold jazz by mail order to hardcore fans throughout America and Europe. Inevitably, perhaps, the company became a focus for the organization of the United Hot Clubs of America. Commodore's owner-manager, Milt Gabler, started the first specialty reissue series by first buying up the remaining stocks of 35-cent OKeh and Vocalion discs which were discontinued in 1935, and selling them with a new UHCA logo to keen collectors prepared to pay a dollar per copy—the price for ten-inch records of classical European music.

Although the Commodore shop was obviously a repository of information about which current or earlier records were worth buying, it was left to a wealthy French enthusiast, Charles Delaunay, to assemble the first comprehensive listing of release details (including documentation of all personnel taking part in each record, where positively identified). Delaunay's *Hot Discography* of 1936, revised in 1948, was, like all reference works, an attempt to catalogue information before it became lost, and before it was overtaken by the need for new information. Yet even as Delaunay was consulting fellow collectors and, in some cases, interviewing musicians for their recollections of who played what, more records were being released which would raise more questions, and so on. This problem dogged the original work and its revision, as it has dogged later efforts by such as Dave Carey and Albert McCarthy, Brian Rust, Jorgen Grunnet Jepsen and, currently, Walter Bruyninckx. But, as the field has expanded at an unbelievable pace, the work of successive discographers has been invaluable in keeping less academic listeners in touch with what is available, and sometimes even in alerting record companies to what they have lying around unreissued or never even used in the first place.

It is revealing that all the major contributors to jazz discography mentioned above have been Europeans and that, for most of the period since the '30s, there has been more consistent and more knowledgeable interest in jazz in Europe (and latterly in Japan and elsewhere) than in the land of its birth. In 1935, Delaunay co-founded the specialty magazine *Jazz Hot* with Hugues Panassié, who was to become president of the Hot Club de France. More importantly, Panassié was already the author of the first serious book to have an influence on collectors in several different countries, called *Le Jazz Hot*. The book and the magazine, and others like the Swedish *Orkester Journalen*, stimulated the collectors' market. These collectors thrived on second-hand American records imported from individuals or from the Commodore Music Shop, as well as those U.S. recordings released by various European labels that had licensing deals with the well-known American companies. Some jazz had, of course, been recorded in Europe. But for a long while, serious collectors were less interested in the works of European-raised jazz players, and only sought after discs made with one or more visiting American musicians. To the Hot Club de France goes the honor of promoting the only group for decades that featured a European jazzman of consequence.

The gypsy guitarist Django Reinhardt may not have sounded temperamentally or idiomatically in tune with jazz as it had been played thus far, and the group sound of the Hot Club Quintet was initially a pale copy of the already pallid Joe Venuti/Eddie Lang discs of the late 1920s. But, simply because Django applied the different idiom of gypsy music to a jazz framework (and had a sufficiently flamboyant technique to carry out the necessary fusion), he was admired by American players of all instruments and all complexions. One of the strongest proofs of its validity is that Django's style rapidly begat imitators in numerous countries, including the U.S., where—apart from one very brief visit in 1946—he could only be heard through his records.

Reinhardt's initial experience of the medium was unpromising, however. After years of accompanying singers on disc (rather like Eddie Lang with Bing Crosby), Django made his first jazz-only recording, which remained unreleased for decades. These two sides by the Hot Club Quintet, billed as "Delaunay's Jazz" because it was he who persuaded the respected Odeon label to hold the session, were rejected because they were considered "too modern." When, three months later, the same personnel made their first issued sides for the smaller Ultraphone company, it was the *engineers* who would have preferred not to release the famous "Dinah." Why? Django's guitar audibly banged against a nearby table during the final chord. The engineers were also dumbfounded by the improvisation for, according to Panassié, "[one of them] came up to me and asked why the musicians had changed the tune, instead of repeating what was on the test pressing."

Django apart, the classic sessions made in Europe in the 1930s tended to be those built around Americans touring or living on the Continent. The two greatest individuals involved were saxophonists Benny Carter and Coleman Hawkins, both originally crossing the ocean for work in the UK. Hawkins had already made a huge impact on American saxophonists, much greater than Sidney Bechet, by virtue of Bechet's European residence during much of the 1920s. When Hawkins came to Europe in 1934, he left the States as the acknowledged king of the saxophone. However, nearly all of his recording had been with Fletcher Henderson, who never featured him on disc to the extent that a later bandleader would have done. Hawkins's declamatory, almost verbose style had not been allowed to dominate entire tracks, except for "Hello Lola" and "One Hour" by the "Mound City Blue Blowers" plus some of those cut by John Hammond for the British market just before Hawkins's UK arrival. The latent ability to carry a whole group, and the even more latent composing and arranging talent which Hawk never fully realized, were brought into much sharper focus on his series of discs with the Dutch dance orchestra, the Ramblers. Even more striking for this period, perhaps, was the way Hawkins could create the momentum for whole performances virtually without any accompanying group, as he did on his duos with American pianist Freddy Johnson (plus a Dutch drummer on one occasion).

Pride of place, though, goes to a session produced by Delaunay and Panassié and issued as "Coleman Hawkins and his All-Star Jam Band." Benny Carter provided his saxophone, trumpet and arrangements; Django Reinhardt led the rhythm section or, rather, is recorded in such a way that he seems to be all the rhythm section that was required. Hawk takes the last and deliberately climactic solos on the medium-slow "Out Of Nowhere"—a beautiful two choruses that foreshadow the stunning "Body And Soul" recorded on his return to the U.S. two-and-a-half years later—and on the up-tempo "Honeysuckle Rose." The session is memorable for another reason: it was done for the major La Voix de Son Maître (His Master's Voice) company and indeed, "Out Of Nowhere" was issued on that label. "Honeysuckle," however, bore the catalogue number "Swing 1" and the brand new logo of Swing Records, the first specialty jazz recording venture anywhere in the world.

Many more American musicians were active in Europe before the onset of war in 1939. A few black Americans settled for long periods—understandably, since in view of the tiny numbers of black residents in Europe at this time, there was little overt racism. Even some of those making fairly short tours, such as Armstrong and Fats Waller, were invited to record with locally-based musicians (including, in both cases, locally-based West Indian-born black musicians). Although the entertainment business stays relatively buoyant in times of great economic uncertainty, the Depression had put considerable pressure on the employment prospects of the more marginal categories of American musicians including, until the Swing boom, most varieties of jazz players. This led to an enforced sense of adventure for those Americans who could find employment overseas, people like Buck Clayton, who went as far as Shanghai.

The tendency of American jazz musicians to seek work abroad led to a corresponding resistance from musicians in the countries they visited. For several years in the early 1930s, the UK Musicians' Union lobbied the government's immigration department to limit the number of visas issued to American performers; the Jazz Section of the French union did the same during the 1960s. In 1935, the British union obtained an almost total exclusion of Americans which lasted, more or less unbreached, for the next 20 years. It is ironic—since the transatlantic traffic had been very much one-way—that it was the American AF of M who first imposed a ban when the British leader Ray Noble (later to compose "Cherokee" and other staples of the jazz repertory) wanted to capitalize on the popularity of his records in the U.S. He was only allowed to do so by leaving behind his British musicians and forming a band of Americans including Glenn Miller, Claude Thornhill and Bud Freeman. Except for the sub-rosa visit of Sidney Bechet in

1949, this situation put an end to Americans and Britons recording together. Nonetheless, Armstrong-inspired trumpeter Nat Gonella went to New York in 1939 and made some tracks with American musicians, as did future entrepreneur Vic Lewis (in 1938) and Leonard Feather, who became a freelance journalist and record producer like John Hammond.

One factor which had kept the American record business alive, if not necessarily the individual performing musician, was the growing practice of playing discs in public places such as cafes. Anything that required complex amplification was liable to be beyond the proprietors' means—indeed, many owners of record-players were still, in the mid-1930s, playing the electrically-cut discs of the past ten years on old acoustic horn phonographs. Yet a small establishment which lacked the space to house "live" performers could play its own selection of recorded music, as an alternative to the radio. A powerful stimulus to this development, especially at first to the jazz side of things, was the popularization of the jukebox.

Demonstrated as early as 1899 but only mass-produced in the early 1930s, this method of having the clientele pay extra for their music caught on rapidly when it was first marketed during the early post-Depression years. The jukebox's wholehearted acceptance in the bars of the black ghettos was responsible for its now accepted nickname (the expression "juke joint" was originally black slang for a brothel, then for any low-class dive). Jukeboxes were also responsible for the recording of much black music. While much of what was cut for the Decca label by black bands might not have justified itself in immediate sales to black buyers, the jukebox became a promotional tool at a time when the number of black artists heard regularly on radio was minimal. As early as 1933, Red Allen started recording again (for ARC) and inaugurated the idea—doubtless suggested by sheet-music publishers—of doing informal and inexpensive small-group versions of current pop songs, with a vocal chorus (by Allen himself) and some casual jazz-tinged instrumental work. This practice was then taken up by such rhythmic singers as Putney Dandridge (also on ARC's Vocalion label) and Bob Howard (on Decca). Each of these nominal session-leaders benefited from what now looks like a floating pool of key sidemen drawn from the important black big bands.

One of the chief beneficiaries of this system, however, soon established his own regular studio personnel, although it was a while before he was in a position to tour with his personal backing group. This was Fats Waller, a superbly talented pianist and songwriter who in both respects took after his mentor James P. Johnson. Fats had already made several recordings for Victor in 1926–30, mostly of piano or organ solos. When Victor producer Eli Oberstein re-signed him in 1934, the small-group series by "Fats Waller and his Rhythm" was born, featuring the hot sounds of trumpet, clarinet, guitar, bass and drums—with the romping piano and riotous humor of Fats himself in the driving seat. Occasionally, this combination was also used with Waller on organ instead of piano. For these dates, it was necessary to forsake Victor's New York studio and travel to Camden, New Jersey, where the company owned the former Trinity Church.*

The popularity of Fats's often satirical and anti-sentimental singing on such Tin Pan Alley gems as "I'm Gonna Sit Right Down And Write Myself A Letter" and "It's A Sin To Tell A Lie" mushroomed and earned him not only his own radio slot,

---

* Fats's first regular drummer, Harry Dial, commented recently, "I always liked to go down to Camden, because that was a $100 deal, whereas those other sessions on 23rd Street were just $20 a time." The $20 per man was for an entire session and a normal maximum of four issuable tracks. The $100 earned Victor a double session (six hours) and eight tracks, for a couple of pieces were recorded in both vocal and instrumental form, issued concurrently.

but guest appearances on the shows of such top white performers as crooner Rudy Vallee. As a result, Waller's casual and
spontaneous studio creations of original instrumentals died
down. He did fewer solo sessions, and even then, he used
well-known standard material like his own songs "Keepin' Out
Of Mischief Now," "Ain't Misbehavin'" or "Honeysuckle Rose"
(whose 1941 remake was subtitled "A la Bach, Beethoven,
Brahms And Waller"). What this rapid success did to the musical personality of Fats—and to the thin person trying to get
out—is a matter for conjecture and possible regret. One can
only rejoice that he crossed over so rapidly to the majority
white audience for swing music (sooner, in fact, than Armstrong) and, posthumously, to the larger middle-of-the-road
constituency unconcerned with and unaware of jazz as such.

Fats's small-group work did much to create the style
which eventually turned into R & B, but which at the time
had no name beyond the general marketing category of "race
records." That term was sometimes softened in the poverty-
(and conscience-) stricken 1930s to the more hip-sounding
"sepia series." R & B originally combined a kind of highly
rhythmic "post-blues" vocal work with a small instrumental
group whose two or three front-line horns simulated the
power and excitement of the black big bands. In the late
1930s, the impetus for R & B lay in an area roughly bounded
by the Harlem Hamfats and Louis Jordan. Both groups
recorded for Decca, to whom Jordan was initially known as a
former saxophonist and featured singer with Chick Webb.
The name of Jordan's group, the Tympany Five, came from
his brief flirtation with tuned percussion in a manner first
used by the former drummer of the Wolverines on the early
records of Red Nichols's Five Pennies (also produced by Jack
Kapp in his Brunswick days). Jordan's most popular style,
however—which was to become highly influential in the late
1940s—had some of the humor of the Fats Waller approach

but, both vocally and instrumentally, was more slick and streamlined.

The much earthier, even cruder sound of the Harlem Hamfats, on the other hand, was created by the conjunction of two blues singer/guitarists (Joe and Charlie McCoy) and some of the lesser-known New Orleans jazzmen based in Chicago. The Hamfats included the Morand brothers, trumpeter Herb and drummer Morris, plus bassist John Lindsay. Herb had recorded with Johnny Dodds in the Beale Street Washboard Band; Morris was briefly a member of Bechet's New Orleans Feetwarmers; and Lindsay had worked with Oliver, Morton and Armstrong. The Harlem Hamfats' limited but lively playing, together with the down-home feel of the blues input, brought success to a specially-assembled studio-only group which never performed together in public. Hits like "Oh! Red" became a second-generation, simplified version of the fusion which Armstrong had pioneered ten years earlier.

Of all the series of discs intended for the jukebox market in the second half of the 1930s, the ones most revered by jazz lovers even today are probably those of the pick-up groups led by Teddy Wilson, the majority of them featuring the vocals of Billie Holiday. Personnel were chosen from the entire spectrum of the big-band field, not just Wilson's employer of the period, Benny Goodman. Soloists from the bands of Ellington, Calloway, Henderson, Chick Webb, Count Basie (when he moved to New York), the Mills Blue Rhythm Band and others worked together, in varying small combinations that would have been tactically impossible outside the studio. The songs were selected on the same basis as for the Fats Waller dates—in other words, the record company's repertoire department had sorted out some potentially usable material from publishers' submissions, for the musicians to examine for the first time at the session itself. If better-selling artists on the same label had already accepted the superior material, then it was not available to the more humble performers.

Holiday was lucky that, after a year of this approach, she was sometimes allowed to tackle standard songs such as "I Cried For You" or even new numbers by Gershwin ("Summertime," of which she did the first improvised version), Porter ("Easy To Love") and Kern ("The Way You Look Tonight"). What Billie brought to any song, even those that were truly dire, was the ability learned from Louis Armstrong to phrase like an improvising instrumentalist. Her phrasing was often so logical, melodically and rhythmically, that the words would make musical sense, sometimes more than they deserved to. These qualities made her, and still make her, an acquired taste, like a lot of the best jazz. John Hammond, who produced the Wilson sessions for Brunswick, later said, "In the mid-30s Billie was so uncommercial that . . . they figured that they were really indulging me by recording Billie and Teddy Wilson." But because the musicians all played for scale, and no arranger had been paid to write something that would take a long time to get down correctly, a sale of 3,000 copies was enough to break even; "I Cried For You," featuring Johnny Hodges as well as Holiday, sold more like 15,000.

Consequently, even before "I Cried" was released, the Teddy Wilson series on Brunswick was supplemented by a Billie Holiday series on Vocalion. The musical policy was identical except that different pianists were used, studio production was by songwriter Bernie Hanighan, and Billie sang the opening and closing of each song (on the Wilson tracks, instrumentalists usually soloed first and last with the "vocal chorus" coming in the middle). At a Wilson session in early 1937, Billie met her musical soulmate—just as she first encountered the songs. These were an above-average bunch of two new Irving Berlin film numbers of unusual construction ("He Ain't Got Rhythm" and "This Year's Kisses") and two older standards

("Why Was I Born?" and "I Must Have That Man"). The man was tenor saxophonist Lester Young. "Prez" had recently arrived in New York with the Basie band, three of whose members (Buck Clayton, bassist Walter Page and drummer Jo Jones) were present on the session; guitarist Freddie Green joined them in the Basie rhythm section a month later.

Lester Young was an acquired taste, too, even for some musicians, for his approach was quite different from the omnipotent Coleman Hawkins and from the heir apparent to Hawk's throne, Chu Berry. For a start, being a former drummer, Lester was an excellent accompanist. With its passionately laid-back quality, his phrasing related closely to the blues philosophy of joyous acceptance of life's adversity. Young's sound was remarkably similar to Billie Holiday's; there was a veiled and grainy texture to the tone with which they voiced their phrases, that sounded like nobody else at all except each other. Rhythmically, Lester's playing has often been compared to that of Bix Beiderbecke and Frank Trumbauer, but he was so much more flexible than either of them that it seems appropriate to look to the same source that Billie acknowledged—namely, the work of Louis Armstrong. Certainly, Holiday and Young also had in common with Louis a fondness for marijuana—on the first recording date of Billie and Lester together, as John Hammond noted, "The session was nearly canceled when one of the top America Record Company officials walked in and sniffed the air suspiciously."

The Count Basie band was only one of a number of black big bands who came to national attention through jukebox hits in the late 1930s, most of them classifiable as "territory bands." These, in record business terms, were groups (black or white) with strong followings in their own region of the U.S., bands whose local hit records then led to them being promoted on a nationwide basis. The Erskine Hawkins band from Alabama had some success on Vocalion, was dropped after the ARC group was bought by CBS, and not long after was signed by Bluebird. In the autumn of 1938, Bluebird was being converted from a "minority music" label only to more of a swing-oriented popular label. Here, Erskine Hawkins had two very successful discs in "Tuxedo Junction," with its restrained but unconventional trumpet solo by Dud Bascomb (the sales were sufficiently big for the highly commercial Glenn Miller band to copy the number), and "After Hours," another precursor of rhythm and blues.

Although Chicago was an important national center, one might also categorize Earl Hines's as a territory band, since until 1940 he was committed by an unequal contract to remain at the gangster-run Grand Terrace Ballroom in Chicago, a building ultimately owned by Louis Armstrong's manager, Joe Glaser. Also dropped by Vocalion, Hines took much longer to be picked up by Bluebird, after which he scored with "Boogie Woogie On St. Louis Blues" and the mildly salacious "Jelly, Jelly" featuring singer Billy Eckstine.

Most of the other big-band hits of this type were on Decca, who signed pianist Edgar Hayes when he led a splinter group from the Mills Blue Rhythm Band. At the last session of this band in 1938 (for some reason, his contract was not renewed), Hayes recorded the definitive version of "In The Mood." This widely-used riff, one of the best-known examples of overlaid three-note repetition, became a cornerstone of the Glenn Miller repertoire. It is a sobering thought that Miller, who has been the subject of more posthumous adulation than all the other protagonists of this book put together, had his finest moments doing straight cover versions of contemporary black bands.

One of the pre-Depression units which had recorded for Brunswick in 1929–30 was re-signed by Jack Kapp for Decca in the mid-1930s. A 1929 field trip by Kapp and Dick Voynow (the one-time pianist with the Wolverines) began the record career of Andy Kirk and his 12 Clouds of Joy, and was directly responsible for a significant change in their personnel. Because the 12 Clouds' pianist could not be found on the day that Kapp auditioned them in Kansas City, Mary Lou Williams—who had already cut some tracks under the leadership of husband John Williams, a recent addition to Kirk's saxophone section— deputized at the audition. On Kapp's insistence, she remained not only for the actual record session, but also for the next 13 years, becoming the band's most distinctive soloist and writing most of the band's arrangements.*

In the five years since their Brunswick sides, Williams effected a virtual transformation in the sound of Kirk's band. They immediately hit their top form with such pieces as her original composition "Walkin' And Swingin'." As a result, she personally went on to do free-lance writing for both Goodman and Ellington. The Kirk band's recording history with Decca, though prolific and lasting ten years, was partially hamstrung by the fact that their big 1936 hit was not an instrumental but a vocal ballad written by Sammy Cahn. (Cahn had his more up-tempo "Shoe Shine Boy" immortalized by Basie in 1936 and wrote "Rhythm Is Our Business" for Lunceford.) "Until The Real Thing Comes Along" featured the high tenor voice of Kirk's singer Pha Terrell in a performance that provided a model for the Ink Spots, the Platters and many more. Jack Kapp kept hoping for Kirk follow-ups—it was Kapp, after all, who had on his office wall a picture of an American Indian, symbolizing for him the lowest common denominator of musical intelligence, and speaking the immortal words "Where's the melody?" Because that was also the level of Kapp's own

---

* Of her early solo piano record, Williams said, "I never received a recording fee nor any royalties from it . . . Many years later, I threatened to sue, and stopped the sale of a record that had been reissued ever since 1931."

musical appreciation, nothing except his company's balance sheet might have alerted him to the qualities of the Kirk rhythm section, whose light but driving feel hinged on Mary Lou Williams' piano and prepared the waiting world for that other Kansas City export, the Basie band.

To gain an insight into the financial dealings of the many bands such as Lunceford's that hooked up with Decca, one need look no further than the documented case of Count Basie. His band signed in 1936 with Music Corporation of America, the same agency which was having success with Benny Goodman. Jack Kapp's brother Dave came to Kansas City bearing a Decca contract that required 24 tracks per year for three years in return for an annual fee of $750, not as an advance against royalties but as a total, outright payment. Basie signed the contract, not having been told by the Kansas City union branch's black section (who may never have had cause to find out) that this was far less than the national scale for recording. Such payment would have amounted to $335 per session including the leader's fee and, with sessions not expected to achieve more than four tracks, that meant six sessions a year, or a minimum of $2,000.

Before the contract came into force, John Hammond recorded for Vocalion a Basie quintet under the pseudonym "Jones-Smith Incorporated." The debut session of both Lester Young and Jo Jones, which created the immortal versions of "Shoe Shine Boy" and "Oh! Lady Be Good," was not without its extramusical problems. As Hammond noted, "The studio [in Chicago] was so small we couldn't use a bass drum, because we only had one mike and I wanted Walter Page's bass to have its proper authority. It didn't really matter because Jo kept such perfect time, so he just used a hi-hat and snare." The Decca agreement eventually went ahead; the union did manage to get the payment increased, but took the line that it was the record company's prerogative not to offer any artists' royalties (neither Teddy Wilson nor Billie Holiday got a royalty from ARC).

It's fortunate indeed that Basie signed a publishing contract with Jack Bregman to handle the band's original material. Jack Kapp also owned State Street Publishing which, for a single down payment, bought the composer rights to tunes Kapp or Mayo Williams had recorded—including many famous blues hits from their days at Brunswick and Paramount, like Leroy Carr's "How Long Blues" and "When The Sun Goes Down" as well as Pinetop Smith's "Boogie Woogie." These songs and others like "Oh! Red," all of them already re-recorded by other Decca artists, constituted the designated repertoire when, at the end of 1938, Basie recorded two quartet sessions with his "All-American Rhythm Section" as a compromise in order to get out of the third year of his Decca term.

During the preceding two years, the glorious relaxed sound of the original Basie band was committed to wax, including most of the numbers still associated with Basie: "One O'Clock Jump," "Swingin' The Blues," "Jumpin' At The Woodside." The Basie sound had much to do with the way the soloists managed to incorporate the blues inflections of all the southwestern musicians who migrated to Kansas City, and how this informed their playing as saxophone and brass sections. Many of their ideas and inflections would have seemed too simple and gutsy for the average Fletcher Henderson-inspired arranger to create, let alone arrangers impressed by Lunceford and Ellington. The band's arrangers (originally all player members) shaped the Basie sound from the riffs that had been created on the bandstand during the Kansas City jam sessions of the 1930s. This explains why the opening theme of "Swingin' The Blues" had already backed the trumpet solo on the first recording of "One O'Clock Jump," and why the brass riff (accenting every third eighth-note) behind the theme of "Woodside" also backed Lester Young on "Doggin' Around."

Melodic originality was not the aim of the band—as opposed to its soloists—but sublime, springy rhythm was. Basie's rhythm section, and particularly the innovative drummer Jo Jones, were crucial in their responsiveness to the rest of the band's insistent freedom from the current norm. Jones once underlined this aspect of the drummer's art: "It's the people you meet who's going to make you play . . . On something like 'Jumpin' At The Woodside' [I would] keep straight rhythm and play the brass figures and also try to play under the soloist." Pretty soon, it was their contemporaries who were copying them, and much of the development of jazz in the coming bebop era was the result of Basie's rhythm section and the way his soloists played rhythm as much as melody. On another occasion, Jones said figuratively of Lester Young, "Do you know that for 20 years after he gave up drums, Lester Young played more drums [on the saxophone] than 14 other drummers?"

· 4 ·

FROM BIG BANDS TO BEBOP

◆

I n the latter part of the 1930s
and the first half of the
1940s, big-band entertainment dominated the popular
music business. All the top bands had their own sponsored
radio shows; made guest appearances in Hollywood films;
played not only for dancing but in stage shows; and often
worked opposite a feature film in the huge cinemas of the day.

At the same time, competition in the record industry
became more intense. The Columbia label—revitalized after
its purchase by CBS—signed up Benny Goodman (from Victor), Count Basie and Jimmie Lunceford (from Decca) in 1939,
with John Hammond becoming a full-time Columbia employee
in order to produce them. In 1939, Columbia also made the

aggressive move of cutting prices on all their releases, reducing the standard popular singles from 75 cents to 50 cents. Shortly afterwards, Duke Ellington left Columbia, to which his Brunswick contract had been transferred, as a result of severing his connection with Irving Mills, who had negotiated the contract. Duke joined the same booking agency as Goodman and Basie and began to record for Victor, enjoying what many consider the peak of his creativity.

Victor and Bluebird were also having amazing successes from 1938 with their new acquisitions. Artie Shaw, for a time, overtook Goodman in both artistic flair and fame, while Glenn Miller soon outstripped everyone in popularity. Charlie Barnet (independently wealthy like John Hammond, but with a talent for playing the saxophone) achieved hit records like "Cherokee" and later "Skyliner" while allowing free rein to his admiration for Basie and Ellington. The whole scene looked so healthy that Victor producer Eli Oberstein left in 1939 to set up his short-lived cheap label, Varsity Records. Oberstein signed, among others, black West Coast bandleader Les Hite (who had a pre-R & B hit with "T-Bone Blues"), as well as the new bands of Harry James and Jack Teagarden.

Many of the bands that proliferated during this period, of course, were offshoots from the established bands. The MCA agency helped various former Goodman sidemen to start up on their own, and did so not only with Goodman's blessing but with the loan of his money (doubtless as a convenient tax loss in one year and an investment for future years). It was in this way that Harry James began his independent career, eventually downplaying his jazz leanings when schmaltzy trumpet ballads brought him several hit records. Gene Krupa, Teddy Wilson and Lionel Hampton received similar financial encouragement.

Unlike James, these three musicians retained the strong association with jazz gained through being featured with Goodman's Quartet. Krupa, the only other white member of the

Quartet, became the first bandleader to follow Goodman's controversial lead and present a black guest instrumentalist in his live appearances—the innovative trumpeter Roy Eldridge, who joined Krupa's band in 1941 (closely followed by trumpeter Hot Lips Page with Artie Shaw). Krupa, though not as subtle as the black drummers he admired like Chick Webb, nevertheless focused public attention on the key role of the drummer; Lionel Hampton (also a sometime drummer, but mainly heard on vibraphone) was even more of a percussive showman. Partly through racial typecasting, but also through genuine inclination, many of Hampton's big-band records for Decca emphasized the trend towards rhythm and blues.

Hampton's famous "Flying Home" exemplified a tendency inherent in the idea of recording. Saxophonist Illinois Jacquet's improvisation on "Flying Home" was seen as such a classic of its kind that Jacquet himself felt obliged to learn his own solo from the disc and repeat it as part of a fixed arrangement. The solo also received the orchestration treatment, and a saxophone ensemble version was included in Hampton's performances from 1945 onwards. Jacquet, then only 19 years old, later recalled the original session: "The horn was bigger than me at the time, so that they had to build a platform so I could reach the microphone. With all this commotion, I didn't know what I was going to play so, luckily, I came out with this solo that caught on to the public so well."

These natural showmen contrasted with several others who found the financial backing (or were pressed into service) to front yet more big bands, but who seemed devoid of the necessary ruthlessness to follow in the footsteps of Goodman and Dorsey. Teddy Wilson was a good example of a fine soloist and arranger capable of excellent musical leadership, but seemed misplaced in this role, except perhaps in the eyes of his band members and a minority of aware listeners. This enlightened or, as they would say, "hip" audience no doubt felt the same way about the equally transitory bands formed by both Benny Carter and Coleman Hawkins on their return from Europe. Neither Carter nor Hawkins was as flamboyant or as populist as the successful black bandleaders of the period.

Similar questions of personality bedeviled the bands of two brilliant white instrumentalists, trombonist Jack Teagarden and trumpeter Bunny Berigan, both of whom attained a measure of popularity through their laid-back but Louis-based singing. Berigan, a prolific studio musician in the early 1930s alongside Goodman and Dorsey, was a star soloist when both of these leaders formed their touring bands. Perhaps he would have been perhaps happier to remain in that capacity—as a leader in his own right, Berigan developed a drinking problem which was the equal of Beiderbecke's and which was also fatal. (Ironically, Berigan's only small-group recordings after forming his own band were three 78 RPM discs of Beiderbecke material, which coincided with the publication of the Bix-inspired novel *Young Man with a Horn*.) Teagarden was made of (slightly) stronger stuff. In his period as a studio musician, he had never been well-featured except on Goodman's first records for John Hammond, despite being possibly the most impressive jazz trombonist then active. After five years of stultifying security with Paul Whiteman, Teagarden started his own big band in 1939. This unit could have been a more jazz-oriented version of the Dorsey band, but a faceless policy and some dire arrangements showed that Teagarden's heart wasn't in it. Unfortunately, a lot of his own money *was* in it and, like other bandleaders, he found himself heavily in debt to his booking agency.

There were many more attempts to break into the now-lucrative big-band field. In order to gain an edge, newer white bands like Teagarden's commissioned some of their instrumental specials from a new breed—the free-lance black arranger, represented by Don Redman, Eddie Durham (ex-Basie,

ex-Lunceford), Buster Harding, Andy Gibson and Fred Norman. (A very similar practice occurred during the white colo-
nization of rock and roll fifteen years later). Even the more
established white leaders soon followed suit; in order to stay
ahead musically and avoid sounding exactly like everyone else,
Benny Goodman and Tommy Dorsey signed exclusive contracts in 1939 with new, individual-sounding writers. Dorsey
had come to admire the power and precision of the Lunceford
band and, learning that Sy Oliver had left, snapped him up on
financial terms which compensated Oliver for each chart
whereas, with Lunceford, he had been just an averagely-paid
sideman. It was a white ex-trumpeter, Eddie Sauter, whom
Goodman lured away from the band of jazz xylophone player
Red Norvo, where he had been producing subtle but swinging
Ellington-influenced scores. For Goodman, Sauter came up
with the classics "Clarinet A La King" (of Swing, naturally) and
"Benny Rides Again."

Benny continued his use of Henderson and other black
writers, which had started the inevitable trend. But it is ar-
guable that his most important work was with the small groups
he featured alongside his big band—and not just because he
was the first to break the taboo against black musicians performing in public with whites.

By using Teddy Wilson in trio and quartet settings, Goodman
knowingly put himself in a situation that was a musical challenge
and that drew from him some of his most committed solos. This
process continued when, after Wilson and Hampton went out
on their own, Goodman employed guitarist Charlie Christian
(from 1939) and, a year later, trumpeter Cootie Williams, who
had been with Ellington for the previous eleven years.

In this side of his activity, Benny was drawing attention to
the lively small-group music which, though often gestated in
Harlem, was paraded before the ears of white fans in the clubs

of 52nd Street. And with the ability of Christian's newfangled electric guitar to create lines reminiscent rhythmically of Lester Young, Goodman was popularizing a trend in small-group playing which would soon lead to the emergence of bebop. The same might be said of some of the studio small groups put together by Hampton in the late 1930s, and of the Ellington offshoots, fronted (again, for recording only) by Cootie Williams, Rex Stewart, Barney Bigard and Johnny Hodges. It could certainly be said of both the permanently-organized John Kirby Sextet—which had graduated from 52nd Street and become slick enough to have its own radio series—and Artie Shaw's featured small group, the Gramercy Five.

Certain of the "band-within-a-band" set-ups existed to perpetuate the classic New Orleans style of the 1920s, shortly to be known generally as Dixieland. This style had a loosely-structured format influenced by 1930s jam-session techniques. The band fronted by singer Bob Crosby, and its small group the Bob Cats, featured second-generation white New Orleans-born musicians such as saxophonist Eddie Miller and drummer Ray Bauduc. Crosby's arrangers, including bassist Bob Haggart, developed excellent adaptations of classic 1920s material recorded by Armstrong and others. Likewise, Tommy Dorsey had his Clambake Seven, which sported white Chicagoans Bud Freeman and Dave Tough, the mentor of Gene Krupa. As Freeman told me, "[Tough] started all of that, that three against four"—that is, Tough took the innovations of Jo Jones and started applying them in a Dixieland context. In this light, the rhythm sections of both Dorsey and Crosby made the bandleaders not so much revivalists as extensionists.

The Bob Cats and the Clambake Seven, incidentally, also promoted the popular interest in boogie-woogie. This was the rhythmically complex 1920s piano style characterized by the eight-note bass patterns of "Cow Cow Blues" and revived by Cleo Brown's 1935 jukebox version of "(Pinetop's) Boogie

Woogie" (her recording was, of course, for Decca). Dorsey featured his pianist in a band arrangement of "Boogie Woogie," ostensibly inspired by Brown and Smith, while the Crosby band did the same on their record of the still famous "Honky Tonk Train Blues," first cut in 1927 for Paramount by pianist Meade Lux Lewis. Lewis had even re-recorded "Honky Tonk Train Blues" in 1935 at the request of John Hammond, who produced sessions by both Lewis and Albert Ammons. Three years later, Hammond featured Lewis and Ammons at the second jazz concert ever to be held at Carnegie Hall, his ambitious program *Spirituals To Swing,* and thereby fueled the kind of excitement about authentic boogie that had been slowly building about Dixieland.

Ironically, it was "modernist" Benny Goodman who gave a boost to Dixieland when, as the star of the first Carnegie Hall jazz concert in 1938, he presented—just like Paul Whiteman in 1924—a segment depicting the history of jazz so far. The success of the concert not only encouraged John Hammond and many others to produce formal presentations in non-jazz auditoriums, but inspired the first viable jazz-only recording venture in the United States. The very morning after the Goodman concert, one of his guest trumpeters, Bobby Hackett, joined pianist Jess Stacy, plus the equally oblique clarinetist Pee Wee Russell and Bud Freeman (shortly to defect with Dave Tough from the Dorsey band to the Goodman band) in a studio group of Chicago-style musicians organized by Eddie Condon. The session included improvisations later titled "Carnegie Drag" and "Carnegie Jump," which appeared as a 12-inch 78 credited to "Jam Session At Commodore" on the newly-founded Commodore label. These and many similar sessions produced by Milt Gabler in the next couple of years (along with the limited editions recorded by the Hot Record Society at this period) defined the sound of Dixieland as it is still played by the fifth- and sixth-generation traditionalist musicians today.

Commodore Records rapidly broadened its horizons, cutting key sides by such players as Lester Young, Coleman Hawkins and Hawkins' erstwhile rival, Chu Berry, who died in an automobile accident in 1941. Oddly enough, the next specialty label, Blue Note (which went on to have an even more diversified and distinguished history), was also inspired by a concert, in this case Hammond's *Spirituals To Swing*. Blue Note founders Alfred Lion and Frank Wolff created the label specifically to perpetuate the concert appearance by Ammons and Lewis with 12-inch discs at the "classical" price of $1.50.

Whereas boogie-woogie inaugurated at least one other small label (Solo Art Records) and gained some coverage for these players from the major companies (Victor, Decca and, in the CBS stable, Vocalion), it was seen by most people in the music business as limited and therefore only suitable for a short craze. But the interest in traditional jazz far exceeded anyone's expectations, including those who most wanted it to become popular. It also turned out to have a built-in factionalism provoked by the differing opinions of serious-minded fans as to what constituted the "real" classic jazz. Such debate soon turned into a crusade against the evils of big-business swing music, and eventually against the even greater evil of small-group bebop.

Before 1938 was out, Hugues Panassié had capitalized on his role as a jazz authority—a role in which his precedence is still being questioned by some American writers—by visiting the U.S., hand-picking groups, and producing sessions which would be issued domestically on Bluebird. The music on these sessions, by players like Sidney Bechet (with James P. Johnson) and trumpeters Tommy Ladnier and Frankie Newton, was vital and highly influential. Everything would have been fine if Panassié had not shot off his mouth about the recordings' alleged superiority over the Eddie Condon approach to Dixieland. Condon's legendary retort ("Do we go over to France and tell the peasants how to jump on a grape?") exemplified jazz artists' age-old resentment of printed evaluations from writers-turned-impresarios like John Hammond. For better or worse, many of the jazz recording opportunities of the next few years were in the hands of just such persons.

George Avakian, then a keen journalist just out of college but destined to have a long career as a producer, persuaded Decca in 1939 to record 12 tracks by Condon and other specially-assembled white Chicagoans, to be issued as a collectors' album of six 78 RPM discs. The next year, he was allowed to follow up with a New Orleans album, which created the last of the rare studio encounters between Armstrong and Bechet plus the final recording of Johnny Dodds. For both of these albums, Avakian provided lengthy and detailed liner notes, as Blue Note had done with their initial issues. So did the young Dave Dexter, whose subsequent writing for *downbeat* overshadowed his occasional record productions and talent-spotting activities for Decca and others. Dexter created a companion volume on Kansas City jazz that focused on figures such as Eddie Durham and trumpeter Hot Lips Page (whom Armstrong's manager had bought off as possible competition for Armstrong by the simple expedient of becoming Page's manager as well). Furthermore, the token interest of major labels in the historical study of jazz, such as Vocalion's boogie-based small groups, followed the lead of the Hot Record Society by listing all the performing personnel in tiny print on the actual record labels. Columbia and Victor were soon doing the same with the entire Basie and Ellington line-ups, respectively.

There was also further acknowledgment of the traditionalist resurgence on the part of record companies. On Blue-bird, Victor recorded two Chicago-style groups who actually appeared as such in public, albeit briefly: Muggsy Spanier's Ragtimers and Bud Freeman's Summa Cum Laude band. Also in 1939, Victor did two Jelly Roll Morton sessions, and the following year they began a series of dates with Sidney Bechet. (Initially, there was no suggestion of an exclusive contract— Bechet also recorded for Blue Note, Hot Record Society and Decca's New Orleans album within the space of a few months.) Despite Bechet's already lengthy career, these early 1940s discs constituted the first comprehensive documentation of his gargantuan ability. Morton, who was in poor health and shortly to die, had been rediscovered by the folklorist Alan Lomax, whose Library of Congress interviews elicited six hours' worth of musical reminiscence and explanation (not issued to the public until a decade later). At the end of 1939, a new small label, General Records, was formed to re-create part of Morton's Library of Congress archive material for an album of five 78 RPM discs entitled *New Orleans Memories.*

Both Bechet's and Morton's band recordings of this period show the continuity of their own individuality, but also an absorption of some rhythmic aspects of 1930s jazz—like the rhythmic use of front-line "horns" in occasional riff patterns. Just as with the Lunceford band's apparently retrograde approach, when creative jazz musicians look back to an earlier style, they perpetuate it in a contemporary manner. Their producers, however, and their ultimate purchasers often look back in a much more simplistic way. Writer Charles Edward Smith, who contributed the sentimental liner notes to the *New Orleans Memories* set, was responsible (with folklorist Frederic Ramsay) for apotheosizing a whole generation of New Orleans players through the enormously influential book *Jazzmen.* Perhaps out of a feeling of guilt that King Oliver had died alone and in abject poverty while their academic research was being carried out, the authors started the search that led to the discovery of another father-figure trumpeter, Bunk Johnson. This provoked several trips to New Orleans by various amateur record producers, the first of which produced four discs of trumpeter Kid Rena featuring Alphonse Picou (creator of the famous standard clarinet solo on "High Society"). Rena's material was issued on the specially-formed Delta label, while several rival sessions with Johnson appeared on labels with crusading names such as Jazz Man, Jazz Information and American Music.

The theory behind this "return to the source" was, that if big-band swing had been hopelessly commercialized—and even white Dixieland-inclined players of the Condon ilk were not considered earnest enough or pompous enough to be accepted by the students of early jazz-record collecting—then there were musicians who had never stirred from New Orleans and who produced "real jazz." (Armstrong and Bechet were avoided as being just too vibrantly creative and alive to fit into any mere listener's concept of authenticity.) The flaw in such scholarly categorization, and the patronizing thought processes behind it, is evident by the fact that Bunk Johnson and others of his generation played in New Orleans-based swing big bands during the 1930s. Also, Johnson's original background was in the ragtime period; once he had a free choice of collaborators and of material (which was rare after his "discovery"), he preferred to perform the rags of Scott Joplin and to apply that rhythmic approach to the current pop songs of the 1940s.

Perhaps because America was being drawn into World War II, it seemed to be a good time to have enmity between different wings of the traditional jazz movement. Meanwhile, two other relevant wars took place, both involving the creators of music. Already during the 1930s, there had been several bitter disputes in various industries involving the right of trade union organization and, where that right had already been earned, about various conditions of employment. It has already been mentioned that the AF of M established basic rates of pay for performing musicians in different situations. They devoted considerable effort to ensuring that promoters and performers did not attempt to operate with fees below the union scale.

Similarly, in the Hollywood film industry, there had already been a brief strike of employees in pursuit of better conditions.

The huge increase in popularity of radio as a medium, and the amount of music used both in sponsored shows and in time-filling "sustaining programs" (such as the John Kirby Sextet's), had made broadcasting fees an important source of revenue for ASCAP. Initially, ASCAP's well-heeled publisher and songwriter members considered radio useful for plugging individual songs and promoting sales of sheet music. But as sheet-music sales started to fall, and as playing at home became less popular than absorbing piped music, ASCAP felt that the royalty rates paid by the radio networks were inadequate. After the breakdown of protracted negotiations, ASCAP withdrew permission for any of their material to be used on the air from January 1, 1941. As this included nearly everything published since 1914 (and, in the case of ASCAP's older composers, much that was written even earlier), the broadcasting industry recognized the seriousness of the threat.

Radio managements responded by identifying areas which fell outside the ASCAP net, setting up their own organization (Broadcast Music, Inc.) to administer the royalties. The areas not covered by ASCAP members, interestingly, included much so-called "minority music" such as blues, country, Latin-American and unpublished jazz items, which naturally tended to gain more air-time. There were also (less creatively on the whole) arrangements of standard material old enough to be out of copyright altogether—for instance, Sy Oliver's version of "Deep River" for Dorsey, or Harry James's "Flight Of The Bumble Bee."

Jazz-trained musicians who wished to continue live broadcasting or recording for radio transcriptions, and even those big bands which had been playing all ASCAP-registered material, were reasonably well-placed to either create acceptable versions of BMI repertoire or, as in the case of Duke Ellington —who played mainly his own compositions—to compose a new library extremely rapidly. (Ellington did so with only the assistance of his co-writer Billy Strayhorn and his son Mercer Ellington—which is how he suddenly acquired a new radio theme-tune in the shape of Strayhorn's "Take The A Train.") The stalemate lasted only nine months, so that live radio was not as hard-hit as were purveyors of printed music, and jazz emerged in a temporarily strengthened position. However, the ASCAP strike had the effect of encouraging radio stations to feature recorded material, thus reinforcing a trend that had been gaining ground since the mid-1930s—youth-oriented "disc jockeys," modeled after Martin Block and his *Make Believe Ballroom* program.

For the musicians' union, disc jockeys were the cloud no bigger than a man's hand poised over a turntable. The union's more immediate concern was the number of jukeboxes replacing bands. The objection by Bunny Berigan to jukeboxes was more on aesthetic grounds: "There's no reason in the world why some stupid son-of-a-bitch with a nickel should have the right to impose his tastes on a roomful of people." Ironically, like other popular bandleaders, Berigan was under pressure from publishers and from his record company to produce a jukebox hit. The record business had been much quicker than the union in expressing its fears about the unpaid use of its discs in public places, and as early as 1933 the International Federation of Phonographic Industries was founded to widen the legal acceptance (already gained in a few countries before that date) of the principle of reproduction rights in recorded sound. IFPI member associations had effectively been able to police the playing of records on the air in their respective countries, and to extract payment from radio stations and jukebox operators.

From the point of view of the AF of M, the key element in both the jukebox issue and the radio issue was that their members' contributions to the records threatened the livelihood of other members. Here was the "new technology" situation that had first surfaced in the Industrial Revolution. In trying to negotiate with the major U.S. record companies for a token payment per recording to be contributed to the union's pension fund, AF of M president James C. Petrillo (the "C" was for Caesar, which was exactly how his opponents and later some of his own members saw him) described musicians who made records as "digging their own graves."

When the record industry refused such compensation, Petrillo obtained the AF of M's co-operation in banning participation on all records of any kind starting from August 1, 1942. The strike was 99.9 percent solid until record companies started caving in 14 months later. One temporary expedient was the re-pressing and re-promotion of items from recent years which might have more mileage in them. For example, one of Frank Sinatra's first records with Harry James, but the last to be issued—"All Or Nothing At All"—had flopped in 1940. But now, following Sinatra's hugely successful discs with Dorsey, "All Or Nothing At All" became a hit. The same company, Columbia, then signed Sinatra when he started as a solo, non-band singer, and from June 1943, recorded him with nothing but a choir in support.*

Another expedient, more interesting from the jazz point of view, had been initiated a couple of years earlier, also by Columbia. George Avakian induced the label to repackage some historic Louis Armstrong sides from the 1920s. In the process, Columbia discovered and issued for the first time a few tracks (and some of Bessie Smith's) which had been passed over at the

---

* Sinatra's move, and consequent redoubled popularity, started the process whereby former band vocalists would outstrip the glamor of the bandleaders who had nurtured them. It has been argued that the AF of M strike delivered the coup de grace to the bandleaders, but this switch in popular taste actually started once Sinatra, a key figure of the wartime era, joined Dorsey.

time of recording. Also significant for jazz was the one authorized exception to the AF of M strike, whereby the American
armed forces were allowed to record musicians for distribution
only to those in the services. There were additional provisos:
the discs would be destroyed when the war effort had been
satisfactorily completed, and the artists would donate their performances on record entirely free. Those musicians who
agreed to record under such conditions constituted a comprehensive roster of stars from the entertainment and classical
music worlds—plus large numbers of jazz artists who would
otherwise have recorded for competing companies.

The V-Disc label ("V" standing for Victory) was directly
run by the War Department, and its sessions extended from
1942 to 1948 in practice, eventually comprising a series of 904
12-inch 78s. A few items were licensed reissues of pre-strike
commercial releases (with no royalties to artists or originating
labels), and some were transcribed direct from live radio
broadcasts. But the great majority of performances were
recorded specially for V-Discs. Jazz and big-band sessions were
produced by George T. Simon, a longtime contributor to
Metronome magazine, and performers included anyone who
was anyone. To help wed minorities like blacks to their war
work, the obvious big-band heroes were convened for V-
Discs. A good deal of more varied small-group sounds also
found a place. (The Armed Forces Radio Service's jazz-
oriented *Jubilee* show for black servicemen constituted better
treatment than what these men usually received in the armed
forces as such.) One source that provided a total of 12 tracks
issued on V-Disc was the 1944 Metropolitan Opera House
broadcast concert of an all-star group selected by *Esquire*
magazine and produced by Leonard Feather. This concert
featured not only Louis Armstrong and Jack Teagarden,
but the equally natural pairing of Coleman Hawkins and Roy
Eldridge, plus the phenomenal piano of Art Tatum.

1. The Wolverines (Bix Beiderbecke, second from right) pose in front of the acoustic sound horn at the Gennett studio, where recording had to be suspended when a train used the nearby railroad line; 1924

2. Jelly Roll Morton with electrical microphone, seen near the end of his career; c. 1939

3. Sidney Bechet plays tenor sax, bass, drums, piano, clarinet, and his favorite—soprano saxophone—on the first jazz overdubbing; April 18, 1941

4. The critic as entrepreneur: Hugues Panassié flanked by Mezz Mezzrow (clarinet) and Tommy Ladnier (trumpet) with James P. Johnson; 1938

5. Artie Shapiro (bass) and Bud Freeman (tenor), with Pee Wee Russell on cigarette, warming up for Eddie Condon's "Windy City Seven"; probably the first Commodore session following Benny Goodman's 1938 Carnegie Hall concert

6. Ben Webster, Benny Carter, Chu Berry, Coleman Hawkins with pianist Clyde Hart; the all-star sax section for Lionel Hampton's September 11, 1939 session

7. Tommy Dorsey and his Orchestra in the RCA Victor
goldfish bowl

8. Benny Goodman and sidemen assessing a playback at
Columbia studio

9. Duke Ellington in working attire; 1950s

10. Count Basie at the piano with (l to r) Buddy Rich, Freddie Green and John Simmons; August 3, 1953

11. An experiment that remained unissued for years: Benny Goodman records his sideman Charlie Christian (electric guitar) with (l to r) Lester Young, Jo Jones, Buck Clayton, Freddie Green, Walter Page and their leader, Count Basie; October 28, 1940

12. Django Reinhardt reunited in London with Stephane Grappelli, with British guitarists Allan Hodgins and Jack Llewellyn plus West Indian bassist Coleridge Goode; January 31 or February 1, 1946

13. Mary Lou Williams recording with one of several wartime
all-women groups; 1946

14. Bobby Hackett visits Louis Armstrong (right), in the studio
with producer Bob Thiele; probably 1970

15. A unique Bessie Smith session with a gospel quartet, tackling a song by Fats Waller lyricist Andy Razaf

16. This famous anti-lynching song was recorded at Columbia, to whom Billie Holiday was under contract—but they allowed Commodore to issue it rather than endorse its sentiments themselves

17. A British reissue of the ODJB hit as recorded for the small Aeolian label, incorrectly dated; Brian Rust's subsequent research obtained exact details of all ODJB sessions from Nick La Rocca's diaries

18. The end of the 78 era: Victor Feldman recorded the session in 1955 before settling in the U.S., but this track was issued late the following year

There is a strong case for saying that these players made their biggest impact on their colleagues at this period. Though widely imitated for a decade or more, they were all about to become venerated as father figures. Armstrong and Teagarden emerged in the second half of the 1940s as the figureheads of an international Dixieland movement, whereas Hawkins, Tatum and Eldridge (while honored in a more roundabout, even dismissive manner) were chief begetters of the burgeoning bebop style. Tatum, who also made a series of solo V-Discs, had the same kind of mobility on his instrument as Hawkins and Eldridge, plus a harmonic and rhythmic virtuosity which seemingly allowed him to approach a tune in any way that appealed to him. Tatum could start a phrase at any part of the bar (or even pretend to suspend the barlines altogether) and still make sense without actually skipping a beat. Such an attitude, and the sheer ability that went with it, could hardly fail to inspire musicians like Charlie Parker and Dizzy Gillespie, who were about to step onto the stage of history.

One other major influence on up-and-coming players, now often overlooked, was Duke Ellington. Gillespie called him "the master" and dedicated to him the big-band composition "Things To Come." Ellington failed to make any studio sessions for V-Disc, but was happy to have his broadcasts used. The result is that his three dozen V-Disc titles (including the *Deep South Suite*, which he never recorded commercially) constitute the first series of live Ellington performances to be preserved and officially released on disc. By the second half of this series, Duke had working for him the bassist Oscar Pettiford, who had already played with Gillespie and Parker (and on the *Esquire* All Stars concert). Pettiford seemed to be passing on the teachings of the departed Jimmy Blanton.

Blanton had died in 1942, the same year as Charlie Christian, and Christian's two short years in the spotlight with Goodman were exactly contemporaneous with Blanton's pioneering work in the Ellington band. Between them, they facilitated most of what has been played on guitars and basses ever since. In jazz terms, Blanton was the more significant because of his pivotal role in the rhythm section. His melodic "walking" lines and springy time-feeling soon rendered the concept of "rhythm guitar" redundant, and enabled pianists in the rhythm sections (guitarists, too, where they didn't drop out altogether) to combine the provocative, freely rhythmic stabs of Count Basie's accompaniment style with the colorful harmonies of Art Tatum. Blanton's influence on fellow bassists also enabled young drummers like Kenny Clarke and Max Roach to capitalize on the responsive, participatory approach of Jo Jones. Most fortunately, Blanton's arrival in the Ellington entourage coincided almost exactly with the leader's move to RCA Victor, which was still far ahead of its contemporaries in the accuracy of its recorded sound—in order to make Blanton suitably prominent in the mono mix, he had his own microphone near the bass bridge (instead of using just one mike for the whole rhythm section).

The brilliance of Ellington's ensemble textures was far better rendered on the RCA Victor recordings than on previous discs. Partly for this reason, Duke's writing of the early 1940s was a profound inspiration to the new school of thought, especially in showing that unconventional melody lines and harmonies could be made triumphantly viable. Nominating a couple of examples from this prolific period is difficult, to say the least; however, "Harlem Air Shaft" and "Ko Ko" (which sounds like the direct predecessor of Gillespie's "Things To Come," along with the Lester Young melody "Tickle Toe") summarize much of Ellington's past as well as his forward thinking. And seldom had the overlaid third-note accentuation been employed so organically as in the ensemble writing of "Ko Ko" and the last chorus of "Air Shaft."

The two long-established major labels to which Ellington and all the big names were contractually bound—RCA Victor and Columbia (CBS)—took until November 1944 before deciding, in tandem, to accept the AF of M terms. A year earlier, they had been somewhat upstaged by their aggressive young competitor Decca, which became the first large company to settle with the union and get back in business. Decca was quickly followed by two smaller but equally ambitious labels established not long before the strike, Capitol and Savoy. Both showed some interest in jazz when they resumed recording; Savoy, aiming as its name suggests at a black clientele, was especially active for much of the next two decades. Two tiny operations from the early 1940s, Keynote and Asch (the forerunner of Folkways Records), had a left-wing/folk-music orientation which, at least while the U.S. and Russia were allies, treated jazz as a sociologically significant minority music. Among the specialty labels that recommenced operations in November 1943 were Blue Note, which has survived more or less continuously to this day; Commodore, whose work became fitful as a result of Milt Gabler finding full-time employment with Decca; and Signature, founded by the young Bob Thiele (although also destined to work for Decca, Thiele had a long career as a jazz producer ahead of him).

With the end of the AF of M strike, the floodgates were open, and numerous small companies were formed to fill the breach in the majors' catalogues. Some of these were deliberately angled towards the jazz collectors' market, such as Continental. Many others were promoting black popular music in general while the war gave it a high profile, among them Philo (which soon became Aladdin) and Apollo. For the first time since the 1920s, it becomes impossible to list all the competitors looking for a piece of the action. By the end of 1945, more than 350 record labels of all kinds had signed the union agreement.

It was the best of times for the jazz musician, especially the jazz musician who was well-established. Leading figures of the traditionalist school recorded for Blue Note, Commodore and Signature (and others), while Coleman Hawkins appeared on nearly all the independent labels mentioned above. Lester Young recorded for several companies, although he was not always available, thanks to his stint with Basie and a less happy one with the U.S. Army. So did two more masters of the tenor saxophone: Don Byas, formerly with Basie in the early 1940s, and Ben Webster, who was with Ellington at the same period.

Each of these four, as well as influencing the work of the bebop generation, could be defined as "fellow-travelers" of bebop—especially if bebop was viewed as the equivalent of some Communist contagion, and several traditionalist commentators were not slow to see it in that way in the late 1940s. These musicians employed and encouraged some of bop's leading protagonists. Indeed, from the viewpoint of the period, there was no distinction (except in age) between them and the boppers. They were all "modernists," and it was only later that members of the various tendencies became aware that, especially rhythmically, the distinctions were discernible. Other influences who pointed towards bebop, but were not part of it ultimately, included Roy Eldridge and Charlie Shavers on trumpet; Trummy Young, featured trombonist with Lunceford for several years; and Nat "King" Cole who, for all his later success as a singer, was at this stage a brilliant, linear-thinking pianist.

It's interesting, though, that when the small record labels mushroomed in 1943–44, bebop did not. The reason is that as late as 1945, rhythm-section players had barely succeeded in working out the most suitable approach. The absence of recording, except of established figures for V-Discs during the AF of M strike, may have deprived us of some archaeological evidence of the faltering steps in this direction; it is a pity that the first communal work by Gillespie and Parker (in the ranks of the Earl Hines big band) was begun and finished entirely within the duration of the strike. But even the big band formed in 1944 by Hines's vocalist Billy Eckstine—which briefly contained Gillespie, Parker and other former Hines sidemen—showed little evidence of bebop on the group's initial records for DeLuxe. A year later, the picture changed somewhat as Eckstine's recordings, and those of many other bands, began to absorb the initial impact of the small-group partnership with which Dizzy and "Bird" startled New York clubgoers in the winter of 1944–45.

Early fragments of both Gillespie and Parker were already on disc before the AF of M ban, from their periods with Cab Calloway's band and the beautifully Basieish outfit of Jay McShann, respectively. Just like the first recorded appearances of Louis Armstrong with King Oliver and Fletcher Henderson, or Sidney Bechet with Clarence Williams, these vignettes immediately gained the attention of young musicians and listeners. The parallel is not perfect, of course: neither Armstrong nor Bechet was keen on reading written music unless absolutely necessary in a particular playing situation, whereas both Diz and Bird had considerable formal knowledge and allowed it to inform but not inhibit their improvisations. Yet the element of surprise, and seemingly strange new solutions to the conventional problems of improvisation, made both Gillespie and Parker appear further ahead of their time than almost anyone who had surfaced since Armstrong or Bechet.

Significantly, Gillespie and Parker played horns, i.e. wind instruments. Their ability to play with a vocalized tone, and to adopt song-like or speech-like inflections, has made horns paramount in furthering and regenerating the jazz tradition and in imparting regular infusions of the blues tradition. By comparison, the important role of the drums and bass has usually been misunderstood, even by their players, during new developments. And innovations on the piano—in the hands of

Thelonious Monk and Bud Powell, who first recorded in 1944 after the strike, with Coleman Hawkins and Cootie Williams, respectively—had a much more delayed influence. This explains to some extent why, when Dizzy and Bird began appearing separately and together on small-group discs in late 1944 and 1945, rhythm sections usually consisted of some players who understood the new language, plus some who didn't. Two examples are the sessions for Guild Records under Gillespie's name which produced his rather schematic melodies "Groovin' High" and "Dizzy Atmosphere" and, on the second occasion, the headlong "Shaw Nuff" written by Parker. A more idiomatic feel to the drumming, thanks to Max Roach, is chiefly what distinguishes Parker's own first date containing the famous "Koko" (not to be confused with Ellington's almost identical title) and his later sessions without Gillespie.

All these and other 1945 recordings demonstrate the tremendous power and vitality of Diz and Bird. Gillespie went on to become more popular and better known than his saxophone counterpart, eventually, like Armstrong, metamorphosing into an ambassador of international goodwill and bonhomie. His trumpet work, however, crackled with dark humor and fantastical phraseology that the general public found—and, without his genial personality, would have continued to find—hard to take. Musically, this was partly alleviated in two ways. First, Dizzy was interested in melodic orderliness, even if such orderliness was of a more complex nature than that of his predecessors, like Roy Eldridge. Second, he had great rhythmic gifts. Even here, there was an element of orderliness, as opposed to the seemingly intuitive feel of Parker; he studied and used Afro-Caribbean patterns, as on the famous "Night In Tunisia."*

---

* Both he and Bird recorded "Night In Tunisia" separately in 1946; Dizzy's own version was for the first bebop record album, entitled New 52nd Street Jazz (produced by Leonard Feather), wherein his four 78 RPM sides were combined with four by Coleman Hawkins.

Almost unconsciously, Gillespie was also a great anthologizer. For instance, with "Salt Peanuts," the main theme (already used in his "Little John Special" for the Lucky Millinder band) is based on a Louis Armstrong phrase from "Ding Dong Daddy" followed by a three-note figure reversing the timing of the "Snake Rag" break; the first ensemble bridge-passage is borrowed from Charlie Christian's solo on "Royal Garden Blues."

Bird, too, had an inbuilt sense of history, quoting the clarinet solo from "High Society" on "Koko" and elsewhere, using the Oliver- and Ellington-hallowed "Holy City" for his up-tempo blues "The Hymn." Parker also had a considerable interest in Latin and Afro-Caribbean music. But unlike Dizzy —who in the early 1940s wanted to become a successful freelance arranger—Bird had no great patience for organizing music on paper. His mind was so prolific that, by the time he finished writing a tune down or teaching it to somebody, he had already thought of dozens of other ways of doing it, none of them exactly simple. On some of his own recordings, he dispensed with an official opening theme altogether, as Hawkins had appeared to do in his famous "Body And Soul," while on others, he created strong yet minimal themes like "Constellation" or "Another Hair-Do." The rhythmic title of the latter exemplified the third-beat accentuations which sprang to life in Parker's improvisations in a way that was as instinctive—and as full of patterns—as Afro-Caribbean drumming. In this regard, Parker's phrasing has influenced all strata of jazz musicians (*and* Latin musicians) ever since.

More so than with the hornmen who preceded him, Bird's written themes closely reflected his improvising style. Many of them were created either just before, or even during, time spent in the recording studio—earlier jazzmen, however, were not allowed to compose on company time. Savoy and Dial, formed by a jazz record-store owner (like Commodore,

Jazz Man and others), were responsible for most of Parker's significant small-group sessions. Both labels were more than happy for him to record original material and so save them from paying publishers' royalties. Savoy's time-honored solution was to become the publisher, with Parker receiving an "advance" of $62.50 per tune in addition to two cents a copy in artist royalties. In a preliminary attempt at "Koko," the musicians are heard being halted in their allusion to Ray Noble's "Cherokee," the previously-published song whose chord pattern Bird had borrowed.* The publishing agreement with Savoy probably explains why Miles Davis's tune "Donna Lee" (based on the even older "Indiana," the first recorded item by the ODJB) was originally credited to Davis on the 78 RPM issue of Parker's recording, but later became an "official" Parker composition because he had pocketed the payment for it.

From the point of view of recorded sound, the best of the Parker Savoys (and of the Dials) were taped at New York's WOR Studio, already used by Commodore and Blue Note, and later the location of dates by Prestige and others. But in the words of Savoy producer Teddy Reig, Savoy's owner, Herman Lubinsky, "was always looking for a bargain," so sometimes cheaper facilities were booked. Lubinsky was also one of the first to make multiple use of the tracks he issued, taking items from Bird's first Savoy session—where he was a sideman for guitarist Tiny Grimes—and re-releasing them with Parker shown as the leader once Bird's star began to rise. Parker's own comment in 1950 about this news was that "Herman Lubinsky does a gang of things he's not supposed to do," while his companion Chan Richardson added, "They say he has eleven sets of books."

---

* Such borrowing had been going on for some fifteen years. But it became increasingly noticeable through the use of more individualistic sequences. Hawkins' "Stumpy" and Gillespie's "Groovin' High," for example, were both based on Paul Whiteman's first hit, "Whispering."

Ross Russell, producer and owner of Dial Records, was hardly in the same moral category as Lubinsky, but he did issue the one performance Parker would have wished to remain unreleased—the 1946 "Lover Man" that creates beauty out of despair and confusion. As a result, he saw Parker revert to recording for Savoy while legally under contract to Dial. Whether or not as a concerted plan, Dial then began to release what are now known as "out-takes"—performances recorded during a studio session which are agreed at the time to be less than satisfactory attempts at "master" versions. Already during the 1920s, it had become standard practice to aim for at least two satisfactory takes of everything recorded, so that the second could be used as an "alternate" source if the first was damaged or had some other technical defect. Sometimes these alternates were released, without any hint of the change, under the same catalogue number as the original issue. On other occasions, especially since the traditionalist revival of the 1940s, alternates were exhumed and issued for the first time (as was done, for instance, at the time of Jelly Roll Morton's death).

To complicate matters further, Dial recordings of original Parker material were not copyrighted by Dial or any other publisher at the time of recording. The individual tunes, and indeed the alternative titles assigned to some of the out-takes, could in time have generated additional revenue as they became standards recorded by others. But this was only taken care of after Parker's death when Dial sold off its material in separate batches, some to Jazztone Record Society and some to Roost. Seeking to make sense of this mess several years later, Aubrey Mayhew, the attorney of Parker's last legal wife, created Charlie Parker Records and issued several albums, registering those tunes still out of copyright for the benefit not of the Parker estate but "Mayhew Music Inc." An indication of Bird's own attitude, however—and the double-edged sword of long-term rights *versus* cash in the hand—is shown by Ross Russell's documented story of Parker assigning half of the artist royalties from his Dial sessions to his personal supplier of heroin.

Gillespie's early dealings with the record business were at least more straightforward, although the first sessions under his own name were for small companies that rapidly went out of business. Guild was sold after a year of operation to the more ambitious Musicraft, who then recorded his first big-band sessions (they also signed Artie Shaw and Duke Ellington, among others). Musicraft in turn sold these tracks to MGM Records. Since MGM only appeared interested in Musicraft's material by Sarah Vaughan, the singer who had updated the approach of Ella Fitzgerald, other Musicraft recordings gradually went into a public-domain limbo where no one worried too much about the original copyrights. As with the Parker Dials, these tracks were reissued over the years by a multitude of budget-price labels and even, in the case of the Gillespies, by Savoy.

Thanks to these business maneuvers, the financial loss to Dizzy over the years is huge if measured against an honest and ongoing royalty agreement. In 1945-6, he achieved a short-term revenge on Guild by appearing regularly on other record labels under such variegated pseudonyms as "B. Bopstein," "Izzy Goldberg" and "Gabriel." The *New 52nd Street Jazz* album was for RCA Victor, who put Dizzy under contract for two years, recording him and promoting him reasonably well. That is more than can be said of his subsequent year with Capitol, where he was expected to be the commercial figurehead of their brief flirtation with bebop.

In the decidedly inhospitable climate of the early 1950s, Gillespie became the first black musician to have his own label, named Dee Gee Records. Nevertheless, he was under pressure to produce jukebox hits in order to ensure adequate distribution for the label, the chief problem to be solved by all small independent companies. "The Champ" was his only success in this direction. Accordingly, after less than two years, Dee Gee was sold (to Savoy), and any profit that might have come from the sale went towards placating the IRS. Gillespie was subsequently able to make a steady stream of recordings, mainly under more favorable financial conditions—he survived to become an elder statesmen whose overall achievement is more significant than any single work of art.

· 5 ·

POST-WAR
DEVELOPMENTS

───────────◆───────────

I n the immediate post-war
years, when swing had lost
its hold on popular taste, the
jazz world was a different
place. For a start, it seemed irretrievably split between modernists and traditionalists. Although both sides valued the interest that the major record labels showed in documenting
jazz—a pursuit which continued sporadically until the end of
the 1940s—such documentation was gradually becoming the
task of the small companies with restricted distribution and
limited lifespans. The intended market for their issues was the
new generation of specialty white fans who had first been
turned on by swing bands and who then discovered hard-core
small-group jazz. The black populace generally recoiled from

94

this "music appreciation" approach, finding Dixieland unbearably old-fashioned and bebop uncomfortably far-out; the wartime period had at least allowed rhythm and blues to gain prominence, and this became the new black pop music.

Of course, there was no firm dividing line between R & B and contemporary black jazz, with those younger musicians already steeped in jazz finding their entry into the profession, from the post-war years onward, through R & B bands. Several established jazzmen had success with music that veered close to rhythm and blues, thanks to the jazz-oriented disc jockeys who started appearing in the mid-1940s onwards and giving equal time to modern jazz and black pop. Lester Young's "Jumpin' With Symphony Sid" and Illinois Jacquet's "Robbins' Nest" (for Fred Robbins) were not only dedicated to the deejays but were featured by them on the same basis as Louis Jordan and Billie Holiday releases.

Before forming his own seven-piece group, Illinois Jacquet was also crucial to the popularity of producer Norman Granz's Jazz at the Philharmonic series. Capitalizing on the slightly hysterical atmosphere of wartime concert performances (heard also in some of the live-broadcast V-Discs), Granz crossed over to the R & B market when 78 RPM excerpts from his mid-1940s concerts were issued, with a single jam session spread over four or six sides. He initially leased most of his product to Mercury Records, rather than working for them directly and giving them ownership of the recordings. Granz went on to create a series of studio sessions, including the albums of Charlie Parker "With Strings."*

---

* In 1944, Billie Holiday became the first black vocalist allowed to have a Europeanized orchestral backing, followed soon enough by Billy Eckstine and Nat King Cole. Bird wanted to be the first black instrumental soloist to be supported by a string section. Granz was later to claim proudly that these recordings "brought modern jazz into places it was never welcomed before, as the public heard it for the first time as pretty music."

The *Jazz at the Philharmonic* discs were sufficiently successful in sales terms to create a market for live recordings, and
to generate imitations like the "Just Jazz" series assembled by
disc jockey Gene Norman (previously involved in production
of the AFRS *Jubilee* programs) as well as the *Hollywood Jazz
Concert* and *Junior Jazz at the Auditorium* albums. (The latter is
one of the earliest instances of musicians being recorded in
concert—by Ralph Bass, later an R & B producer—with their
knowledge but without the promised payment for the issue of
the records.) Rather like the more jazz-oriented organizations
of the dying big-band era, the tours and recordings by these
all-star groups conveyed some of the genuine excitement of the
jazz itself to fans attracted initially by the atmosphere of the
event. For instance, one Jazz at the Phil concert provided a
young Clint Eastwood (director of the film *Bird*) with his first
opportunity to hear Parker in the flesh.

The importance of white big bands as a funnel through
which new jazz influences could flow to a wider audience did
not cease overnight, either. As late as 1949, Benny Goodman
and Charlie Barnet's bands (both of them recording for Capitol) incorporated some temporary bebop elements, as did Artie
Shaw, before all of these leaders were obliged to break up their
groups for lack of a sufficient public response.

Music publishers, still extremely powerful, were highly
resistant to bebop versions of popular standards. Barnet's "All
The Things You Are," briefly available in the U.S. and the UK,
was withdrawn following their protests; three years earlier, an
intended Kern memorial set of four tracks by Dizzy Gillespie
was banned before its issue, and only resurrected in the 1970s.
Nonetheless, it is easy to understand how composing a new
jazz-based melodic line on a given chord sequence would seem
more rewarding—creatively and possibly financially—than retaining the standard melody and title.

The more persevering Stan Kenton and Woody Herman were consistently influential in broadening the white audience for modern jazz sounds, with their individual blends of updated swing and younger improvising soloists. Kenton, whose initial direction came from the power-for-power's-sake aspect of Jimmie Lunceford's band, was for many years the most "progressive" of the big-band leaders. The Capitol label's aggressive promotion and brash recorded sound served him well—in fact, one texture particularly associated with him, the spread chords of a five-piece trombone section, would hardly have been so effective without Capitol's combination of depth and echo. Many of Kenton's ventures, such as the 1950–51 "Innovations in Modern Music" ensemble of 40 musicians, seem more pretentious and bombastic than Paul Whiteman ever was. Still, tracks like "Jolly Rogers" or "Young Blood" satisfactorily balance the ensemble with solos by keen second-generation beboppers.

Woody Herman, like Kenton, took over his first band back in the 1930s and achieved his first popular success with "At The Woodchoppers' Ball." This jazz perennial had a Basie-like feel and was based on the same third-note repetition as the brass riff from "Jumpin' At The Woodside." In the middle and late 1940s, Herman developed quite a flair for blending this approach with allusions to bebop, as on his version of Louis Jordan's hit "Caldonia" and its would-be Gillespiesque trumpet ensemble. Interestingly, Herman's drummer at the start of this dramatic period was the adaptable Dave Tough, and hints of third-note accentuation are heard from both Tough *and* bassist Chubby Jackson on Herman tracks such as "Apple Honey."

"Apple Honey" forcibly illustrates the post-war approach to rhythm. In previous decades, the overlaid cross-rhythms accented every third of the eighth-notes in a fairly obvious way. Yet from the bebop era onwards, this technique served as a standard resource for the underlying rhythm section instruments to draw upon, but often at a different part of the bar from each other, just as it did for the improvising front-line musicians. For listeners, the challenge of trying to respond to apparently conflicting cross-rhythms, as opposed to simple syncopations of a single figure against a steady ongoing beat, soon separated the sheep from the goats. The goats were stubbornly confident of keeping the beat in their head without losing their footing, whereas the sheep who could only respond with their feet turned to R & B or (if they were white) to second-generation Dixieland.

The other aspect of the bebop generation which affected the Herman band and many other groups, was the epidemic of heroin addiction among musicians both black and white. Although marijuana has been a fairly constant aid to players' relaxation, from Louis Armstrong onwards, alcohol was the usual crutch for those earlier jazzmen who needed one, and many addicts such as Lester Young had their lives shortened by its side effects. Billie Holiday and Charlie Parker, however, were the first highly visible performers to advertise (however unwittingly) the superior power of heroin—its ability to alter states of consciousness and turn the user into a junkie. The epidemic was so linked in the popular press with the jazz milieu that when the late-1950s experimental play *The Connection* depicted a cross-section of addicts, it included the character of a failed jazzman, plus several professionals performing music in the Charlie Parker style. Many of those who survived a period of dependency are still active today, but many others died in their youth—including ex-Herman sideman and bop baritonist Serge Chaloff, as well as the dazzling trumpeter Fats Navarro.

Fats had a bright and optimistic sound contradicted by a certain caution in the phrasing, which, while harmonically sophisticated, was rhythmically somewhat conservative and less interesting than Dizzy Gillespie's phrasing. Navarro was part-black and part-Cuban, and was sometimes to be found sitting in with Cuban bands before this practice became commonplace. This influence is not reflected in his records with the sole exception of composer Tadd Dameron's "Jahbero," based on "All The Things You Are" (but without a doubt indecipherable as such to Jerome Kern's executors). One can only regret that his short career went unnoticed, and that his earliest disciple, Clifford Brown, though admirably cleanliving, also died in his mid-twenties in a car crash.

Navarro's sometime collaborator, Bud Powell, achieved in his youth the seemingly impossible goal of conveying the urgency of bebop on the piano. Bud also wrote a few isolated Afro-Cuban pieces, of which "Un Poco Loco" is especially notable. Driven by Max Roach's cowbell cross-rhythm, which divides eight beats exactly into three, "Un Poco Loco" is a perfect blend of jazz and mambo, with dynamic improvisation based not on a chord sequence but on a single scale. No other keyboard player matched this level of energy and invention, except Earl Hines and later figures such as McCoy Tyner and Cecil Taylor. Regrettably, Powell was another of bop's ill-fated individuals, the last episode of his life forming the inspiration for the 1986 film *Round Midnight*.

Thelonious Monk was known in the late 1940s more as a writer ("Round Midnight," "52nd Street Theme," the latter recorded by both Gillespie and Powell) than as a pianist. The intensity of Monk's playing was obvious less on the performing level than on the intellectual level. His distant point of departure was the work of Art Tatum, from which he derived and schematized the principles of harmonic substitution, often sounding as if the already sparse piano of Ellington was being played with only two fingers of each hand. Powell and Monk both began recording under their own names in 1947, each creating a trio version of a favorite chord sequence of the boppers, Gershwin's "Nice Work If You Can Get It"—Bud accompanied by Max Roach, Thelonious by Art Blakey. Powell's, unfortunately, was for one of the many small companies that went out of business that year. His tracks were eventually released by Roost Records, the label founded by Teddy Reig in 1949. Monk was luckier in being invited to do three sessions in five weeks for Blue Note. Having just decided to make the switch to modernist jazz, Blue Note needed to do a lot of recording before the threatened start of the second AF of M strike—again, over scales of payment—on January 1, 1948.

Two other pianists whose careers began between the two recording bans were most influential as popularizers. Oscar Peterson and Erroll Garner shared a swing-era rhythmic approach with an ear open to the melodic lines of the beboppers. Peterson recorded his first sessions in Canada from 1945 onwards, but following his signing by Norman Granz, he went on to become the most recorded pianist of the 1950s. His first hit, "Tenderly," was sufficiently successful for him to have to repeat it note for note at a 1952 Jazz at the Phil concert. Erroll Garner, on the other hand, had already had a hit record in 1945 with another slow ballad, "Laura," as done for Savoy; he turned out a huge amount of music for the rest of the decade, working for dozens of small labels. In 1950, Garner obtained an exclusive contract with Columbia, re-recording "Laura" almost right away (this was well-timed, since from the 1940s on, contracts usually called for material not to be covered by the same artist within a five-year period). Garner was prolific at individual sessions, often taping 20 tunes or more in an afternoon. During a long dispute with producer Mitch Miller, when an album of such marathon recordings was issued without his consent, Garner set an important test case in asserting the artist's right of approval or rejection of his own performances.

The second AF of M ban, of course, found the managements of individual record labels better prepared. Any artists under contract were encouraged to stockpile as much of their repertoire as the label considered necessary before the deadline, with studios and engineers eventually working 'round the clock right up to midnight on December 31. Naturally, the major companies were more able to make investments of this kind, since most studios and pressing plants belonged to them but were rented out to small independent labels. When the strike became effective, the majors were also more cunning in finding ways around it. They were able to finance the recording of backing discs for some of their vocalists in Mexico or even in London, where the musicians had no common cause with AF of M members whose imported "hit-parade" discs were more and more squeezing out their own local product. RCA, noting the response to the jazz/Afro-Cuban fusion generated by Dizzy Gillespie's work for them, began domestically releasing the mambos originally intended for the Cuban home market by Perez Prado. Although they had less need this time around, the majors also checked their vaults for material worth re-releasing or which had been overlooked for some reason. RCA, for instance, discovered an unissued Sidney Bechet version of "12th Street Rag" (which had become a hit in the deliberately corny rendition by ex-Casa Loma trombonist Pee Wee Hunt) and bought up the privately-recorded discs of Louis Armstrong's Town Hall Concert from the previous year.

An interesting development was that many of the specialty jazz labels did some new recording during the strike. Teddy Reig said long afterwards, "You have to remember that in the first ban there were very few independent labels . . . [The musicians] didn't gain anything from the first ban. The musicians—the jazz guys—said the hell with it and made records anyway." Reig's own occasional productions during the second ban included some sessions in Detroit and the Bird classic "Parker's Mood." Norman Granz did some of the recording for a mail-order album set called *The Jazz Scene* which included some undercover Ellington, some entirely un-accompanied Coleman Hawkins and Parker's longest studio track to date, entitled "The Bird." Blue Note recorded Monk again and Navarro twice (including "Jahbero"). At least one company—Sittin' In With, the second of many independent ventures by young enthusiast Bob Shad—seems to have been founded expressly to steal a march on other labels, large and small. Another relevant development was the issue of three 78s of Charlie Parker guesting at a Dizzy Gillespie concert in Carnegie Hall. The totally unauthorized nature of the record-ing (apparently taken from the hall's P.A. system) was tacitly admitted by the absence of the players' names and by the very name of the pirate label, Black Deuce. Presumably Teddy Reig, as co-producer of the concert, knew something of the owner-ship of the source material, for it was reissued on the Roost label after Parker's death.

All of this activity seemed remote from the concerns of the major labels. Columbia's effort to disguise the lack of agree-ment with the AF of M was the launch of their first 33⅓ RPM long-playing microgroove albums in July 1948. Not long after, RCA brought out its competing 45 RPM records. Although both slower speeds and pressing on vinyl rather than shellac guaranteed superior reproduction to the 78, the seven-inch extended-play sides only lasted about twice as long as a 78. At least there were no exclusive patents involved: the 33⅓ RPM speed had been in use since the early days of film soundtracks, before adoption of the optical method. 33⅓ had also been the standard speed for both radio transcription discs and publicly-licensed background-music services like Muzak.

As early as 1932, RCA had released a few 33⅓ RPM items consisting of medleys of hits by Ellington and others, but since this was during the depths of the Depression, what seemed like a bright idea went nowhere. However, Columbia had cut all of their sessions since 1939—particularly with a view to

European classical music, but to all other material, too —at 33⅓, recording at 78 RPM for the issued versions. As a result, even before the days when recording on tape became standard, Columbia had a series of long-play performances ready for issue. After a year or so of heavily promoted competition between RCA and Columbia, the obvious fact was established throughout the industry: 45s were suitable for short pieces and for microgroove issues of "singles," whereas 10-inch and 12-inch 33⅓ discs (lasting up to 15 and 25 minutes per side) were ideal for longer works.

The initial impact of this development on jazz recording was virtually nil. Although a few jazz musicians had contravened the wishes of the AF of M during the strike, they were not rewarded when the record companies agreed to higher scales for individual sessions in November 1948. The greater cost of recording started a gradual trend towards concentration of both production and promotion resources on material that could sell in high quantities, and towards the eventual marginalization of jazz in the industry. At the end of the strike, jazz was already a much lower priority than it had been in 1943. For instance, Count Basie, though still under contract, was not invited to record for another five months; Armstrong (who did not even have a recording contract by this stage) and Ellington were not allowed back into the studio until September 1, 1949.

The major labels did not lose interest in jazz entirely. On the contrary, they discovered a demand for jazz at 33⅓ and 45 RPM which could be fed by reissues, with superior sound, of earlier 78s. Few producers considered the possibility that jazz might be capable of creating its own long works, although Columbia did have Ellington record the marvelous "Tattooed Bride" in late 1950 and "Harlem" a year later, in each case alongside his new extended arrangements of earlier pieces. Columbia's enthusiasm for the LP format was bolstered by the issue for the first time in 1950 of Benny Goodman's *Carnegie*

Hall Concert of 1938. Recorded privately by Albert Marx (who was now running the small Discovery label), this best-seller was edited to fit on four 25-minute sides, and it captured the public's imagination as an event that might have been made for the long-playing record.

This was the start of a 1950s swing-era revival—not at the live concerts and on the dance floors where the action had once been, but in the home. Television was beginning to supplant radio, with the high-fidelity record-player already on the horizon. Nostalgia for one form of jazz induced a vicarious glow, whereas the traditionalist revival had appealed to those too young to have need of nostalgia. The Carnegie Hall release has been in print almost continuously for 40 years; its initial success led to follow-ups of historic material, such as a Goodman *Treasure Chest* of late 1930s broadcasts, which Benny himself had recorded off the air. Similar albums from RCA poured forth— broadcasts from Tommy Dorsey, Glenn Miller and Artie Shaw, plus Fats Waller transcription material. The mid-1950s response of the film industry, in the shape of Glenn Miller and Benny Goodman biopics, also popularized the process of re-recording original big-band arrangements (sometimes even with the former band members who had now become versatile sessionmen), a practice which continues to the present day.

While the first deliberately conceived live recording may have been done in 1940 by pianist Art Hodes, probably the earliest retrospective issue of unreleased but historic sounds was a 1946 78 RPM album of the late Charlie Christian jamming with Thelonious Monk and Kenny Clarke at Minton's in Harlem. In the later 1950s, Columbia even discovered on one of their early 33⅓ RPM duplicates some informal studio playing by Christian, which they issued for the first time as "Blues In B" and "Waitin' For Benny." A couple of years later, Charlie's contribution to the *Spirituals To Swing* concerts was released in album form. With the release in the early

1970s of all the Goodman alternate takes, many broadcasts on which he appeared and a 15-minute jam session, Christian became the earliest of the prematurely deceased jazzmen to have his recorded output so significantly expanded after his demise.

Until the boom in albums of reissued 78s which occurred during the middle and late 1950s, there was little consolation for fans of early classic jazz—the reissues on 78 which had been trickling from the major companies dried up at the beginning of the LP era. As a result, one or two new bootleg labels appeared, specializing not in newer live recordings, but in dubbed copies of rare 78s from the 1920s, often credited pseudonymously. When it came to the attention of RCA that material owned by them had been pirated by "Label X," they sued retailers and distributors in order to get the pressing withdrawn; ironically, evidence was offered in court by the defendants that the pressing plant used to produce the offending discs was RCA's own! A happy outcome was that the editors of *Record Changer* magazine, Orrin Keepnews and Bill Grauer, programmed a series of official RCA reissue albums (some including the use of alternate takes) which came out as 10-inch LPs released on RCA's "X" label. In 1953, Keepnews and Grauer also started Riverside Records, one of the companies which, before moving on to modern jazz the next year, was founded in order to record new material by traditionalist players like ex-Bunk Johnson sidemen Jim Robinson and George Lewis.

For the next decade or more, it became the accepted orthodoxy, especially in Europe and eventually Japan, that Bunk Johnson's survivors epitomized what was most authentic about New Orleans jazz. Non-American white revivalists like Chris Barber started from this premise. By the early 1950s, other bandleaders who had started out before the George Lewis hegemony had moved on either to modern jazz or to extensions of Dixieland and small-group swing. Humphrey

Lyttelton, for instance, spearheaded a short-lived collaboration with UK-based calypsonians.

The renewed interest in recording swing-era improvisation was boosted by several sessions taped in December 1953. Norman Granz's Clef label held a two-day marathon by Art Tatum leading to a series of solo albums, plus group dates with veterans like Roy Eldridge, Lionel Hampton and Ben Webster. Almost simultaneously, the Vic Dickenson Septet inaugurated the jazz series of another former folkmusic label, Vanguard Records—produced by John Hammond. This introduced to a wider audience the U.S.'s first important young white swing-era extensionist, Ruby Braff. The Buck Clayton Jam Session on Columbia (produced by George Avakian with Hammond) featured extended solo work by big-band sidemen mostly of an earlier generation, backed by all of the original Basie rhythm section except the Count himself. Soon, many dates with such players backed by "modern" rhythm men, especially bassists, were being recorded, with none of the resulting music doing violence to anyone's stylistic continuity.

These sessions and their numerous follow-ups helped to rehabilitate the "mainstream" of stylistic approaches born in the 1930s, revitalizing a mode recently squeezed in the enmity between traditionalist and modernist fans. The recording opportunities all used the microgroove technology that allowed individual numbers to last five, ten, or twenty minutes. This freedom was in turn aided by the new practice of recording everything on reel-to-reel tape rather than on acetate disc, an innovation which—along with the new generation of German-made microphones—was one of the more beneficial by-products of World War II. Until the mid-1950s, however, the great majority of bebop-derived jazz was still being recorded as it had been in the mid-1940s, before the advent of these new techniques.

Two of the underground influences of the turn of the decade—recordings by Miles Davis and pianist/theorist Lennie Tristano—were cut with only 78 RPM issue in mind during Capitol's brief involvement with bebop. In each case, some tracks remained unreleased until appearing on microgroove a few years later. Even one of the original issued tracks by Tristano, "Intuition," would have stayed on the shelf but for the efforts of Symphony Sid in broadcasting the test-pressing, which had been rejected by Capitol as being too "way-out." Certainly, this unpremeditated group improvisation was as far removed from bebop as it was from the collective improvisation of New Orleans jazz and from that to come in the 1960s. It was also somewhat less interesting than the normal work of Tristano and his key disciple, alto saxophonist Lee Konitz, in which they attempted rather cerebral extrapolations of the harmonic and melodic shapes of bop. Their work was fatally undermined by the deliberate isolation of the cross-rhythms of contemporary (and indeed, earlier) black jazz. Both Konitz, who remained active, and Tristano, who did not, affected the occasional individualist such as Paul Desmond and Bill Evans. Thanks to both Desmond and Evans, Konitz's and Tristano's serpentine solos slowly became more widespread from the 1960s onwards.

Their other 1949 session together, set up to feature Konitz but issued as being Tristano's (without either of them giving their consent), launched Bob Weinstock's New Jazz label. New Jazz quickly evolved into Prestige Records, the stable of so many key figures of the later 1950s, including Miles Davis. Miles's Capitol recordings, however, were immediately influential among a coterie of musicians and, as a result, were eventually overpraised by writers. When the tracks were reissued on a 12-inch LP in 1956, they were given the album title *Birth of the Cool*, and it has designated both the music and the band ever since.

The young Davis had just left Charlie Parker's quintet when he became involved in the *Birth of the Cool* project, one of the many detours (or, as some would say, blind alleys) of a fascinating career. Miles had perfected the first of his frequently-imitated trumpet styles: an almost vocal, laid-back sound far removed from Dizzy Gillespie, and deriving rather from Lester Young and Bix Beiderbecke. By an odd coincidence, the instrumentation of the medium-sized *Birth of the Cool* band closely resembles that of the eight- and nine-piece groups in which Frank Trumbauer featured Bix on "Singin' The Blues" and others. The oppressively detailed, bottom-heavy arrangements have a surface similarity, too, except that this time it was the harmonic language of bebop that was being overelaborated. Indeed, it was as an arrangers' workshop that this band was first conceived and is best remembered. It helped focus the talents of John Lewis (formerly with Gillespie), Gil Evans (who had scored Parker tunes and Miles's "Donna Lee" for the innovative Claude Thornhill dance band) and Gerry Mulligan—all of whom went on to longer-lasting things.

There was a brief period in the early and mid-1950s when Cold War politics and "cool" jazz seemed to go hand in hand, and when anything played hand on heart (i.e. most of the creative black jazz) was willfully ignored. Once again, just as when the majority population had tired of hearing bad news in the mid-1930s, it became possible for jazzmen of the white persuasion to achieve some wide popularity. As well as those whose only ambition seemed to be emulating the *Birth of the Cool* band, such as Shorty Rogers, one of the chief architects of cool jazz came to the fore in the person of Gerry Mulligan. A couple of his early 1950s sessions perpetuated the slightly ponderous arranging style he had contributed to Davis's group (ironically, scores he wrote for Kenton and other big bands were simpler), but the sound for which he became famous was spare and almost light-hearted by comparison. The combination of Chet Baker's trumpet and Mulligan's baritone saxophone with the sole accompaniment of bass and drums on originals such as "Bernie's Tune" and "Walkin' Shoes" not only caught the public's imagination, but helped found another new independent label.

Pacific Jazz was formed by Richard Bock, formerly with the Discovery label. To distribute the original singles and LPs by Mulligan, Bock operated on the same principle as small R & B labels like Atlantic—i.e., he delivered the stock to local retailers in the trunk of his car. He also avoided the cost of hiring either major studios or radio-station facilities by holding his first sessions in the home of a sound-engineer friend, and solved one or two other problems by seeing some of the creative uses of recording on tape. Speaking of Chet Baker's early technical deficiencies, Bock said, "When we made the first quartet records he was still pretty immature and I had to do a lot of editing and splicing to make up complete solos without any fluffs."

Editing of a primitive kind had been available before tape, and had been employed on some of the Jazz at the Phil and Just Jazz issues. But such editing required playing back copies of the original recording on two different turntables, and split-second timing in stopping one turntable and starting the other while cutting the master disc "live." Now it became absurdly easy for any producer with a musical ear and a steady hand on the razor blade to alter the order of, or even omit, solos during longer performances, as George Avakian did on the Buck Clayton Jam Sessions. One could also alternate between sections of different takes of a piece, provided that any differences of tempo were undetectable. (Paul Desmond once wrote of Avakian, "George usually smiles serenely through the most disastrous takes imaginable, hoping that something good will somehow happen and he'll be able to splice it in later.") This method was particularly useful for perfecting ensemble arrangements, where in earlier days, even minor flaws in performances with perfectly adequate solo work had necessitated recording a whole new take. Now, rather than re-do the whole piece, with inspiration gradually dwindling in the solo passages, it was sufficient just to re-record the offending ensemble section.

Another creative facility offered by tape was what was then known as "multi-tracking." With two tape machines or with the new two-track machines, it was possible to record a whole performance and embellish it afterwards while playing back the original. After the commercial success of "over-dubbing" in the hands of former jazz guitarist Les Paul, this technique had been used by Tristano on a 1951 single for his own short-lived Jazz label. Overdubbing also figured on the 1953 debut album of saxophonist Teo Macero, who five years later—after understudying for Avakian—began his career as a renowned producer for Miles Davis, Ellington and others.

The two established jazz producers who raced to find applications for overdubbing were Avakian and Bock, with the latter (now able to afford the high-fidelity Capitol Studios) creating a 1954 album of Chet Baker as a vocalist accompanying himself on trumpet for one number. Even on the other pieces, voice and trumpet were not performed at a single sitting. Consequently, a year later, Bock could easily remove Baker's vocal from one of the alternate takes and substitute the clarinet of Jimmy Giuffre. Bock included this track on an instrumental-only sampler album—one of the earliest of its kind, and compiled from unissued takes—called *Jazz West Coast*. Avakian's East Coast response was to have Louis Armstrong back *his* vocal with a trumpet obbligato on a track of *Plays W.C. Handy*, an early example of the LP devoted to a single composer.

The new conservative jazz emanating from Los Angeles, and much imitated elsewhere, was frequently rather jolly and uncomplicated, like the white jazz of the 1920s. At the same time, the music could have a wan and even cerebral side, enabling transparent-toned Swedish saxophonist Lars Gullin to find favor with U.S. fans for a cool minute. West Coast jazz was also celebrated in the popular press, with first Mulligan and then Baker being written up in *Time* magazine, while Dave Brubeck went one better as the first jazz musician to appear on its cover. He, too, had helped start a small label which soon became part of Fantasy Records.

Brubeck also benefited from the use of tape. By the early 1950s, it was possible to buy home reel-to-reel machines which were far more flexible than the so-called portable disc recorders that had captured the Charlie Christian jams and other sessions at Minton's, or the early Jazz at the Phil concerts. The first widely successful albums of Brubeck's quartet with Paul Desmond were taped at concerts in 1952–53, where an onstage recorder was stopped and started by Brubeck himself. The same technique was used by Charles Mingus and Max Roach for the *Jazz at Massey Hall* concert, at which they played and which immortalized the last public reunion of Parker, Gillespie and Bud Powell. Of course, Brubeck's later albums were more impressive in the eyes of many commentators, but he might never have had the chance to make them were it not for the buzz created by the early live albums.

The main problem with Brubeck at this stage was that his rhythm section was unintentionally heavy and stiff, while the progressive element on which the performers prided themselves consisted of pseudo-Baroque counterpoint of a distinctly unpolyrhythmic nature. Much other West Coast music of the period fell into the same trap, being played and written by ex-big-band musicians whose main ambition was to earn a comfortable living as sessionmen in the film and television studios, working with totally non-jazz music. To be sure, Shorty Rogers was commissioned to arrange some sequences of *The Wild One* and *The Man with the Golden Arm* (whose respective motorcycle-thug and drug-addict themes gave later film directors the cue to link jazz with crime). Nonetheless, the average movie score was still based firmly on 19th-century European music. As a consequence, even the off-duty work of the sessionmen was not exactly overflowing with the influence of the blues. Indeed, at this period, musicians such as Rogers or Jimmy Giuffre could only get close to blues by making fun of it—as on "Block Buster," credited pseudonymously to "Boots Brown."

This type of jazz was, of course, not all that was happening on the West Coast. But it was getting onto more and more records because it was selling. As a result, its faults were not restricted to the Californian context. Many albums recorded in New York were done the same way: cute arrangements of the old standard pop-songs and conveyor-belt originals, nearly always with eight three-minute tracks per 10-inch disc or, on the 12-inch discs that became the norm from 1955 onwards, with 12 tracks, retailing at $3.95 and $4.95, respectively. Especially with the new pictorial album covers and written blurbs occupying the back cover, the format seemed acceptable for popular material, whether new or reissued. It also worked for earlier jazz, though the stronger the material, the harder it was for younger listeners to digest a whole album of 78s end to end.

The production of new jazz material on this basis showed the severe limitations of most arrangers and composers, and also unnecessarily restricted those soloists who would have been capable of playing at greater length. It is hardly surprising that the creative black jazz of the 1950s on record tended to consist of simpler arrangements and longer tracks. Many of these averaged around five minutes; with Blue Note and to some extent Prestige, items were excerpted from their album sessions to be released as singles for jazz radio play and for jukeboxes in black areas.

Radio and jukebox play, though, was hardly the aim with the Modern Jazz Quartet; their music and their marketing was squarely targeted to the intellectual white audience. The MJQ's efforts eventually inspired a premature fusion with symphonic performers in the movement known as "third stream." With original material and Baroque-style arrangements crafted by John Lewis, the Modern Jazz Quartet often sounded like a musically superior version of what the Brubeck quartet was driving at. Fortunately, their stance tilted away from total preciosity, thanks to the lyrical and blues-inflected playing of Milt Jackson on vibes. The MJQ's early work, in which the solid virtues of bassist Percy Heath were matched with drummer Kenny Clarke, balanced the disparate backgrounds of Lewis and Jackson on classics like "Django," a tribute to the deceased guitarist. Clarke had spent part of a year in 1948 with Lewis residing in Paris; he eventually followed the example of Don Byas and Sidney Bechet, who had settled in Europe after World War II, by moving there permanently in 1956.

Before relocating to Europe, Kenny Clarke had been a key player in Prestige's and Savoy's move toward the bebop equivalent of mainstream jam sessions. Four or even fewer tunes would fill a whole album, extended versions by a quintet or sextet; often, the group would be assembled just for one session. This collection of musicians would be unnamed or officially leaderless; the Savoy album *Opus De Jazz*, which featured Kenny and Milt and which has since been reissued with Jackson as leader, took its name from the Horace Silver piece "Opus De Funk." Like many musicians, Silver has pointed to specific records as formative listening experiences, like Tommy Dorsey's "Boogie Woogie" and Earl Hines's "On St. Louis Blues." Along with Clarke, Silver was often a member of the all-purpose New York session rhythm section in 1954–55—as was Percy Heath, before they both became too heavily committed to touring with the Jazz Messengers and the MJQ, respectively. The other vital figure in the proliferation of the spontaneous-sounding "blow-ing session" album was a no-nonsense recording engineer, Rudy Van Gelder. A former optometrist of equal aural accuracy, Van Gelder set up his first studio (in Hackensack, just outside New York City) in his own living room. From 1953 onwards, he was favored by Blue Note, Prestige and Savoy for his strikingly spa-cious but detailed sound.

One of the few long-lasting jazz series not involving Van Gelder was started in 1955 by Atlantic Records. Atlantic moved into jazz when Nesuhi Ertegun joined the family (brother Ah-met was already producing highly successful R & B with artists like the jazz-associated singer Big Joe Turner). The son of a ca-reer diplomat, Nesuhi had in the 1940s recorded traditionalists for the Jazz Man label, then began doing albums by Shorty Rogers, Lennie Tristano, the Jazz Messengers and, for nearly two decades, the Modern Jazz Quartet.

Both the MJQ and the Messengers were initially co-operatives, each with no leader but with a musical director. Horace Silver's involvement in the latter group led to both him and drummer Art Blakey eventually signing long-term contracts with Blue Note Records. Silver and Blakey culti-vated the roots of a trend drawing on the ideas of "funk" and "soul." These words became marketable as defining the links between post-bop and the broader spectrum of black music, including blues, rhythm and blues, and especially gospel. Some years before such marketing—designed for a white au-dience sated with the West Coast sound—Silver's new blend was reawakening the interest of blacks who had turned away from jazz in the dazzling glare of early bebop.

The reasons are clear from Silver's first quintet album, featuring fellow members of the Messengers. "Doodlin'" is a 12-bar blues so basic that one of its cover versions was by a catalyst of 1950s vocal music, Ray Charles. Its catchy theme is a figure that repeats on every third beat; Blakey, in his highly melodic drum solo, accentuates every third half-beat (i.e. eighth-note) several times. On Silver's own accompaniment to the theme of "The Preacher," his piano might just as well be a gospel-music tambourine; an implied eight-to-the-bar feel is contrasted with a bass-line harking back to the two-to-a-bar of Jimmie Lunceford and early New Orleans. It's especially a polyrhythmic kick to hear Blakey using third-beat accentuations in some of his backings to Clifford Brown (for instance, "Split Kick" and "Confirmation") on the earlier Blakey quintet session *A Night at Birdland.* *

A mere few weeks after the Birdland session, Clifford Brown co-led the first live date of the other main mid-1950s drummer-oriented group, the Max Roach/Clifford Brown Quintet. Roach, too, referred to third-note accentuation in his solo contribution to "Clifford's Axe" and (appropriately) "All God's Children Got Rhythm," as well as displaying his usual interactive style of accompaniment to others' solos. The Roach/Brown Quintet went on to make a fine series of studio sessions for a new jazz subsidiary of Mercury Records, started by Bob Shad, who was now on the label's staff. This connection may be the reason why all the famous originals written by Brown—including "Daahoud" and "Joy Spring"—were registered with an in-house publishing company, Brent Music. Brownie's former colleague, Benny Golson, who later composed "I Remember Clifford," had his "Junior's Arrival" (a.k.a. "Step Lightly") recorded by Brown/Roach, only to see it unreleased for 20 years because he insisted on retaining the publishing rights himself.

Drummer/journalist Art Taylor, who worked with many of the musicians mentioned in this chapter, has pointed out

---

* *A Night at Birdland* was the longest specifically-commissioned live recording to be originally released as a series of three 10-inch LPs. Nearly five years later, Blakey went one better and did three 12-inch LPs in one evening at Paris's Club St. Germain, with an edition of the Jazz Messengers that featured Clifford Brown follower Lee Morgan.

that Golson and Horace Silver were among the earliest jazz composers to form independent publishing companies and insist on handling all their own material. One of Golson's saxophone influences, Lucky Thompson, had already done so in the late 1940s. Duke Ellington, after breaking with Irving Mills, had founded a small organization to register those obscure instrumental works which the standard publishers considered uninteresting compared to his song output. Around the same time as Silver, Charles Mingus and Max Roach started an in-house imprint for material on their own Debut Records, the only reasonably long-lived label of the 1950s to be owned and run by musicians.*

Interestingly, when Bob Shad left Mercury, he formed Time Records and issued a compilation that included two incomplete alternate takes of Clifford Brown done for Mercury. Shad's later venture, Mainstream Records, put out in 1972 an entire album of Brown/Roach material, disguising the fact that some of it had already appeared on Mercury (and that all of the recordings might be considered to have belonged to Mercury). Mainstream claimed that "a contract was signed [with Roach], including a royalty arrangement for Clifford Brown's widow."

Aside from Brown, the other important soloist featured by the Roach quintet—and one of the most significant of the decade—was Sonny Rollins. As well as dismantling and reassembling some of Parker's methods, Rollins enjoyed special relationships with several other drummers on record. Using first Blakey and then Roach on his own albums, he went on to work in one-off situations with Shelly Manne (who, like Gerry Mulligan, was seemingly untainted by his identification with the West Coast), with Philly Joe Jones, then Elvin Jones. Elvin

---

* When Debut ran into trouble and disappeared from circulation, Mingus assisted the reissue of the original tapes by selling them as a form of alimony —by contrast with a small 1970s label which foundered when a "marriage partner" denied the label owner further access to his stock of records.

played on Rollins's stunning live set *A Night at the Village Vanguard,* and the chemistry between the two excited Blue Note so much that they delayed release of *Newk's Time* — a session with Philly Joe that had been recorded six weeks earlier — until a year after the Village Vanguard album.

Prior to this, Rollins had been under contract to Prestige. Though the difference was perhaps less noticeable with such a confirmed improviser as Rollins, there was a marked difference of approach between Blue Note's producers and Prestige's. Alfred Lion of Blue Note paid for pre-recording rehearsals by the performers; according to Rudy Van Gelder, he "did his homework better than anyone. He'd come to a date with the musicians rehearsed and he'd know the precise routine for everything. Bob Weinstock was a lot looser. His approach was always very low-key." Without ever implying that he didn't know what was going on musically, others have pointed out that Weinstock's shrewdness was of a different order. Post-Parker altoist Jackie McLean described Prestige this way, but his comments could apply just as to many independent labels, particularly in R & B and rock and roll: "They give you a little bit of front money, and then they tell you about the royalties you are going to get after the record is released . . . But all they ever do when you go to them and ask them for some money you figure you've got coming to you, they just tell you that things are bad, that this or that album didn't do too good." In order to terminate a Prestige contract, Thelonious Monk had to pay the company's undefrayed expenses ($108.27). All too often, this meant, as with McLean, that "I paid for the whole thing: engineers, the notes on the back of the album, the color photograph, the whole thing, out of my money."

Miles Davis, who indirectly introduced both McLean and Rollins to Prestige, recorded for both Prestige and Blue Note, with an exclusive Prestige contract from 1954–56. This arrangement allowed all the original material Miles recorded to be published by Prestige Music, which presented no inter-personal problems if he used tunes by Rollins ("Oleo," "Out Of The Blue") or by McLean ("Dr. Jackle," "Dig") because they were eventually offered contracts, too. But the same thing that had happened to Miles's own "Donna Lee" now happened with Eddie Vinson's pieces "Four" and "Tune Up," as well as with John Coltrane's "Vierd Blues" (a.k.a. "Trane's Blues," which Trane had already recorded under yet another title). These titles officially became Miles Davis compositions, published by Prestige and still owned by Prestige's successors. In Miles, Weinstock had almost met his match. A later Wein-stock employee, producer Bob Porter, has written that "Miles would stare blankly at Weinstock, and Weinstock would stare sweetly at Davis, and not a word would be exchanged for 20 minutes! It was a question, eventually, of Miles trying to con money out of Weinstock, and Bob trying to con more sides out of Davis."

The outcome of these conferences was that, to fulfill his obligations to Prestige, Miles recorded two 1956 sessions con-sisting of an almost non-stop performance by his quintet. In addition to getting the job out of the way as quickly as possible, Miles used this situation to diminish the normally tense atmo-sphere of the recording studio—as he had done in 1954, when he taped "Blue Haze" with all the studio lighting turned off. Davis organized his sets as if he were on the bandstand and ignoring any applause, as was his wont.

The two dozen tracks were spread over four-and-a-bit albums which Weinstock released gradually over a period of five years. The first two albums were sequenced to reflect the informality of the occasion: *Cookin'* consisted of the last five numbers in the order they were recorded, with the opening trumpet notes of "When Lights Are Low" almost overlapping the cymbal which closes "Tune Up." *Relaxin'* went so far as to include fragments of the musicians' conversation (in the manner of the contemporary Eddie Condon jam-session albums for Columbia). The musicians in this henceforth legendary quintet exerted an enormous influence in the coming years—not only John Coltrane, who was still in 1956 searching for his mature style, but the members of the rhythm section. Red Garland took the widely popular step of wedding the Bud Powell style with the prebop (two-to-the-bar) approach of Erroll Garner and Ahmad Jamal; Philly Joe Jones and Paul Chambers immediately became the most in-demand drummer and bassist for free-lance recording sessions.

Miles himself had refined his trumpet work since the late 1940s, so that it was more intense, more terse, more lyrical and more gripping. In addition, he treated his carefully selected repertoire of standard songs and bebop classics of ten years earlier with a good deal of freedom. If Miles had, like Beiderbecke, died within a few years of his first classic records, he would still be celebrated for them, but celebrated as a doomed loser. Davis, however, had emerged from a period of heroin addiction ready to take on the music business and win. A year before the conclusion of his Prestige contract, his quintet had begun recording, without Prestige's permission, for a major label, rather than waiting until he was technically free.

George Avakian at Columbia not only re-signed artists like Ellington, Armstrong, Condon and Buck Clayton in the 1950s. He also kept a keen eye on those jazzmen who were winning a broader reputation in the modernist field, picking up Brubeck, Blakey and the trite-and-polite trombonists J.J. Johnson and Kai Winding after their successes on small independent labels. Columbia's invitation to Miles came (as did Ellington's) after an impressive—and newsworthy—appearance at the recently founded Newport Jazz Festival. This annual event, like the college concerts of Brubeck and others, was helping to focus the renewed respectability of jazz; the only Miles track issued on Columbia before the completion of his Prestige commitment was used to illustrate the recorded lecture by composer/conductor Leonard Bernstein (another sign of the times) called *What Is Jazz?*

But Miles had a special project in mind with Columbia, one dear to his heart, much like his recordings with strings were dear to Charlie Parker. This would be a reunion with *Birth of the Cool* arranger Gil Evans. Davis's collaboration with Evans led to a famous series of big-band albums that a smaller label would clearly have been unable to finance. On the other hand, as Gil said to me when noting the contributions of the New York sessionmen involved, "It didn't cost them that much. We did the whole album [*Miles Ahead*] in four three-hour sessions with no rehearsal. The reason we could do it, I guess, was because the musicians all were so familiar with the style. So a man like Ernie Royal, he could just play the lead on those things exactly the way you wanted it." What Miles recalled about the album was that it was initially marketed as a middle-of-the road mood-music album: "The first time it came out, it had a white woman with a little boy on the cover . . . I told 'em to take it off."

Although the later *Sketches of Spain* was allowed to go over budget in terms of studio time, Evans has pointed out that he got a total payment of $500 for writing that particular album; even back in the 1930s, arrangers were often receiving $75 per three-minute track. Columbia has had almost continuous revenue from *Sketches* for over 30 years, and by 1980, the album was reckoned to have sold a million copies.

Gil naturally pays tribute to the work of Davis himself at the period of *Miles Ahead*: "He was just beginning to play in a sustained style. When he played a slow tune, usually he played it in a mute. But to play open and on the flugelhorn too, it wasn't easy for him to do the first time, it was a tough challenge."*

Miles Ahead also marked the point at which Davis became more conscious than ever before that an album could be not merely the documentation of a developing soloist or group, but an artifact. Previously, the amount of material recorded, or the conditions under which it was recorded, were less in his control; now Miles could have a large say in what was taped and how much it was issued. Typically, he became less conservative and more adventurous in the studio, crafting one of the most influential albums of all time. The 1959 *Kind of Blue* album, though possibly overvalued like *Birth of the Cool*, is extraordinary because it combines a regular, organized small-group with the recording circumstances of the typical blowing session. Miles's compositional contributions—so skeletal that they placed enormous reliance on the input of the other performers—were first seen by those players during the course of the recording session itself.

---

* It should be noted that recent reissues of *Miles Ahead* include, unannounced, some portions of inferior alternate takes. All the tracks except "The Duke," "My Ship," "Blues For Pablo" and "The Meaning Of The Blues" show slight differences from the original issued versions, mainly during Miles's solos. Since this album, too, was produced by George Avakian, these inferior takes could represent complete unedited performances, as they were before Avakian spliced in passages from other takes.

· 6 ·

FREE JAZZ
AND THE
AVANT-GARDE

———————◆———————

I f anything underlined the
late-1950s consolidation of
bebop—or "hard bop," as
the Horace Silver/Art Blakey
approach tended to be called—it was the record companies' renewed interest in Charlie Parker. Bird's death in 1955 focused
the attention of musicians and fans, as with Beiderbecke earlier,
on what they had missed or taken for granted. But the complica-
tions of his estate also made it possible for both authorized and
unauthorized recordings to be issued and reissued with im-
punity, and with a profit at the end of the day. Bop in its pristine
form had stayed at the minority cult level; in nine years of releases under his own name, Bird had substantially fewer issues
than Ellington did in his four years at the end of the 1920s

(Gillespie's output would have been comparable, but for two extremely prolific visits to Paris).

However, as already noted, some Dial alternate takes were made available during Parker's lifetime. Immediately after his death, Savoy issued a 12-inch LP of all the music from his "Koko" session, including incomplete performances terminated by mistakes, together with much brilliant but otherwise unusable improvising. This eventually became a series of five Savoy LPs collecting nearly all the out-takes, followed by eleven on the Clef label (now renamed Verve) and such things as an unissued Miles Davis session with Parker on tenor saxophone. Not until 1977 did Savoy, by then under new ownership, conclude a revised royalty agreement with Parker's heirs. These releases increased the amount of his official studio work by around 50 percent.

All of Bird's studio output added together has been dwarfed by the unofficial recordings that have appeared steadily in the last three decades and more. The quality of these "bootlegs" varies wildly, from the three albums put out in 1961 on Le Jazz Cool Records—mostly taken off the air from reasonably engineered broadcasts—to two late-1950s LPs on Jazz Workshop (the second of Charles Mingus's labels). The Jazz Workshop performances had been captured on a wire-recorder at live gigs with a single microphone, the impromptu balance being matched by improvised editing—the recordists saved time and money by turning off the machine whenever Parker himself was not playing.

Naturally, none of the live Bird was in two-track stereo, which became standard for new recording from 1957 (after being patented back in 1931). Nonetheless, even the incomplete performances were often longer than 78 RPM sides, and thus only "made sense" as LP tracks. More importantly, they tended to confirm the impression of earlier concert albums that live recordings, even by less brilliant musicians, conveyed an intensity missing from most previous studio sessions. And, as taping longer performances in the studio became the norm, conscientious artists such as Miles Davis began making their studio recordings much more like live gigs.

In the late 1930s, the revival of interest in traditional jazz had been sparked by white listeners while some musicians had kept the faith throughout. Similarly, the groundwork for the bop renaissance of the late 1950s had already been laid by the continuing activities of players like Art Blakey and Max Roach. A year before Parker's death, Blakey's *A Night at Birdland* had reinterpreted three Bird-related melodies, while Roach and Sonny Rollins each later recorded a whole album of Parker material, in between their more distinctively hard-bop tunes.

Thelonious Monk was continuing to play his own pieces, including those written ten or fifteen years earlier. He enjoyed a personal revival at this period through his 1956 album *Brilliant Corners* (with Sonny Rollins), his 1957 quartet (with John Coltrane) and his 1959 Town Hall concert. Although Monk's material was still regarded as too challenging by younger players —just as his piano style had few disciples compared to that of Bud Powell—it became evident that many of his earlier originals had pioneered the idea of minimal chord movement, which Miles Davis was now championing in his late 1950s "modal" approach. Examples are two train depictions, "Locomotive" and "Little Rootie Tootie." While Ellington's "Caravan" or even Luis Russell's "Saratoga Shout" are also relevant, Monk's rhythmic designs had specifically forecast the punchy, hard-bop ensemble sound. More than that, his pianistic playfulness with specific phrases, also incorporated into some of his written lines, inspired much of the writing and improvisation of the new avant-garde about to burst on the jazz world.

Charles Mingus, who was known to include bop classics in live performance, also concentrated on recording his own pieces, including a series of musical portraits such as "Reincarnation Of A Lovebird," "Dizzy Moods" and "Jump Monk." In this respect, he may be likened to Duke Ellington (to whom he also dedicated original compositions) and indeed, there was also a parallel in his compositional approach; Monk's forward influence was closer to that of his own idol, Art Tatum. In other words, Mingus was far more successful than his contemporaries at taking a group of soloists versed in the bebop vernacular, and molding their abilities to extend the language —and loosen the structures—of bop. The *Pithecanthropus Erectus* album illustrates how he was already doing this in 1956, while a comparison with *East Coasting* shows the wide emotional range of which Mingus was capable.

Both *Pithecanthropus Erectus* and *East Coasting* capitalize on the intensity of playing "live in the studio." Even when working with his usual players, Mingus sought to put them on the spot musically. Pianist Bill Evans was not a regular colleague but a last-minute replacement for *East Coasting*, and had to be ready to cope. "You sort of met the players in the studio sometimes," he told me years later, "and you did the whole album in one day's recording. You know—*new* music. And yet, many times they really came off remarkably, because everybody could respond to that type of challenge. [Mingus] is like a catalyst, he can just generate a lot of sparks and vitality, and things just get going when he's in command."

As well as running Debut Records with Max Roach, and attempting another self-organized label in 1965, Mingus had a close association (as did Roach) with Candid, an unusual jazz series that was more short-lived than even most specialty jazz labels. Archie Bleyer had made his reputation in the late 1920s by writing "stock arrangements" for publishers (recorded by Fletcher Henderson and others) before becoming a publisher himself. In the 1950s, he founded Cadence Records, which had pop hits with Andy Williams and others. Attempting to plow his profits back into something more esoteric, Bleyer initiated his Candid jazz and blues subsidiary in 1960, entrusting all supervision to former *downbeat* editor Nat Hentoff (Hentoff had done some album production for Contemporary, one of the best West Coast companies).

Within a few of months of recording, Hentoff had facilitated two epoch-making LPs, *Charles Mingus Presents Charles Mingus* and Roach's *We Insist—Freedom Now.* Both of these works contain strong musical statements about racial injustice. Soon these two albums were in release; Roach's had the distinction of being banned in South Africa. Hentoff was told that no further Candid recordings could be contemplated, apparently because he was spending money faster than it was being recouped, as if that could not have been expected. The result was to place *Freedom Now* and the other Candids among the many "collector's items" of the early LP era—Hentoff later wrote of the Roach album that "the few copies offered for sale from time to time could almost have been made literally of gold for the prices they have commanded." As a postscript, the entire Cadence operation was later bought by Andy Williams, by then a respectable middle-of-the-road star, in order to prevent repackaging of his early foibles. Only in 1971, after he was persuaded they had little to do with his personal reputation, did Williams allow the historically significant Candid albums to be reissued.

By 1960, the first shock waves of the avant-garde had hit. John Coltrane, who increasingly dominated the period from 1957 until his death ten years later, had made his reputation in fairly conventional modern jazz circles and was therefore well-placed to lend authority and respectability to the movement. But this would never have been effective had it not been for Coltrane's increasing commitment to the cause. Initially noted as a sideman with Miles Davis's quintet and sextet (especially on *Milestones* and *Kind of Blue*), he had been signed as a leader by Prestige shortly after Davis had left them; there he recorded a large number of albums, some of them blowing sessions which, although "leaderless," were issued with great prominence given to Coltrane's name.

Becoming reluctant to use his own compositions on Prestige because of their usual publishing contract, Coltrane left the label after two years. He took with him a backlog of original material—some of it very involved harmonically—for his first albums on Atlantic, *Giant Steps* and *Coltrane Jazz*. During the Atlantic period, Coltrane formed his own quartet with McCoy Tyner and Elvin Jones, making some marathon recordings of their simpler, regular repertoire. As at Prestige, he left Atlantic a considerable pile of tapes to issue after his departure.

At the end of his two-year contract, Trane spent the rest of his career with Impulse, a jazz subsidiary founded in late 1960 by the ABC-Paramount company. ABC had already released a series of jazz albums organized by their producer, Creed Taylor, who left shortly after setting up Impulse (to work for Verve, recently sold by Norman Granz to MGM). Taylor's replacement at Impulse was Bob Thiele—he of the Signature label, briefly revived in the late 1950s, after a long spell at Decca. Thiele took over Coltrane's recording so successfully that, in the six years from 1961, Coltrane's annual advance rose from $10,000 to $40,000, briefly overtaking even Miles Davis's sums. Impulse packaging (created by Creed Taylor) in gatefold sleeves with beautiful artwork, priced at $5.98 instead of the then standard $4.98, obviously helped create an aura of high seriousness about Coltrane's work.

Coltrane's association with Thiele was so conducive to prolific creativity—and therefore to posthumous releases—that in the ten years from his first album, Coltrane far exceeded even the present-day total of Parker's recordings of all kinds with just the material he officially taped under his three contractual commitments as a leader. Parker's studio career was of a similar length but was barely affected by long-play recordings; Coltrane's, on the other hand, took place virtually entirely during the LP era, with the addition of Trane's sideman appearances plus unauthorized releases more than doubling his output.

What is fascinating, however, is how Coltrane's style gradually changed according to the developments going on around him. An early album such as *Blue Train* shows him already one of the masters of his instrument, with an amazing facility of execution and an eerie spine-tingling tone which, though unique, reflected his experience in rhythm and blues bands. The material chosen is admirably balanced with two driving blues at different tempos, two of Coltrane's original and complex harmonic designs, and a standard ballad of the kind that "soulful," blues-based saxophonists still used for jukebox consumption. The group's performance is of such heightened intensity throughout that it is easy to overlook a certain stylistic disparity between Trane and the brilliant rhythm team of Paul Chambers and Philly Joe Jones, which makes the tenor man sound either rather static or on a different spiritual plane, depending on how you view it.

Coltrane's effort to combine surface serenity and inner turbulence in his music was triumphantly realized once he teamed up with drummer Elvin Jones. Their first recorded appearance together was 1960's *My Favorite Things* (whose soprano saxophone solo made the title-track into a hit single); the apotheosis of their collaboration came in 1964 with *A Love Supreme*, which, like Miles's *Sketches of Spain*, was a million-seller by the end of the 1970s. The opening piece of each of these landmark albums combines Coltrane's incantatory and open-ended improvisation with drumming based on Afro-Latin cross-rhythms, but in a remarkably loose and dense-sounding counterpoint. On *Supreme's* "Resolution," Tyner's solo is partly devoted to an extended series of third-note accents, which then recur during Jones and Tyner's backing of Coltrane.

In the last few years of his life, and coinciding with the mid-1960s maturity of the free jazz movement, Trane continued to increase the rhythmic complexity of his music. He sought greater melodic counterpoint by adding extra reed players like Archie Shepp, Marion Brown, Donald Garrett and, on a permanent basis, Pharoah Sanders. Even before the eventual addition of extra percussion, several of these players took part in an extended collective improvisation which marked the start of Coltrane's last period, *Ascension*.

To these and many other musicians of the free-jazz generation, Coltrane was a kind of father figure, an established star who nonetheless encouraged younger and more radical practitioners. Coltrane's colleague and contemporary Eric Dolphy was viewed in the same light, and would have played a greater role in bringing forward new players, had he not died in 1964. Equally schooled in the basics of jazz but interested like Coltrane in seeking new avenues (he had also worked with Charles Mingus), Dolphy had ears that were as well-trained harmonically as Trane's. There were differences in their methods, however. Trane ran rapid-fire scales and broken chords, which even those unable to follow note for note could observe were being played accurately and logically. But Dolphy's more angular phrasing was harder to hear, and therefore took longer to absorb. The ensuing decades have seen the influence of this phrasing continue to increase.

Significant, too, is the fact that Dolphy was equally proficient on alto saxophone, bass clarinet and flute. Prior to the example of Eric Dolphy, the only reason for a jazz saxophonist to "double" on woodwind instruments was in the hope of undertaking studio work of a non-jazz nature. The Dolphy approach, though, has since become the predominant way of adopting these instruments in a jazz context. And, more than that, it has been Dolphy's example, more than Coltrane's, which has taught succeeding generations that there is a valid reason for such doubling.

Coltrane's position after the death of Dolphy was roughly parallel to that of Coleman Hawkins more than twenty years earlier. Hawkins, too, had encouraged and employed people like Kenny Clarke, Max Roach and Thelonious Monk. But the man who rode out of the West with a completely unexpected and seemingly oblique approach to what jazz was thought to be about, was Ornette Coleman. Like Lester Young, Ornette had an approach that was simple in some ways, melodic and virtually non-harmonic, yet rooted in the blues. Like Young, he had no in-group reputation based on his apprenticeship with the recognized greats. And he had nothing at all on disc, until he found himself finally with sympathetic colleagues and a chance to record.

The impact of Coleman's debut album *Somethin' Else!!!!* —recorded in 1958 with Don Cherry and drummer Billy Higgins for the Contemporary label—was as unsettling as Young's arrival with "Jones-Smith Incorporated." To the harmonically sophisticated musician who heard Coleman (on record in most cases, since he had not yet left the West Coast), there was a strong suggestion of someone who "didn't know his chord changes." Yet to those listeners who were ready to respond, there was a new and refreshingly unpedantic approach, even compared to Coltrane or Dolphy, together with a personal sound which lent it conviction. Mingus's reaction was on the whole favorable, and his *Charles Mingus Presents Charles Mingus* album translates this response into the terms of his own music. In addition to younger players in many corners of the world who began immediately picking up on the Coleman style, John Coltrane went so far as to record some of Ornette's tunes, including "The Blessing."

The Tatum Group Masterpieces

Louis Bellson
Benny Carter
Red Callender
Buddy De Franco
Bill Douglass
Harry Edison
Roy Eldridge

Lionel Hampton
Jo Jones
Barney Kessel
Buddy Rich
John Simmons
Alvin Stoller
Ben Webster

8 LP set 2625-706

19. Long, open-ended jam sessions made possible by the advent of the LP; boxed-set reissues like this have been described as the last innovation of the vinyl era

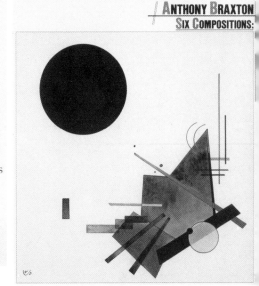

ANTHONY BRAXTON
SIX COMPOSITIONS:

20. The Kandinsky reproduction suggests that Anthony Braxton's music is seen as classically avant-garde

21. One of the many classic bits of vinyl whose CD reissue does indeed contain *Somethin' Else*—a newly-discovered bonus track

22. One of a growing number of sessions recorded for CD release only

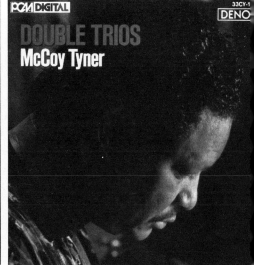

SOMETHIN'
ELSE
CANNONBALL
ADDERLEY
MILES DAVIS
HANK JONES
SAM JONES
ART BLAKEY
BLUE NOTE
MILES DAVIS PERFORMS BY COURTESY OF COLUMBIA RECORDS

PCM DIGITAL
33CY-1
DENO
DOUBLE TRIOS
McCoy Tyner

23. Charlie Parker in full flight with (l to r) Charlie Shavers, Ben Webster, Johnny Hodges, Flip Phillips, Benny Carter; June 1952

24. Milt Jackson, Miles Davis and Bud Powell, probably at the Royal Roost, January 6, 1949; many of the live recordings of these musicians with Parker are broadcasts from this venue

25. Kenny Clarke (left) returns from Paris to reunite with Percy Heath and Horace Silver outside the old Birdland club, at the instigation of Bruce Lundvall, then president of CBS Records; 1978

26. Sonny Rollins with a lyricon (an early synthesized wind instrument), listening to producer Orrin Keepnews; c. 1979

27. Thelonious Monk in action; c. 1959

28. Charles Mingus at a mixing session with producer
(and former Mingus sideman) Teo Macero; 1971

29. Ornette Coleman (back to camera) with Jimmy Garrison, Bobby Bradford and Charles Moffett at Atlantic studio—no recordings by this line-up have yet been released; c. 1962

30. John Coltrane (left) with Jimmy Garrison, Rashied Ali and Alice Coltrane, greeted with flowers on arrival in Japan; 1966

31. Bill Evans (right) drops in during a playback of
Oliver Nelson (seated) and Jimmy Smith; 1960s

32. Albert Ayler recording for Impulse; 1960s

33. Archie Shepp (left) with Alan Shorter, Roswell Rudd and John Tchicai
at Rudy Van Gelder studio to record *Four for Trane;*
August 10, 1964

34. Gato Barbieri on tenor and Don Cherry on pocket-trumpet; 1960s

35. ECM founder/producer Manfred Eicher serenades
Keith Jarrett; undated

36. Hariprasad Chaurasia, Jan Garbarek, John McLaughlin
(seated) and Zakir Hussain, former tabla player with Shakti,
during recording of Hussain's *Making Music;* 1986

The material from Coleman's successive early-1960s albums on Atlantic—*The Shape of Jazz to Come, Change of the Century* and four others (plus three albums of out-takes, inevitably issued much later)—was all of a piece. These recordings showed a remarkable consistency of style on the part of Ornette's quartet, as well as considerable variety of mood. If in retrospect they seem less than revolutionary, there are good reasons for this, just as there are good reasons why it was Coleman's influence that was decisive in the radical developments that were to follow.

For a start, Ornette's alto playing was disarming in its apparent simplicity; his instrumental tone was the most direct expression of this. Whereas Coltrane's sound mirrored the strained intensity of contemporary electric blues guitarists, Coleman played more like a rural throwback to pre-Louis Jordan saxophone. Indeed, his sound was reminiscent of the older unsophisticated folk-blues *singers* (who, coincidentally, were being discovered or rediscovered by folklore enthusiasts as a supposed antidote to rock and roll at exactly the same period). Although Ornette's material deliberately omitted standard songs, it consisted mostly of only slightly modified versions of the accepted 12-bar and 32-bar song forms. His compositions almost invariably started with saxophone-and-trumpet unison statements popularized by Parker and Gillespie, followed by solos with each instrument leading in turn, then a restatement of the theme.

In both his written themes and his improvised solos, Ornette was far more diatonic, and therefore more direct melodically, than Parker. Rhythmically, too, he was familiar enough with Bird's style to appear unattracted (not merely daunted) by the kind of bar-by-bar linear complexity his predecessor had perfected. Instead, a little like Rollins in the 1950s, Coleman spread the complexity over longer phrases of non-standard lengths; perhaps this is one reason why Rollins himself employed Don Cherry and Billy Higgins for some later work, like *Our Man in Jazz*.

Ornette's harmonic aspect, or the lack of it, was even more noticeable at the time. Although the diatonic melodies meant that Coleman's playing was ruled by the traditional system of major and minor keys or scales, the rate of change was far slower—and decided upon spontaneously during the course of performance, not dictated by a given chord sequence. The bassist (usually Ornette's long-time collaborator Charlie Haden) thus had the responsibility or the freedom to affect the direction of the group, while the unpredictability of the phrasing afforded both the bassist and the drummer increased interplay. All of this dramatically expanded the scope for varied interpretation of the same introductory material.

Coleman's most far-sighted early work proved to be *Free Jazz*, by a double quartet with two bassists and two drummers. *Free Jazz* was the first album to consist of a single continuous piece spread over both sides of the disc, broken only by a brief fade-out at the end of Side One which was then reversed at the start of Side Two. The LP was thus historically significant in both recording and marketing terms. But three months later, when Ornette came to the end of his two-year Atlantic contract with a lot of material left "in the can," he laid down stringent financial conditions for any future recordings and live appearances. The result was his doing little of either.

In the long run, Coleman has gained considerable success and respect with this approach. In the following five years—during which he used a new rhythm section, also adding expressionist violin and trumpet playing to his alto achievements—the only albums of his music were issued in Europe and/or made at public performances. One of these live recordings, *Town Hall Concert 1962*, was announced for release on Blue Note, with whom he later signed a contract, but appeared instead on another label. Ornette explained the situation in the late 1960s: "Right now I've got three records on the market made from my own tapes which were deliberately taken from me, and I haven't received a penny . . . Then they tell me, when I ask about it, 'Do you think Atlantic Records are straight?' There is an establishment that says, 'If you do this here, we'll give you four dollars, and the government gets some of that.' But there's another establishment that says, 'You do this here and I can get it from you without giving you anything.'"

Alongside the creative turmoil of Coleman and Coltrane, who were pioneering the movement towards free jazz, there were further developments in relaxing and extending the formulas of bebop. Such changes, often of a rhythmic nature, were less obvious than in hard bop and more subtle than the changes still to come in the avant-garde area. Scott LaFaro, the second bassist on Coleman's *Free Jazz* album and briefly Charlie Haden's replacement with Coleman, spent the longest part of a tragically short career working in the Bill Evans Trio. Piano trios have seldom been the forum for innovation, more often indeed for ossification, but LaFaro found a perfect vehicle for extending the participatory bass-playing favored by Mingus. Evans, despite having played in the Miles Davis "modal" group, did not attempt such material by and large, but allowed the scalar approach to strongly influence his improvisation on standard songs.

Moreover, Bill Evans's lines were so sure rhythmically, even when enunciated with delicacy, that they encouraged sophisticated counterpoint between his bassist and drummer (Paul Motian). Such interplay was greater than the counterpoint one usually heard in piano trios, but also greater than that of *any* group in 1959, except those of Mingus and Coleman. The extraordinary freedom with which the Evans Trio kept the basic beat between the three instruments—sometimes by implication rather than direct statement—was to have a considerable effect on most subsequent groups working outside free jazz. And it is a back-handed compliment to Evans the pianist that his lyrically distinctive style, which revitalized some of the techniques of Lennie Tristano, became so rapidly imitated in the more populist arena of "cocktail piano."

Similar factors have militated against serious consideration of some of the derivatives of bebop in combination with Afro-Latin rhythms. This fusion has, since the late 1940s, exerted a considerable influence on the music played for Latin audiences—either those living in the States and dancing to bands now containing bop-tinged soloists, or those in Latin-American countries whose pop music (as in Europe) had become more and more affected by U.S. recording and arranging techniques. The most dramatic example of this fusion was the Brazilian "bossa nova" of the early 1960s. The international circle was completed yet again when the style and its material was picked up by North American jazzmen like Herbie Mann, Dizzy Gillespie and Stan Getz.

Stan Getz was one of the generation of white Lester Young followers who originally surfaced during the bop era, often in the ranks of the big bands such as Woody Herman's. Getz shared honors with his colleague Zoot Sims during their gradual journey to musical maturity through the 1950s and 1960s. Having shown no previous interest in Latin styles, or even any particular rhythmic expertise compared to Sims, he developed a stronger sound and more dynamic thrust through his espousal of the bossa.

Getz also enhanced his earning power considerably as a result of two Top 40 singles drawn from his Creed Taylor-produced Verve albums. It is greatly to his credit that he refused to coast on the crest of the wave. After all, as he quipped, "When you have a contract that involves half a million dollars over five years, and calls for three records a year, you don't have to worry about money." That renewed contract with Verve began in 1967; by the start of 1969, Getz was being wooed by Teo Macero at CBS with discussion about the terms of an even better contract that could only become operative three years later!

Though Getz continued to focus strongly on spontaneous and mostly non-Latin jazz, especially in live appearances, many of his albums reflected the ways in which technology was beginning to cushion the star performer by the mid-1960s. Recording was still only done on three-track or at most four-track machines. But whereas the star was under contract and could devote unlimited time to perfecting his part, accompanying musicians were now employed at a scale of $60 per three-hour session. Rather than rely on the chemistry of the moment, as with *Miles Ahead*, producers became more inclined to prerecord any large-scale written arrangements and bring in the soloist later. One of Getz's Verve recordings, in fact, featured him against backings which had been originally taped for the use of guitarist Wes Montgomery.

Wes Montgomery left Verve as the jewel in the crown of Creed Taylor when Taylor started his own CTI Productions in 1967. Whether the guitarist, whose hit records usually had a soft Latin background, would have reasserted his excellent jazz playing is a moot point, for he died the following year. At that stage, both Verve and Pacific jazz, reversing the above procedure, took earlier Montgomery recordings done live with a small group and added a posthumous big-band accompaniment to their memorial album "reissues." Fortunately, perhaps, the monophonic Montgomery tracks could be surrounded by the new backing in a fairly realistic way. This was possible because by 1968 (and first of all in Europe) record companies stopped producing parallel stereo and mono issues of the same material, learning how to master stereo albums that would not be damaged if played on the mono equipment still used by some consumers.

While Montgomery's most remunerative work was determinedly middle-of-the-road, it was successful because in the

1960s the Afro-Latin eight-to-the-bar rhythms had invaded the entire pop music field. The "uneven" phrasing of early rock and roll—with its shuffle beat derived through R & B from jazz—had been displaced by elements from Mexican, Cuban and Brazilian music which relied on interplay with essentially "even" timing. Such timing had not been heard in any new North American styles since the days of early New Orleans jazz. Naturally, the Latin singers and instrumentalists made brilliant and complex use of the available rhythmic counter-point, whereas North American pop vocalists mostly sounded stone dead by comparison. One or two exponents of the Twist, the archetype of the pop-Latin beats, were reasonably rhythmic and soulful singers, but the most interesting development was in the soul-jazz field.

The Latin feel was being tried out *alongside* the jazz shuf-fle beat as early as Lou Donaldson's 1958 "Blues Walk," featur-ing subsequent Latin-crossover star Ray Barretto on congas. Jazz musicians who were selling their records partly to a black post-R & B audience, such as Cannonball Adderley, found Latin a natural *alternative* on certain numbers. Adderley, a brilliant Parkerish alto saxophonist, became more particularly noted for this use of Latin rhythm in the late 1960s. In 1960, his "Sack O' Woe" was played partly over a straight jazz beat and partly over a rhythm "that's common when you're dancing." It's no great surprise to learn that this rhythm—equally common to the bossa nova, the Southern folk-dance known as "hambone" and to many Afro-Caribbean styles—relies on a third-note accentu-ation in the rhythm-section accompaniment.*

---

* Adderley's recordings for the Riverside label had by then become so suc-cessful that he formed a production company and became the first jazzman, outside of the small musician-owned labels, to produce albums by others. The following year, Quincy Jones became a vice-president at Mercury and, among others, produced the work of stylistically omnivorous reed-player Rahsaan Roland Kirk.

Similarly, Horace Silver had long been interested in Latin beats. While his piece "Ecaroh" (from 1952!) alternates between a Latin feel and a jazz feel, his 1964 "Song For My Father" was simply the most popular in a long line of fully Latinate pieces stretching back a decade. A much younger pianist who took this leaf out of Silver's book was Herbie Hancock, whose debut album included "Watermelon Man." This tune later became a hit in a Latin-jazz rendition by Mongo Santamaria. Billy Higgins, who played on Hancock's own version, was acknowledged for his creative cross-fertilization in the comments of Ron Carter: "Billy Higgins is a fine example of a New-Orleans-beat drummer. He's just playing funeral street beats. But if you listen to the record he made, *The Sidewinder*, with Lee Morgan, it sounds like a rock beat. It is not rock. It is only classified as rock for the commercial value of the term."

Just as early rock and roll had confounded the music business—with artists like Chuck Berry and Fats Domino "crossing over" from R & B (by the 1950s a catch-all term for black popular music) to the so-called "popular" (i.e. white) category—Lee Morgan's and Horace Silver's hits showed up on the pop chart of the trade bible, *Billboard* magazine. Silver commented recently, "Jazz had a little better shot than today precisely because they would take a jazz tune and put it on the jukebox where it had more potential for people hearing it. Also because [the tunes] had that danceable thing, it maybe meant more cover records."

Always an important consideration for a composer who received royalties through publishing his own material, cover versions confirmed the wide acceptability of such material. In Silver's case, soul figures like James Brown as well as big bands like Woody Herman's recorded his material. As a result, Blue Note came under pressure, not from artists but from retailers and distributors, to produce more albums of a similar nature. This at least made them temporarily enough of a force in the marketplace to be bought out in 1966 by Liberty Records, one of the many medium-sized companies attempting to become a major.

The sale proved to be a well-timed move for Blue Note's original owners, who remained on the staff for a while. In the mid-1960s, unit sales in the popular field were increasing dramatically, making the average jazz item seem even less desirable to the large distributors. Riverside Records, despite their own efforts in the soul-jazz area, went bankrupt in 1964. In 1966, Pacific Jazz followed Blue Note into the arms of Liberty. A few years later, Liberty itself was bought by United Artists, another medium-sized company attempting to become a major until they were absorbed by a real major—the British-based EMI, which in 1979 became the subsidiary of an electronics company. As often happens, it took a couple of years before Blue Note's lack of independence really took effect. At that point, producer Alfred Lion retired, leaving the label to become the home of black jazz-disco music in the mid-1970s with, for a while, former trumpeter Donald Byrd as its president. But while still riding high in 1965, Lion made a stylistic move similar to the one he made in 1947: he started recording the now-mature avant-garde.

Almost ten years before his appearance on Blue Note, pianist Cecil Taylor began his studio career in a rather small way on an obscure Boston label, Transition Records. Transition, the brainchild of an enthusiast named Tom Wilson (later the only black producer to work with Bob Dylan), went bankrupt in 1957. Although some of Transition's material was reissued by the equally small yet longer-lived Delmark Records, Taylor's tracks were lost until the mid-1970s. Cecil's bassist, Buell Neidlinger, noted that Wilson paid the musicians $41 each instead of $150 for their eight hours' work; Taylor said, "I had to bring him up on charges before the union for not fulfilling his contractual obligations. Of course the union decided against me."

Wilson had the chance to produce Taylor again when he moved to United Artists in 1958. Presumably under pressure to please his bosses, Wilson insisted on the use of well-known sidemen rather than Taylor's own choice for the first album. *Hard Drive* featured former Jazz Messenger Kenny Dorham, Horace Silver's drummer Louis Hayes, and John Coltrane. Within four years, the album had been re-released under the title *Coltrane Time*.

Of the Taylor sessions which were produced by Nat Hentoff, two important examples appeared: one for Contemporary, one for Candid. A second session for Candid fell victim to the foreclosure of that series, and did not see the light of day until 1972. By then, Taylor was preparing to operate his own label, Unit Core Records, having not recorded since 1966, when even some Blue Note dates were not without incident. Both *Unit Structures* and *Conquistador* were taped at Rudy Van Gelder's studio, where Taylor fought to group his musicians together and avoid both the close miking and the separation of the drummer favored by Van Gelder. When Cecil attempted to dangle some tiny bells against the piano strings while recording *Unit Structures*, Van Gelder protested about this treatment of his piano. Taylor threatened to call off the entire session, until Alfred Lion persuaded Van Gelder to tolerate the bells.

The music on these albums is typical of the mature compositional style of Taylor; the organization of the rhythm section with two basses and drummer Andrew Cyrille is highly suitable to his needs. On all the early sessions, some standard songs were re-interpreted. In spite of soloists like Steve Lacy on soprano or Archie Shepp, there was considerable unease caused by the relatively straight-ahead playing of bass and drums *versus* the leader's energetic and angular phrases, most often entirely voiced in tight Monkish clusters rather than single-note lines. The same discomfort is apparent on the recordings of Eric Dolphy and, to some extent, the early albums of Ornette Coleman. But perhaps because the piano is also a rhythm-section instrument, the disparity here seems more alarming. In short, Cecil's pre-1961 players are of their time, while he is ahead of his.

Taylor found his ideal partnership with the pioneer free-jazz drummer Sunny Murray, who claimed that Cecil's playing had been less rhythmic until the two worked together. Taylor, for his part, noted that Murray "developed into an immensely important drummer because he could do certain things with time that were not regulated by meter." The documentation of their relationship began with a half-album commissioned by, and issued under the name of, Gil Evans (the producer was Creed Taylor). *Into the Hot* included only original material and briefly featured Cecil's largest group on record so far, a seven-piece, looking forward to the methods of the 1966 Blue Notes.

More striking still is the live session in 1962 *At the Café Montmartre* (in Copenhagen), done with just Murray and Taylor's long-time altoist Jimmy Lyons, because no suitable bassist was available. If there are sections of Coltrane's records where, despite audible contributions by piano and bass, the musical event taking place seems to be a duet between Trane and Elvin Jones, this is even more true of the work of Taylor and Sunny Murray here. Probably the first historically significant recording to be made in Europe since the 1937 "Coleman Hawkins Jam Band," *At the Café Montmartre* is also the most important recording without a bass-player since Armstrong began working with a big band in 1929.

Fellow pianist and bandleader Sun Ra is a full generation older than Taylor, yet made his impact very much in parallel with him. Once again, the influence of pianists like Ra and Taylor was delayed compared to that of the charismatic horn-players, perhaps because of their relatively slow development away from conventional material. Ra (named after the Egyptian sun god, naturally) did not record standard songs until later in his career. His earliest album has him directing his own compositions in fairly straight-ahead performances by a boppish ten-piece band. Like Taylor's debut, this LP was made in 1956 for Transition, as was a second album which only appeared a decade later on Delmark.

Almost simultaneously, Sun Ra began a unique contribution to discographical history by regularly documenting his work and issuing, often in limited editions, a series of LPs on his own Saturn label. This activity commenced in the late 1950s; by 1980, there had been at least 50 albums released on Saturn, plus one or more on the related Thoth label. There were also quite a few LPs commissioned by other concerns like Savoy, Atlantic and Impulse; the latter company also reissued some of the early, out-of-print Saturns in the mid-1970s.

Ra's piano work has often remained closer to the previous tradition than Taylor's, but his contributions to musical history include the creation of whole pieces entirely through collective improvisation, without even the briefest of organized ensemble material. This approach characterizes several long tracks as presented on record, but these are often excerpts from even longer improvisations. Thus, the actual form of the piece is fixed only by the choice of where to fade into the performance and where to fade out again. This production technique has become very much a fact of life in the free-jazz era, and it presents an ideological problem: the greater the freedom allowed the players at the time of recording, the graver the apparent distortion caused by later decisions about what to release and what to scrap.

It's worth mentioning here the problem of composition versus improvisation, not in the artistic sense discussed in Chapter Two, but as regards the law of copyright. It may have been perfectly justified for Ellington, say, to incorporate phrases coined by his sidemen and then claim credit for the overall composition. Even "themeless" versions of popular songs (such as Coleman Hawkins's remake of "Body And Soul" titled "Rainbow Mist") have their identity established by the chief improviser rather than the creator of the initial chord sequence. But the more communal the improvisation, the less significant any element of prearrangement becomes, and the less sense—and less justice—there is in listing the bandleader's name as "composer," as per Coltrane's *Ascension* or Ornette's *Free Jazz*. A legal fact of life is that, in order to protect the "intellectual property" of a piece of music (as opposed to physical ownership of a taped performance), it is necessary for it to have a composer or composers. Therefore, for recorded group improvisations not to be beyond the law, it has become common more recently for all the performers to be listed as joint composers. Failing that, the group leader allows his name to be used, and the other members of the group hope that he passes on some of his composer royalties.

Both Cecil Taylor and Sun Ra at this period occupied a similar niche to Monk in the 1940s—allied to the developments of the day, but at one remove because of their roles as composer/ organizers, and because their influence was often on pianists with similar priorities (the new vernacular for those specializing in the keyboard was drawn from McCoy Tyner and/or Bill Evans, the Bud Powells of the 1960s). Viewed according to these 20-year parallels and those mentioned earlier in this chapter, the avant-garde rhythm section now had its act together, and the time was ripe for a front-line musician who had ridden the recent tremors to step forth and signal the start of the full-scale earthquake.

My Name Is Albert Ayler was the first widely-distributed album by the saxophonist who had played with Cecil Taylor and (like Ornette) with rhythm and blues bands. Ayler epitomized the radical re-think that his contemporaries had been searching for. The tonal vocalization, the lurching phraseology and the complete rhythmic freedom of his improvisation contrasted wildly both with the standard material on that initial album, and with the simple folky melodies he created as starting-points for his subsequent releases. There seemed to be few precedents for Ayler's music even in the recent activities of those musicians mentioned above, although it is highly significant that Ayler formed an immediate partnership with Sunny Murray, and later with free drummer Milford Graves. Commentators or fellow musicians, when not seeking to deride and dismiss Ayler completely, had to look back to the New Orleans styles of relatively untutored post-Bunk Johnson players in order to explain and understand Ayler's combination of emotional commitment and apparent stylistic naïvete. Every aspect of Ayler's contribution seemed to be extreme, even his capacity to make people like Coltrane and Coleman sound conventional and stilted by comparison. For this reason, Ayler's impact on the mid-1960s can only be likened to that of Charlie Parker.

There are one or two parallels between Parker and Ayler in their respective recording careers as well. The first time that either saw the inside of a recording studio was in order to do a broadcast—what was different was that Ayler's was in Europe, and that European interest in free-thinking black Americans was sufficient for Ayler to be the star guest on this first broadcast. (This then became the *My Name Is Albert Ayler* album which was issued by the still functioning European branch of the Mingus-founded Debut label, who also put out Cecil Taylor's live recording of seven-and-a half weeks earlier.) A further difference was that the Danes then recorded Ayler in New York but for issue in Denmark, after which he prompted the formation of the first small U.S. label to specialize in free jazz—rather as Dial Records had been formed principally to record Parker.

Writer Valerie Wilmer has noted that Ayler was advised by Cecil Taylor and others not to record for fledgling producer Bernard Stollman because the financial consideration was unsatisfactory. Nonetheless, Ayler went ahead and ensured the controversial success of Stollman's label ESP-Disk. The first of Ayler's several ESP albums was entitled *Spiritual Unity*. At that session, recalled Wilmer, "As soon as the musicians started to play, the engineer fled the control room and did not return until the tape had almost run out . . . The tape had been made in monaural because the frightened engineer thought it was only intended for a demo." ESP-Disk was launched in 1965 and sponsored a promotional concert at New York's Town Hall, subsequently recording, among many others, Sun Ra, Steve Lacy and Gato Barbieri. The label also acquired Ornette Coleman's Town Hall Concert, plus live recordings by Charlie Parker, Billie Holiday and Bud Powell.

From the end of 1966 until his untimely death four years later, Ayler had a financially more rewarding contract with Impulse, thanks to the enthusiasm and advocacy of John Coltrane. This resulted in several better-recorded albums, but Ayler's last two Impulse sessions were controversial in a new way. The first was done with studio musicians, including session vocalist and songwriter Rose Marie McCoy, who once recorded with Fletcher Henderson. *New Grass*, like its successor, included some solo singing by Ayler, and tempered his tenor playing with stiff eight-to-the-bar rock rhythms. This album effectively widened the audience for Ayler's work in the same way as Parker's recordings with strings did. Only ten years later, *New Grass* inspired the tenor solo of a British number-one hit ("Hit Me With Your Rhythm Stick" by Ian Dury); the formerly unacceptable saxophonist himself turned up on the soundtrack of a TV documentary about skateboarding.

The pursuit of Ayler's kind of popularity preoccupied record producers for much of the 1970s. Meanwhile, Don

Cherry had initiated the search for another, more profound fusion. By the mid-1960s, Cherry's wide-ranging activity had made him a notably broadminded Gillespie-like figure: he had worked in turn with Ornette Coleman, Sonny Rollins and Ayler. His own group, which recorded for Blue Note and briefly featured Pharoah Sanders, had been founded during his first period of living in Europe. In addition to forward-looking European musicians like bassist Jean-Franvois Jenny-Clark and vibes player Karl-Hanns Berger, Cherry uncovered the talents of another Aylerish saxophonist, Gato Barbieri.

It was typical of Cherry that he should encourage such players. During the next few years, he worked with many more Europeans, South Africans Johnny Dyani and Abdullah Ibrahim (Dollar Brand), and even Turkish musicians like percussionist Okay Temiz. More than that, Cherry incorporated folk melodies from far-flung countries, collecting and using instruments such as the gamelan, cheng, doussn'gouni, tambura and a huge variety of ethnic flutes. This development had been anticipated by other black Americans like Yusef Lateef and encouraged by Coltrane. It might have been considered somewhat irrelevant to jazz, in the way that Gillespie's involvement with Afro-Latin music was dismissed by some. But in the hands of Don Cherry, this movement became something to be taken seriously. By the time it was christened "world music," it was one more trend to put in the melting pot of the 1970s.

· 7 ·

JAZZ AND ROCK

◆

From the mid-1960s onwards, the huge increase of unit sales of pop records had far-reaching consequences for jazz recording. Ironically, this pop success was directly caused by what the U.S. industry termed the "British Invasion" (which had itself been fueled by a British blues movement, in which many jazz musicians had been involved at least peripherally). Undoubtedly, the search for the "next Beatles" inspired the expenditure of untold millions of dollars, in advances and promotional activity, by the major companies and by medium-sized companies wishing to retain a share of the pop market.

The stakes were sufficiently high for the accounting

executives at the major labels to view jazz as increasingly irrelevant. Jazz as marketed by these same companies had traditionally been treated with a certain respect for its past reputation. But jazz still didn't carry the same prestige as European classical music, because of its close links with old pop music and black people, who were still thought of as inherently non-prestigious. Insofar as jazz records sold to a wide, white audience, they sold surely but slowly—it took nearly 20 years for *Sketches of Spain* and *A Love Supreme* to achieve their sales levels of a million copies. With the new achievements in stock turnover, many worthy jazz issues no longer justified the warehouse space required for an economical minimum print-run. Even attempts to make reissues (with their very low initial outlay) into more prestigious, academically acceptable purchases—like CBS's early 1960s boxed sets of Fletcher Henderson, the *Thesaurus of Classic Jazz* and other projects—had eventually proved unprofitable. And though the picture didn't change immediately, the process had begun whereby the majors' involvement in jazz recording—more or less continuous from the late 1910s until the late 1960s, despite a few hiccups—would become the exception rather than the rule.

The change was delayed, however, by the very circumstances which made it inevitable. The youth market that made the pop scene seem infinitely expandable was cultivated so assiduously that it developed its own minority tastes. Along with the widespread and fairly mindless addiction to popular music and fashion, a small but sizeable counterculture developed. Following the example of the black civil rights movement, this group espoused radical politics or opted out of mainstream society altogether (or even pretended to do both at the same time, which is hardly very effective). The beginnings of "progressive rock" were supported by these record-buyers, so that the major labels were soon selling lengthy improvisations either by groups such as Britain's Cream or by San Francisco's Jefferson Airplane, and the Grateful Dead (whose slightly jazz-leaning work was condemned by Cream's Eric Clapton "because they hadn't listened to the right records," i.e. blues records).

Since no one, especially no one employed by the large companies, knew exactly what was progressive, music much closer to jazz was also targeted to the same market. RCA artist Gary Burton abandoned the acoustic-jazz framework of his earlier albums in 1967, forming a quartet that blended his vibes with electric bass guitar by former acoustic bassist Steve Swallow and with the genuinely blues-influenced guitar of Larry Coryell. A year earlier, ex-Cannonball Adderley saxophonist Charles Lloyd set up his own quartet with future stars Keith Jarrett on piano and Jack DeJohnette on drums, in order to imitate and exaggerate some of the techniques of the current Miles Davis and Coltrane groups.

Charles Lloyd's producer and manager was George Avakian, now free-lancing after quitting Columbia first for Warner Bros. and then RCA. Avakian signed Lloyd's group to a lucrative contract with Atlantic; part of the deal was that the company would put as much money into promotion as they would with a new rock group. After two years, Lloyd and Avakian split, doubtless because Lloyd wanted more of the proceeds. Atlantic issued numerous concert tapes done during the contract, and Avakian continued recording the Keith Jarrett quartet with Dewey Redman, also for Atlantic.

Having realized belatedly that the steady sale of Coltrane's records was due as much to this "progressive" audience as to the conventional jazz-buying public, ABC-Impulse, upon Coltrane's death, signed up both Pharoah Sanders and Trane's widow, Alice. Bob Thiele's comments at the time openly linked the signing of Ms. Coltrane the keyboard player to arrangements for continued release of the backlog of Coltrane recordings. Shortly after her husband's death, Alice had issued a tape (or a copy tape) of material recorded during his Impulse contract as *Cosmic Music*, the one and only album on the Coltrane Recording Corporation label. This LP was reissued by Impulse, and Alice herself began a series of albums which, with the introduction of her harp and organ alongside her piano work, nullified the playing of respected sidemen such as Charlie Haden and Ron Carter. Records like *Journey in Satchidananda* made it evident that the direction from jazz via world music would eventually lead to the spineless New Age jazz of the 1980s.

The aim of Pharoah Sanders, who also played on some of Alice's albums, seemed to be to harness the energy of the former Coltrane group on his own more commercial recordings. The cosmic consciousness of the age ensured that his second Impulse album, *Karma*, sold close to 200,000 copies within a few years, according to a later executive of the company. Musical reservations about his efforts at the time, of the kind that would normally be expressed in a magazine article, recently found their way onto the cover blurb of a new Sanders album (a most unusual place for criticisms of an artist) by Kevin Whitehead. "On Pharoah's LPs," Whitehead wrote, "the Coltrane quartet's spontaneous polyrhythms were reduced to a busy hubbub of static grooves. One aspect of Sanders' style was hailed as distinctive: his mastery of extended techniques, particularly split-tones and a precise, hoarse falsetto . . . came to sound empty and formulaic." One could certainly say the same—especially as to rhythmic unadventurousness—of the Sanders imitations popularized by Gato Barbieri, whom Bob Thiele signed up when he left Impulse in 1969 to start his own label, Flying Dutchman. It is equally evident that this started another watering down of jazz elements, this time into fusion and disco music.

The development of first fusion and, later, New Age, parallels rather closely the way the counterculture was neutered; those fond of conspiracy theories would say that the music was actually used for that purpose. One of the most successful attempts to make jazz serve the cause of radical politics was Charlie Haden's *Liberation Music Orchestra,* which Thiele produced shortly before leaving Impulse. Haden's solo bass feature was entitled "Song For Che" (Che Guevara was then becoming a posthumous hero). The longest track, "Circus '68 '69," was a rare attempt at programmatic jazz, musically depicting the chaos at the 1968 Democratic Party convention.* Apart from brief, overdubbed extracts of folk songs from the Spanish Civil War, though, Haden's album was entirely instrumental, with strong improvisation couched in mordant arrangements by Carla Bley which she has never bettered. Haden's 12-piece group, which featured Barbieri and Don Cherry, was the nucleus of a large, occasional assemblage called the Jazz Composers' Orchestra Association.

The Jazz Composers' Orchestra Association had its roots in various collectively-organized concerts in 1964. Under the effective management of Carla Bley and her husband, trumpeter Mike Mantler, the JCOA became one of the earliest collectives to obtain funding for its concerts and for setting up a JCOA record label. The label's first release consisted of a 1968 double-album of compositions by Mantler, performed by large ensembles featuring the above-mentioned musicians plus a variety of others, including Larry Coryell, Steve Swallow, Pharoah Sanders and Cecil Taylor.

JCOA went on to sponsor concerts and albums by Bley, Cherry, violinist Leroy Jenkins, and Archie Shepp associates Roswell Rudd, Clifford Thornton and Grachan Moncur III. On these later LPs, rather than working under the standard arrangement whereby the composer/leader earns a royalty and

---

* The anti-war protestors at the convention, in the moment of their defeat, sang the black spiritual "We Shall Overcome Some Day." Is it entirely a coincidence that, a few years after Haden's recording, a famous folksinging duo had a mega-hit with another spiritual, "Bridge Over Troubled Water"?

everyone else is paid a session fee, all the performing musicians received an equal royalty rate. The JCOA also took the significant step of setting up New Music Distribution Service, in order to identify interested retailers; supply them with product from the host of small specialty record labels beginning to spring up in the U.S.; and, on a reciprocal and non-profit basis, to handle the equivalent labels in various European countries and in Japan. Interestingly, Bley, Mantler and Haden are white, but their interest in alternative politics was, at the time, at least as genuine as their interest in alternative distribution. (It was alleged that ABC-Impulse was less than assiduous in promoting the *Liberation Music Orchestra* album, making it more of an underground venture than had been hoped.)

The musician who was the most visible advocate of the new black consciousness, Archie Shepp, had been publicized by the music media because of his prolific association (facilitated by John Coltrane) with Impulse. Not only Shepp's printed statements, but his music as well, was intended to further the cause. Whereas Louis Armstrong and all the greatest soloists up to Coltrane and Coleman spoke to the heart of their listeners, Shepp went straight for the jugular. His recording career had begun with Cecil Taylor in 1960, and he had appeared in a rather low-profile avant-garde series on Savoy Records produced by trumpeter Bill Dixon. He then got the nod from Thiele, who had him tape an album of tunes by Coltrane, then appear on a couple of albums on which Trane's group also performed.

In terms of his straight-ahead rhythm and choice of material (most of his records from this period included one or more standards), Shepp's approach often seemed closer to Ornette or even to R & B saxophone than to either Coltrane or Ayler. Only during his second Impulse contract were "message" albums like *Things Have Got To Change*, *Cry of My People* and *Attica Blues* released, in 1971-72. Before that, Shepp had toured

Europe several times, recording in Denmark in 1963, in Germany in 1967 and making numerous albums from 1969 to 1970. By the start of the 1970s, he had the highest profile of a large group of black Americans resident for several months in France.

While in France, these black jazzmen were repeatedly recorded in shifting combinations either by Musidisc (on their America label) or by BYG Records. Like ESP-Disk before them, BYG quickly acquired a bad financial reputation. Even by holding back the royalty payments promised to group leaders, BYG soon went out of business. At one point, the label was offered for sale to U.S. Columbia, whose own brief and half-hearted attempts to record the free jazz of the late 1960s still remain unissued. The very nature of the BYG recordings' European origin, and the fact that many Americans of the bebop generation had also recently emigrated to Europe, eventually earned these players greater interest and respect in their own country.

The BYG label more or less restricted its activities to taping itinerant American musicians. But the arrival of free jazz had already revolutionized the performance, and the recording, of young European musicians as soon as it began to appear on disc. Alto saxophonist Joe Harriott, one of a group of players born in the British West Indies who settled in London at the start of the 1950s, was probably the first European-based jazzman to move away from fixed-time playing and fixed chord sequences. Harriott's vital Parkeresque work in the 1950s had already stood out from that of most of his copyist contemporaries on the British scene; his exploration of free jazz only began (in 1959) after the appearance of the first Ornette Coleman album. Interestingly, and rather prophetically, neither his methods nor his individual alto sound had much in common with Ornette's—one could almost say he was more inspired by the liner notes than by the music on Coleman's album—but this development might not have happened without the influence of recording. In addition, Harriott helped pioneer the fusion of jazz with Indian music in the mid-1960s, a move clearly influenced by the popularity (on records, initially) of the sitarist Ravi Shankar.

Similarly, German trombonist and Harriott contemporary Albert Mangelsdorff had already established a sizeable reputation in conventional—in his case, Tristano-influenced—jazz before making a definitive shift to free jazz in the early 1960s. Mangelsdorff's international influence only became a reality in the next decade, by which time Harriott had passed away. Both of these players received some critical attention for their early free albums, in the shape of reviews in *downbeat*. As with Lars Gullin a decade earlier, this recognition from the homeland of jazz was possible only because of records, for there was still no way these musicians could be heard live in the U.S. unless they became permanent immigrants.

Younger players all over Europe were beginning their careers just as free jazz was reaching its heights. In the words of saxophonist Peter Brötzmann: "About the same time in Holland, in Germany, and a little later in England, musicians began working with the same material—which was the mid-1960s, the same time free music was really happening in the States." The development was aided by the 1960s movement of Americans to Europe and the wider circulation of those on shorter visits. As in the 1930s, there were several recordings made of visitors with European musicians, such as the Eric Dolphy *Last Date* album with drummer Han Bennink and pianist Misja Mengelberg. (Bennink and Mengelberg went on to become leading lights on the Dutch free-jazz scene.)

In common with British drummer John Stevens, Bennink has retained an involvement in the time-based playing of earlier American jazz; so has the saxophonist Evan Parker. Even though the flow of Stateside visitors into the UK was still more restricted than on the Continent, Parker found parallels and inspiration for exploration in key recordings from the U.S. Recently, he described an out-of-time passage in Coltrane's 1965 "Brasilia" in these terms: "The accommodation they make for each other in the piece is amazing, and the tension that comes out of that is tremendous . . . Then it becomes just a matter of interaction of phrasing, and really is very close to the procedures that are at the basis of [European] free improvisation."

Despite the generalized example of records, procedures which would have been dutifully copied by Europeans of an earlier decade were now worked out in playing, often in such intensely focused situations as the duo. With only two musicians, even if one has a rhythm instrument, there is no longer a rhythm section or a front line. Examples of these duos include Parker and John Stevens (active in 1967 but only recorded as such in 1975), and the team of Parker and guitarist Derek Bailey. Although of the Harriott/Mangelsdorff generation, Bailey renounced conventional playing in the mid-1960s in favor of free improvisation.

The attempt to get such music on to disc was frustrated by the general lack of independent record labels in Europe. European multinationals such as EMI and Decca/Telefunken —the only others of consequence were Polydor and Philips, who in the 1970s would merge as Polygram and buy out Decca —had leasing arrangements for all the popular American product. As a result, these companies had the market tied up at least as tightly as had the U.S. majors before 1943. Even CBS and RCA did not set up their own European offices until the 1960s, with the powerful Warner/Elektra/Atlantic (WEA) and MCA following suit in the next decade. The majority of American independents, including all the significant jazz labels mentioned in the last two chapters, leased their product to the European majors until the early 1960s, when the first moves were made to import American pressings of labels such as Blue Note, Riverside and Candid.

In the case of European music, until the 1960s, what jazz was recorded on specialty series like Swing and Vogue (in France) or Tempo (in England) was financed and distributed by the major holding companies. The very few jazz-inclined independent producers—like Denis Preston, who recorded Chris Barber, Acker Bilk, Humphrey Lyttelton, and Stan Tracey—leased their material to the majors. As for uncompromising avant-garde jazz, there was occasional interest from small labels; the fledgling Island Records, for instance, released a 1968 Spontaneous Music Ensemble album with John Stevens, Evan Parker, Derek Bailey and bassist Dave Holland. One or two historic, and now extremely rare, sessions were issued by tiny operations set up expressly for that purpose.

In the later 1960s, the same "progressive" outlook that developed in the U.S. induced the European-based majors to start issuing minority product, in the hope of discovering a trend that would be financially rewarding. New jazz recordings appeared briefly on subsidiary series belonging to Decca (John Surman, Michael Gibbs, Mike Westbrook), RCA (Westbrook, Chris McGregor), Polydor (McGregor, Spontaneous Music Ensemble), CBS (Tony Oxley, Howard Riley) and Philips (Keith Tippett, Nucleus), to name only some British examples. Even EMI's Apple label, run by the Beatles and their entourage, not only featured the Modern Jazz Quartet but recorded Yoko Ono performing live with Ornette Coleman.

Even this reasonably broad range of progressive music, however, was too strong and too badly promoted to earn any visible income for small companies. One result was a second SME album for Island and a second Chris McGregor for Polydor (each including a visiting American musician, as it happens) being left on the shelf. With the majors' interest in even conventional jazz at its lowest ever by the end of the 1960s, it was obviously going to be the responsibility of small labels to document the new European music. The most dedicated and resilient ones were those which the musicians themselves played an active part in running.

The Instant Composers' Pool, a Dutch collective organization, launched the ICP label with *New Acoustic Swing Duo*; as duo member Han Bennink has said, "When I did the first record with [reedman] Willem Breuker, there were 500 copies and I drew all the covers by hand." Meanwhile, a label based in West Berlin, Free Music Production, made its debut with *European Echoes*. This album featured a 15-piece group assembled by trumpeter Manfred Schoof and containing players from several different countries—Bennink, Enrico Rava, Evan Parker, Derek Bailey and Alex Schlippenbach. The latter musician's own large-scale Globe Unity Orchestra had first recorded for the middlebrow jazz label MPS (Musik Produktion Schwarzwald), with many of their albums produced by critic Joachim Berendt. Later, Globe Unity recorded prolifically for FMP. Peter Brotzmann, a regular member of the group who has made over 20 of his own albums on FMP, asserted that "behind FMP there is one crazy person that has been working for it since the beginning, Jost Gebers. Without him, FMP would have died as a record label."

The man behind Incus Records is Derek Bailey, who founded it in 1970 with Evan Parker (until recently still a director) and Tony Oxley. According to Bailey, "If you happen to be a musician who doesn't need to make records, you've got no reason to have a record label, because the whole thing is a pain in the arse." As one minor example of the difficulties encountered, the label's second Bailey/Parker duo, *The London Concert*, does not acknowledge that it took place at the Wigmore Hall. Why? For the simple reason that the venue would have charged the record company a "facility fee" for the use of their name.

Obviously, having your own record label is better in many ways than being hired to create x minutes of music for a big, impersonal organization. Actually running one, however, is something that few musicians have a taste (or even a talent) for. As already noted, there were isolated attempts in the U.S. during the 1950s; the companies mentioned above had also been preceded by Charles Mingus's latest label in 1965 and by an album issued in 1966 by PG Records, run by and featuring Don Pullen and Milford Graves. Yet in the 1960s, the American record industry at least proved somewhat more receptive to the new jazz than the European industry was to the European avant-garde. So performers who were at home behind a fretboard or a mouthpiece had to start supervising the editing of their tapes, the test pressings of their discs, and the designing and printing of their record sleeves. Not only that, but storing the finished albums, advertising their availability, packaging and mailing them to the few interested stores, or (a more time-consuming effort) to interested individuals around the world. Plus, of course, there is all that paperwork—not for their own satisfaction, but for the taxman, or for that useful intermediary, the jazz-loving accountant whose only payment might be a couple of free albums.

Nonetheless, the satisfaction of seeing one's work documented, and of retaining control over its use, has led many more musicians since the late 1960s to go this route. Germany's Gunter Hampel (Birth Records) and Willem Breuker (BV Haast) are early examples. An interesting collective variant was attempted in the U.S.in 1971 by trumpeter Charles Tolliver and pianist Stanley Cowell. As co-leaders of the quartet "Music Inc.," Tolliver and Cowell started a record label named Strata-East. This set-up was described as a condominium whereby artists (including Pharoah Sanders, poet Gil Scott-Heron and the Heath Brothers) used the company umbrella to put out self-produced albums while retaining their rights to the material and any profits arising therefrom. Unfortunately, that innovative arrangement broke up in some acrimony five years later. It's hardly surprising, then, that even among the huge number of small labels that have been started in the last two decades, the great majority have been run by non-players. Such non-musicians occasionally had a less exploitative—and more collaborative—relationship with the performers than did some of their predecessors.

It is also no surprise that the jazz-rock movement which hit its stride during the late 1960s should be associated with the major multinational companies. RCA had signed Benny Goodman and Tommy Dorsey just as they were about to achieve great fame, and CBS had picked up Dave Brubeck at the right moment in the 1950s. In the same way, CBS shelled out large sums of money to bands like Chicago and Blood, Sweat and Tears once it became clear that fusions of jazz and rock music could be a viable, popular, money-making activity for the 1970s.

By coincidence, the leading black pioneer of jazz-rock was already under contract to CBS: Miles Davis. It is somewhat to the credit of the company, but also typical of the times, that CBS dared to promote the work of a black artist along with the upstart young white bands that achieved greater success. Even so, it took Miles himself to exert pressure (as he had with Bob Weinstock) before this came about. According to Clive Davis, then a CBS vice president, Miles insisted at one point that "'if you stop calling me a jazz man . . . and just sell me alongside those other people, I'll sell more.'" One might say that Miles spoke not a moment too soon—in 1972, Clive Davis dropped Charles Mingus, Ornette Coleman and Keith Jarrett (who had all been signed the previous year) in one fell swoop.

There is still an element of controversy as to whether CBS exerted some undue artistic influence on Davis at this period. As singer Betty Carter said at the time, "He'd made money for Columbia for years. How come they didn't respect him enough then to put his picture on the trade magazine? But he had to join them [i.e. become stylistically acceptable] and do what they

wanted him to do before they put his picture on *Record World.*"
Miles's producer from 1959 to 1984, Teo Macero, disagrees,
noting that "there were other things that were done before that,
1965, 1967, 1968 . . . Go back and you'll see the source, and
you'll see it in the music." As early as 1963, for instance, drummer Tony Williams—on *Miles Davis in Europe,* his first full
album with the band—briefly introduces an eight-to-the-bar
backing figure straight out of the pop-music field.

More so than his colleagues in the mid-1960s Davis group
(Wayne Shorter, Ron Carter and Herbie Hancock), Tony
Williams was young enough not to have an automatic prejudice
against pop. Nor did he think twice about playing a front-line
solo while the horns played a repeated, rhythm-section-like
role on "Nefertiti"; his backing parts were especially unpre-
dictable and, throughout his six-year tenure, his drumming
had a creative tension between rhythmic simplicity and Elvin
Jones-influenced complexity. The virtuosity this required was
more than matched by the all-encompassing ability of the other
Davis sidemen, who walked a similar tightrope between familiar chord sequences and Tristanoesque, abstract improvisation.

A few of Miles's 1967 albums showed such abstraction
and complexity as predominating. The 1968 records, including
subsequently released out-takes, revealed the pendulum swinging the other way, with the introduction of electric piano and
bass (including George Benson's guitar on one session) seeming
far less out-of-place than it would have been earlier. The following year, Miles opted definitively for the electric context—
with large rhythm sections consisting of multiple keyboards,
two bassists and eventually additional percussion—for *In a
Silent Way* (Tony Williams's last with Davis) and its double-LP
follow-up *Bitches Brew.* The latter album sold 70,000 copies in
its first two months; after this success, Miles became, in the
eyes of CBS, not merely a status symbol but a "hot property."
In 1971, his contract was renewed, guaranteeing him $300,000

for three years, the equivalent of what Stan Getz had been offered nearly five years earlier.

One of the interesting aspects of Davis's work at this period, apart from the crucial way it defined the parameters of jazz-rock fusion, lies in the manipulation of studio technology. Since at least the end of 1967, Teo Macero would sometimes leave the tape rolling continuously, so that a piece which only came together gradually would be captured without the musicians having to wait for the red light to start a take. Creative editing and repetition of parts of a taped performance had already been a feature of Charles Mingus's *Black Saint and the Sinner Lady* in 1963. Yet these techniques were never used as extensively as they were on *In a Silent Way*. The original session had produced about two hours of music, subsequently edited down to some 80 minutes by Macero; he claims that Miles then reduced it to two pieces lasting a total of 18(!) minutes, which was finally expanded to fill two LP sides by repeating the opening section of each track to end the track.

Davis's interest in studio techniques did not, instructively, extend to recording himself separately from his accompaniment, except for brief portions of the *Jack Johnson* film score and a short throwaway track called "Red China Blues." He did occasionally employ such effects like the electronically-created echo on his trumpet for *Bitches Brew*, which may have been produced live in the studio via an amplifier. On the track "Go Ahead John," Miles's original trumpet solo was, after recording, fed in again a few bars later to create the effect of a long trumpet duet.

Not only were the details of Miles's own playing highly influential but, as in the past, so were his sidemen. During the mid-1960s, Herbie Hancock, Wayne Shorter and Tony Williams were each recording their own versions of the current Davis compromise in albums under their own names. All of them did so on Blue Note; indeed, it was *their* efforts, rather than the label's work with Coleman, Cherry and Cecil Taylor, which at the time characterized the "Blue Note School" of avant-gardism.

Again, as in the past, Miles's sidemen were in an excellent position to form their own groups once they left Davis, and easily obtained lucrative recording contracts. Hancock did three albums on Warner Bros. before making the same affiliation as Miles himself—with CBS. For that label, he has cannily alternated back and forth from increasingly commercial ventures to serious (if somewhat glib) acoustic small-group jazz recordings, for all the world like one of those popular bandleaders of the swing era. Some of his jazz work has involved duos with his successor in Miles's band, Chick Corea, whose mix of activities has been comparable. Hancock has also hooked up from time to time with his colleague from the Davis period, saxophonist/composer Wayne Shorter, and his late-1970s VSOP quintet reunited all the Davis group, with Freddie Hubbard replacing Miles.

Weather Report was formed in 1970 by Shorter and keyboardist Joe Zawinul. Never a member of the Miles touring group, Zawinul collaborated with Davis on virtually all his studio sessions of the *Bitches Brew* period. Like Hancock, Shorter and Zawinul's group enjoyed a fifteen-year relationship with CBS. In view of the musical distance Weather Report traveled, it's fascinating to compare the last pre-Weather Report albums by the co-leaders, both made in August 1970. Shorter's *Odyssey of Iska* session features his own saxophone plus a joyous yet complex rhythm-section blend of Brazilian and Milesian approaches. *Zawinul* includes more horn-players (and an expanded rhythm section) but keeps them at the service of an impressionist's ear for effects and atmospheres. Zawinul's "Arrival In New York" was created by taking 30 seconds from Cannonball Adderley's "Country Preacher" (a Zawinul tune) and replaying the 15 i.p.s. tape at $3\,^3/_4$ i.p.s., thereby eliciting other-worldly sounds suggestive of an ocean liner's horn. Zawinul's work in Weather Report, especially after the advent of the synthesizer, eventually came to dominate the group at the expense of Shorter, but he also blended influences from funk, Latin-American rhythms and from European composition in such a way as to give "fusion" a good name. Weather Report came to define a whole genre, just as the Modern Jazz Quartet had in the 1950s.

It is tempting to attribute Zawinul's sensitivity and detachment about his compositional approach to his being European. He emigrated from Austria in 1959, and it's certainly worth noting that Weather Report's original bassist, Miroslav Vitous, was from neighboring Czechoslovakia. Vitous's debut album under his own name, incidentally, had been produced for a "progressive" subsidiary of Atlantic—as had Chick Corea's and an early Ron Carter feature—by their employer, Herbie Mann. Mann's Latin-Jazz "crossover" music had been marketed so successfully by the late 1960s, with consumer surveys and the like, that he could afford to indulge his sidemen as long as their albums were not issued under his name.

Another European associated, like Zawinul and Vitous, with the Miles Davis school of the late 1960s and early 1970s was British guitarist John McLaughlin. Invited to New York to work with Tony Williams' post-Davis group Lifetime, McLaughlin recorded two albums under his own name for Alan Douglas's small Douglas label. (In 1962, Douglas had done some jazz production for United Artists, including the unique piano trio session Money Jungle by Ellington, Mingus and Max Roach.) One side of McLaughlin's second Douglas LP, My Goal's Beyond, was a trial run for the quintet he formed in 1971, the Mahavishnu Orchestra; there were Indian elements in the drone of the tambura and the hand-drumming of the tabla. Either because of his spirituality or because he was anxious to establish himself, McLaughlin accepted a total fee of $2,000 for these two albums. But when his contract passed to CBS, the Mahavishnu Orchestra became the first popular success of the fusion field—playing Brubeck to Weather Report's MJQ, so to speak.

The Mahavishnu Orchestra's original line-up contained another Davis associate in drummer Billy Cobham—who had been on part of *Jack Johnson* and toured with Horace Silver—as well as three Europeans: McLaughlin, Vitous's former colleague Jan Hammer on keyboard, and Irish bassist Rick Laird.* A subsequent edition of the group included French violinist Jean-Luc Ponty, while McLaughlin's later acoustic group Shakti consisted of just McLaughlin and three Indian musicians, among them the violinist Lakshminarayana Shankar. The commercial failure of Shakti, however, showed that the fusion audience was less interested in the musical fusions as such than in the virtuoso techniques (and virtuoso decibels) pioneered by McLaughlin's electric group.

Now that Latin-jazz and jazz-rock had made eighth-note rhythms acceptable in improvised music, and not merely in pop, it was not sufficiently challenging for some musicians to play eight-to-the-bar (although there is a lifetime of rhythmic variety to be had thereby). Fusions not only with Indian but with Central European music made possible unusual rhythms of seven, nine, thirteen, fifteen, seventeen beats to the bar. Inevitably, everyone but cult followers eventually stood by and watched such intellectual games in dismay. Meanwhile, the musicians who relished these challenges were often the same musicians who became heavily involved in exploiting the new complexities of studio technique.

Four-track tape—standard by the mid-1960s—was superseded within just a few years by eight-track, sixteen-track

---

* Laird's previous American work had been with Buddy Rich, the last swing-era veteran to form a big band that was, in the late 1960s, open to contemporary influences of a reasonably conservative nature. So was most jazz-rock, pre-Mahavishnu and pre-Weather Report.

and twenty-four-track studios. For the dedicated fusionists, it would have perhaps been logical to use thirteen or seventeen tracks. But it was overdue for *any* musician with jazz connections to investigate the benefits that might accrue from what was already available in the pop field. It was rumored that with one particular single, King Curtis had overdubbed sixteen possible tenor solos to choose from. The opportunities presented by such technology enhanced the mystique of recording engineers, who could now become virtual co-producers. For instance, Billy Cobham's second album under his own name was recorded in New York, but the tapes were mixed and edited in London by Cobham and Ken Scott, who had engineered the early Mahavishnu Orchestra albums. As a result, Cobham was able to audition a section of "Flash Flood" and choose between alternative Randy Brecker solos recorded over the same backing, on parallel tracks. The wholesale use of close miking and separate tracks for each instrument at this period explains why even conventional big-band re-creations sound nothing like 1930s originals, which were sometimes recorded with a single microphone for the whole band. As Brecker said many years later, "My generation is used to overdubbing and not recording live. Musicians have separate booths and headphones in the studios. As a result, people tend to overplay and play loud. And the music becomes too intense."*

The company that became most identified with the use of technology in a jazz-influenced context was Creed Taylor's CTI, which graduated from being an independent production

---

* The Brecker Brothers, trumpeter Randy and saxophonist Mike, were among the top sessionmen of the 1970s. Despite their strong jazz credentials—both had toured with Horace Silver, for instance—their reputations were really made through studio work on other people's record dates. Like David Sanborn, who later made his own albums on Warner Bros., the Brecker Brothers assembled a band of studio notables (all of whom also appeared on each other's albums) and made a series of successful LPs for Arista.

company to a full-fledged label in 1970. The whole philosophy of the CTI approach was an outgrowth of what Taylor had envisioned for Impulse ten years earlier: arty and extremely expensive gatefold sleeves (and no liner notes) plus a list price to match. The recorded sound, courtesy of Rudy Van Gelder, was equally glossy, and invariably relied on being created in stages, like pop and middle-of-the-road productions. A backing track, taped first, was worked on by the star soloist, whose efforts were eventually "sweetened" with brass or strings as arranged by Don Sebesky or Bob James.

CTI's star soloists did include some notable instrumentalists—Freddie Hubbard, George Benson and, in decreasing order of musical significance, saxophonists Stanley Turrentine, Hank Crawford and Grover Washington.* All of these players had an inbuilt populist streak to their playing, which the CTI process managed to enhance at the expense of anything else, especially with edited-down singles destined for radio play. The results were records that became desirable consumer products; this mood music even took the Monk-influenced pianist Randy Weston (for one album only) and sold him to vastly more consumers than had ever heard his name before.

The performers, while often laughing all the way to the bank, were sometimes unhappy about CTI's methods. Producer John Snyder, then an assistant at CTI, has said, "George Benson told me that when he made *White Rabbit* he had driven all night from Detroit. When he got there Don Sebesky presented him with tunes that Benson didn't know and consequently played tentatively. After the session Creed told Sebesky to fill in the gaps . . . Taylor was successful in exposing jazz artists to an audience twenty or thirty times larger than they had been exposed to before. This talent eventually cost him the loyalty of

---

* Washington got his highly successful break by recording solos over backing tracks originally intended for the indisposed Crawford.

the musicians who went on to record for 'major' labels as soon as their CTI contracts expired." Turrentine, for instance, went on to Fantasy, which after the late 1960s commercial success of Creedence Clearwater Revival, had expanded into a major group of labels; Benson moved to Warners, Washington to Elektra (both part of WEA); and Hubbard joined his former Blue Note colleagues at CBS.

In the mid-1970s, CTI agreed to have the enormously powerful Motown corporation distribute their product, an arrangement that called for 24 new albums a year. Despite issuing many previously unreleased tracks by artists who had already left CTI, Taylor failed to deliver. He became the defendant in litigation for breach of contract, and the CTI logo vanished from the record stores—while Grover Washington's early material reappeared on the Motown label.

In some respects, the transatlantic equivalent of CTI has been the European Contemporary Music label, also founded in 1970, but in Munich. ECM began life as a small concern dedicated to recording a cross-section of sounds, even doing two albums by Derek Bailey. They started to pick up steam with Chick Corea, then running his avant-garde quartet Circle with Dave Holland and Anthony Braxton. During the same European stay, Corea also taped two LPs' worth of impressionistic piano solos; the following year, he formed his popular group Return to Forever, which made its debut on ECM. Return to Forever's contract was subsequently bought by Polydor (ECM's first distributor) for a tidy sum which went towards expanding the smaller label's activities.

Improvised piano solos henceforth became the province of Keith Jarrett, the ex-Charles Lloyd virtuoso who had followed Corea in the Miles Davis band. Jarrett had done some session work for CTI and, alone among the Miles alumni, had expressed a strong preference for the traditional "acoustic piano" over the various, increasingly sophisticated electronic keyboards. Jarrett did take it for granted that, even without a rhythm section, the "even" eight feel was as much a part of jazz as the "uneven" twelve feel. His actual playing, as in the case of Oscar Peterson, is often a case of manner over matter, and appeals to a similarly wide audience; the 1975 double-album of his *Köln Concert* had five years later sold 600,000 copies, and was followed by a triple album, a single album and a boxed set of ten albums, all of solo piano.

The label's sales triumph was matched by their packaging (a sort of pastel equivalent of CTI) and professionalism. Trumpeter Enrico Rava (a member of the 1969 *European Echoes* group and of Globe Unity, described his ECM experience this way: "It was the first time I worked in full collaboration with a record label that could help me in specific ways, not only putting at my disposal ultra-modern studios, with perfect sound but also doing a proper promotion on my records. I think in New York my first album for ECM . . . stayed in the shop windows for a month." The company was able to ensure that its U.S. distributors also arranged concert tours for even its European musicians, which was hitherto unheard-of.

ECM's most consistent success has been with middlebrow American artists like Jarrett, Gary Burton and post-McLaughlin guitar impressionists Pat Metheny, John Abercrombie and Ralph Towner (of the group Oregon). Considerable artist loyalty has been achieved sometimes without the benefit of an exclusive contract; Jarrett, for instance, was for several years free to continue recording for Impulse. In addition, ECM features Europeans who have gradually refined a style in which the guts of American jazz are progressively curdled by a distinctively European lyricism. Saxophonist Jan Garbarek, who actually started out as a Coltrane/Ayler imitator, found his true role in two quartet recordings with Jarrett; he is now often heard in tandem with his fellow ECM leader, bassist Eberhard Weber (whose earlier group, Colors, made great capital of the Europeanized American, Charlie Mariano).

Many more artists have enjoyed long associations with ECM founder/producer Manfred Eicher—most of the above-mentioned for fifteen years or more. Even Pat Metheny notched up ten years and eleven albums before defecting to the WEA group in 1985. These musicians seem to have enjoyed an uncommon degree of autonomy in working out their projects. Equally, there are many stories about performers who did not particularly enjoy their experience of working with Eicher—or whose one album for him was never released, because it did not match his stylistic tastes. Yet this is no more than saying that some artists are suitable for ECM and some are not, which is surely true of any label with a strong identity.

If any one aspect of ECM's activity defines the label's identity, it is the sensitivity with which the music is recorded (and the high-quality noiseless nature of the vinyl on which it is pressed). For those musicians whose aim it is to sound as mellow and ungritty as they do on an ECM album, the production style is a faithful reproduction of their intent. But sometimes a different approach is required. Pat Metheny's keyboardist Lyle Mays said of the group's last ECM album *First Circle*, "We were in the studio by ourselves. It was an opportunity for us to get a version of our music that was not so much processed through Manfred Eicher. So we were going for a little hotter sound; basically, for better or worse, something that represented how it sounded to *us*, and how it sounded live." Eicher's relationship with his two favorite engineers (Martin Wieland in Ludwigsburg and Jan Erik Kongshaug in Oslo) sometimes seems more a determining factor than his choice of musicians; certainly, the ECM style of recording has become as influential internationally as have players like Garbarek and Weber.

After their great success in the mid-1970s, ECM began to take on board some more avant-garde Americans, some of them for one album only. Chicagoan drummer/composer Jack DeJohnette, who first recorded for ECM in 1971—with Keith Jarrett, while both were members of the Miles Davis band— introduced to the label one of the many editions of his own group which included Lester Bowie, trumpeter with the quintet known as the Art Ensemble of Chicago. By then a decade old, the AEOC was born from the Association for the Advancement of Creative Musicians, perhaps the most important, and certainly the longest-lived, of the many black collectives organized in different cities in the 1960s. Not coincidentally, the Art Ensemble had found their first response from the international jazz audience through working in Europe. They had made two albums in Chicago for the tiny but still active Nessa Label, run by a former assistant at Delmark Records, Chuck Nessa. One LP was issued under Bowie's name, and the other, recorded without Joseph Jarman, was credited to the "Roscoe Mitchell Art Ensemble." These albums, though, had only enjoyed limited distribution.

Recognition, if not overwhelming in financial terms, was certainly more forthcoming when the Art Ensemble of Chicago moved to Europe in 1969-70. Thanks to BYG and other labels (plus a French feature film in which they appeared), the AEOC taped 15 albums in the same number of months. Some of these found their way back to the U.S., though few were actually reissued there. When the musicians themselves returned, they did a couple of albums for Atlantic; the second one, *Fanfare for the Warriors,* had a guest appearance by the leading light of the AACM organization, pianist Muhal Richard Abrams. They then ran their own AEOC label. As with Sun Ra earlier, almost a decade had passed since the group's first recordings in Chicago before they successfully imposed their presence on New York. From the mid-1970s on, it was belatedly acknowledged that the Art Ensemble of Chicago had not only added to the language of jazz, but had also effectively become standard-bearers of the avant-garde.

By this point—when a third generation of free-jazz players like saxophonist Chico Freeman was already emerging from Chicago—the AEOC had signed with ECM. The group's superior recordings for ECM drew attention to the mastery of saxophonists Mitchell and Jarman, and to the panstylistic provocation of Bowie (who went on to do separate albums for ECM with his Brass Fantasy). It also became apparent, as with Sun Ra, that the AEOC's exotic effects and multiple use of miscellaneous instruments—as well as their theatrical stage presentation—were less significant than their ability to draw on various periods of jazz and prejazz history, building convincing and compelling performances from disparate materials.

Much the same might be said of saxophonist and composer Anthony Braxton, except that his concept is possibly even more all-embracing. He has written a number of works which are fully scored, leaving no apparent room for improvisation, and some which go far beyond the free-time playing introduced in the 1960s and which are completely out-of-time. On the other hand, far more so than his close colleagues—the members of the Art Ensemble—Braxton has recorded a considerable number of jazz standards (from "Maple Leaf Rag" onwards) in a manner that distantly reflects his early admiration for Paul Desmond and the Tristano disciples.

Braxton's recording career is roughly similar to the AEOC's. One of his two late 1960s projects for Delmark became a much-imitated milestone: the double album *For Alto*, which consisted entirely of unaccompanied solos and featured pieces dedicated to Cecil Taylor, John Cage and violinist Leroy Jenkins. Braxton recorded with Jenkins and with trumpeter Leo Smith in Chicago, in New York, and in his Paris period—unlike the eagerly-received Art Ensemble, this was a group without bass or drums. He also worked for a year, mostly in Europe, with Chick Corea's Circle.

Braxton's espousal by a serious and well-equipped record company came in 1974 when he returned from Europe and signed a contract with Arista. The executive producer of several of their jazz projects, Steve Backer, was involved in classic reissues; he had pushed Arista to buy the rights to the Savoy label after the death of Herman Lubinsky. Backer also recorded fusion by the Brecker Brothers and other artists on Arista/GRP (GRP has in the 1980s become an independent label). But the performer who got the most favorable treatment was Anthony Braxton, recording nine albums in five years despite the fact that his records were "only marginally profitable for the company." Backer suggested to Braxton that his first Arista albums should "deal with time and meter. Then we [would be] able to make more people in the jazz community embrace his music."

The most unusual and doubtless the least profitable Braxton project was 1978's *For Four Orchestras*. This work required 160 musicians and ran for 114½ minutes (on a three-LP set). Backer noted, "I can't think of another instance where a black musician, coming from the jazz tradition, has been allowed that kind of liberty, where that kind of money and that kind of energy have gone into a project with such limited commercial appeal." Proud, promotion-worthy words indeed. Yet in an Italian interview not long afterward, Braxton revealed that he had put up some of the money himself as "co-producer." "I had to, because Arista didn't want to risk it on their own and I definitely wanted to do that project," he revealed. "I spent so much money, and I owe so much that I came to Italy to escape my creditors and get as far away from them as possible!"

·8·

THE FUTURE OF
JAZZ RECORDING

———————◆———————

The mid-1970s coming of age of free jazz was signaled by the gravitation of new players to established centers such as Chicago, New York, Berlin, Amsterdam or London. For the most part, these were musicians young enough to be aware only of the most recent styles, people for whom free jazz represented the classic "hard" style compared to which jazz-rock/fusion was a popular "soft" option. For most of them, bebop, if familiar at all, would have sounded quaint and outmoded, despite the occasional references to it by mentors like the Art Ensemble or Anthony Braxton. This was somewhat less true, however, if they had been affiliated with one of the black collectives organized in cities like Chicago (where newcomers included Chico Freeman, Henry Threadgill and the trombonist George Lewis); St. Louis (Oliver Lake, Hamiet Bluiett, Julius Hemphill); Los Angeles (David Murray, Arthur Blythe); and New Orleans.

As usual, New York was more of a competitive free-for-all where "free-jazz concert" often meant the musicians didn't get paid. But even there, more solidarity was evident in this style of music than in many others. The idea of collectively-produced, or self-produced, albums reached a peak in the mid-1970s, mirroring the approach to producing live performances by the avant-garde musicians. Such concerts took place in even the largest of the other cities; the copious loft spaces of New York had housed such performances since early in the 1960s. The "loft scene" trend was given greater impetus at the end of the decade by Ornette Coleman and reedman Sam Rivers, who both opened their own premises and set up organizational structures (including applying for grants from foundations and from the city) so that countless other musicians could make their appearances there.

The few recordings of this music that were done for American labels during the 1970s were either closely connected with the loft scene, or actually taped in such venues. They show that, just as it took nearly two decades from the unexpected arrival of Lester Young to the apotheosis of hard bop, the same length of time since the startling debut of Ornette Coleman had brought about further stylistic consolidation. The series of five albums from one week's performances at Sam Rivers' Studio Rivbea in May 1976—collectively called *Wildflowers* and done for the Douglas label (which had lately enjoyed success with its posthumous issues of Jimi Hendrix material)—covers a catholic collection of second- and third-generation free players. As well as demonstrating that the language is well-established, the recordings feature congas or other additional percussion in a way which, although inspired by late-period Coltrane or the Art Ensemble, is more rhythmically conservative than either. The rhythmic approach of the music on *Wildflowers* might be termed post-fusion.

Similar elements of relative conservatism can be heard in albums recorded around the same time at other lofts for the small India Navigation Company. One India Navigation track is a virtual anthem of this movement, David Murray's "Flowers For Albert." The dedication to Albert Ayler highlights a direct influence on Murray's tenor sound yet a considerable distance in rhythmic terms from Ayler's early trio and quartet albums. In the same way that the 1950s had seen the first attempts at "third stream" music, the mid-1970s witnessed the arrival of musicians like Anthony Davis and James Newton, whose post-free compositions involve a more natural blending with European classical techniques. Another development paralleled in the 1950s (by the Modern Jazz Quartet) was the musically formalist approach adopted when Murray, Hamiet Bluiett, Oliver Lake and Julius Hemphill began working together in 1977 as the World Saxophone Quartet.

It is noteworthy that a group like the World Saxophone Quartet was immediately in the position to start touring in Europe and to make their recording debut for Black Saint Records—an Italian specialty label that sells 70 percent of their albums of American artists elsewhere than in the U.S. All four of the WSQ members had worked for Black Saint as individual leaders, as had a lengthy list of progressive musicians: Archie Shepp, Steve Lacy, Lester Bowie with Arthur Blythe, Don Cherry, Don Pullen, Leroy Jenkins, Anthony Braxton with Max Roach, Cecil Taylor (with and without Roach), Chico Freeman, George Lewis, Henry Threadgill and others. Shepp commented, "The fact that for some years I've recorded solely and exclusively for European and Japanese labels has brought forth the wrath of the monopolistic [American] record companies that use their power over magazines like *downbeat* . . .

A few years ago, in 1975, I was negotiating a contract with Arista, but we couldn't reach agreement about money. I don't see why I should sign a contract now at 1960 rates." So Shepp's only appearances on Arista—like Anthony Braxton's first album on the label—was by courtesy of the London-based Black Lion/Freedom Records, whose product was leased for U.S. sale to Arista for a while in the mid-1970s.

This marked one of the first instances of European-financed recordings of American musicians being sold back to their country of origin. (The English have a proverbial expression about "carrying coals to Newcastle," of which selling jazz to the States must be a contemporary equivalent.) The practice has, though, become increasingly common, with ECM being distributed for a long time by WEA and Black Saint now marketed in the U.S. by Polygram. Indeed, the advertising muscle of such distributors in periodicals and elsewhere has, in the 1980s, outdated the first part of Shepp's statement.

Yet Shepp's complaint about working for low pay may still have some validity. One British jazz critic, sent to New York to record American players for a British label, was told while in the States that the union scale for recording (geared mainly to the requirements of sessionmen) was now so high that one could often persuade jazzmen to record for less than scale. Otherwise, the reasoning went, they would price themselves out of work for small specialty labels altogether. Interestingly, since jazz critics and jazz photographers often have another full-time job, they, too, often work under scale, and full-time practitioners tend to miss out if they demand the professional rate for their efforts.

It is the Japanese labels, though, that have had the most beneficial influence on the international jazz record scene. At the start of the 1970s, the Japanese branches of RCA (known there as Victor or JVC) and CBS/Sony—plus smaller companies like Denon, Trio, and later East Wind, Seabreeze and

WhyNot—were already taping the specially-commissioned sessions that seldom appear in the U.S. or Europe, except as high-priced imports. In addition to Japanese musicians, some of whom have gained worldwide reputations, these sessions have often featured Americans or even Europeans of repute, but strictly for Japanese consumption. Herbie Hancock and Miles Davis, for example, have made albums in Japan which have never been released in their own country. It was a Japanese label that virtually founded the German ENJA label by agreeing to co-produce their 1971 recordings of American pianist Mal Waldron and of Japanese trumpeter Terumasa Hino's Berlin Festival performance, as well as by taping Albert Mangelsdorff in Tokyo.

Japan's jazz audience has grown at such a phenomenal rate in the last 25 years that their record companies have also led the way in reissuing either historical items or newer items originally done for other countries. Although in the 1980s it has become widespread to follow the Japanese trend of releasing reissues in facsimile reproductions of the original packaging, it was the viability of earlier Japanese reissue programs that inspired a similar explosion in the U.S. during the 1970s. Another cause of American "reissue-mania" was the example set by chronological, comprehensive compilations from overseas. Collections of Louis Armstrong on OKeh (in Britain and France), of the Parker Savoy sessions (first organized in this way by the UK label Realm) and of the Parker Dials (on the British Spotlite label)—established new standards of thoroughness and completeness in terms of presentation, inclusion of alternate takes, and remastering of the recorded sound (in mono when originally done in mono).

The insatiability of the Japanese market also motivated the search for historic material that was legitimately recorded under a valid recording contract but, for a variety of reasons, never previously released—like the two further LPs' worth of Sonny

Rollins at the Village Vanguard in 1957. The Fantasy label, acting on the advice of their "minister without portfolio," music columnist Ralph J. Gleason, acquired the Prestige label in 1971 and Riverside the following year. They then launched an influential series of double album reissues selling at two-for-the-price-of-one.* Another sign of the times in the 1970s was the setting-up of the Trip label. Trip did not purchase any of the material it reissued, but leased it for specified periods from the major labels which could not profitably use it themselves.

Of course, all this reissue activity helped to encourage a movement that was already hinted at by the now more backward-looking work of people like Archie Shepp. Twenty years earlier, the response to West Coast Jazz had created the hard bop consolidation on the one hand and, on the other, a swing/mainstream revival. Now the reaction to the rapidly degenerating fusion movement was the previously noted (but not yet critically pigeonholed) "free consolidation"—and a bebop revival.

Once again, it was discovered that bebop, a style which had been considered marginalized, or at least neglected, was still full of vitality, and that some of the relevant musicians had been playing all the time. Some records had even been made during the dark years: in the last days of Prestige, and then, with former Prestige producer Don Schlitten, on first Muse Records and later Xanadu. Revived bop sounded nowhere near the same as original bop, not only because of more modern recording techniques, but also (as before, with the swing revival) because of the incorporation of modern rhythm-section techniques. As a result, younger musicians and younger listeners were drawn in.

The bebop revival found its focus in 1976, the year of *Roots* and the American Bicentennial, when Dexter Gordon

---

* In the 1980s Fantasy has also purchased Contemporary and Norman Granz's 1970s venture Pablo, which itself had influenced reissue trends by repackaging Granz's Art Tatum material in two boxed sets: one of eight albums and one of thirteen.

returned to the U.S. His American manager, Maxine Gregg, played her trump card with the new president of CBS. "I knew that Bruce Lundvall had been a tenor player," Gregg recalled. "So I invited him and the people from the other record companies to the Vanguard, and they all wanted to sign Dexter." CBS made the best offer, and recorded a double album live at the Vanguard called *Homecoming*. A later studio date, *Sophisticated Giant*, sold around 100,000 units.

The return to full professional activity of Art Pepper a few months later—culminating in his first-ever New York club date, also at the Village Vanguard—had a similar impact on listeners who had lived through the West Coast period. Pepper had once commented that until his 1957 session with the Miles Davis rhythm section, "I had never recorded with musicians of that caliber before." With this remark, he inadvertently wrote off the entire West Coast phenomenon—but his fans didn't mind. Like the later Coleman Hawkins and Ben Webster works of the swing revival, the "modern mainstream" purveyed by Dexter, Art and other surviving beboppers touched a whole generation who had never been encouraged to listen to them until now.

During his time at CBS, Bruce Lundvall was in an excellent position to ensure that jazz was represented in its output. He has since done the same at Elektra, where he started the Musician sub-label, and then at EMI, to which he was lured by the promise of being allowed to reactivate the dormant Blue Note series. Another former tenor player, Michael Cuscuna—freelance producer for Dexter's *Homecoming* plus hundreds of others, and now working full-time for Lundvall—has described Lundvall as "probably the only person to rise to the highest echelon of the record industry, and remain both honest and remembering that he loves jazz."

Record fans consistently underestimate the extent to which single concerned individuals have been able to, or have been obliged to, influence record company policy. Record fans also conveniently overlook how many non-jazz labels suddenly start a loss-making jazz series as soon as they make a too-sudden profit on their pop output. This "single-man theory" can be demonstrated by pointing to the number of CBS projects put on ice as soon as Lundvall departed, and the rapid disbandment of the Musician series when he left Elektra.

Lundvall's vital role in recorded jazz is represented by the label switches of a number of artists. After the expiry of his CBS contract, Dexter Gordon moved to Elektra, and later re-signed with Blue Note. Stanley Turrentine, Mose Allison and Bobby McFerrin were with Elektra and followed Lundvall to Blue Note. So did Jimmy Smith, who first applied soul-jazz to the electric organ and has returned to the label that first discovered him in the 1950s when it was still an independent.

Guitarist James "Blood" Ulmer made his first albums for small independent labels, then joined CBS. After a period without a record deal, he currently records for Blue Note. Ulmer may also be considered representative of a stylistic trend associated with the band Prime Time, led since the mid-1970s by Ornette Coleman. Prime Time combined some of Coleman's earlier principles with heavily amplified guitars and bass-guitars (two of each) plus, more recently, electronic drums.

This movement was, in one way, another consolidation of the language of free jazz, but in a populist framework which was definitely post-fusion. If the generation of musicians mentioned earlier in this chapter may be likened in the historical ebb-and-flow to 1950s hardboppers, the "free-funk" of Ulmer and of drummer Ronald Shannon Jackson (who also worked with Prime Time) may be the 1980s equivalent of late-1950s modal jazz. A simplified and very influential dialect, but hardly a new language, this school is an obvious precedent for the younger players whose music was named M-BASE by altoist Steve Coleman (no relation to Ornette).

Oddly enough, the first recorded appearance of Prime Time, on the 1976 Ornette Coleman album *Dancing in Your Head*, was released on the Horizon label. This label was a division of decidedly middle-of-the-road A & M Records, co-owned by Herb Alpert. Horizon was another series which abruptly changed direction and then was discontinued altogether, after A & M fired Horizon's founder/producer, John Snyder. Snyder then formed a new label named after Ornette's loft venue, Artists House, which issued further items from the Prime Time session and extra unreleased Horizon material by Paul Desmond and by Charlie Haden (in duo performances with pianist Hampton Hawes).

Artists House issued several more newly-recorded albums, covering various jazz styles. What all Artists House albums had in common was a new relationship between artist and record label: the artists would lease their material to the production company for five years, rather than sell it in perpetuity. This idea was probably borrowed from top-name rock groups who had the clout to insist on renegotiation or return of their master tapes for reissue by another label. Rock groups would get (on paper at least) a royalty of as much as 17 percent or more. But royalties for jazz players were often still as little as five percent of the list price—by then, usually $7.98.* Snyder pointed out that "publishers are paid on every record now, but the artists, because they have no one organization that represents their interests, are subject to whatever record companies give them." The Artists House contract gave them 67 1/2 cents on each copy printed, including those given free to potential

---

* However, as revealed by writer Michael Ullmann, this royalty was only paid on 90 percent of records, since, back in the 78 RPM era, records were so easily breakable. Further deductions were made for container costs, with a whopping 30 percent allotted for "free goods" (which meant that distributors of major labels paid for 1,000 records and were given an extra 300 records free as an incentive).

reviewers. (Not even book publishers are usually so generous to their authors.)

Obviously, few of the smaller specialty labels had initially set out to rip off their artists. But if they became successful enough to seek major distribution deals, they would be liable (at least in the U.S.) to be drawn into this system and to dilute their ideals accordingly. Small labels founded from the 1970s onwards, however—whether musically uncompromising or more mainstream—are used to the total lack of interest from conventional distributors. Therefore, they use specialty distributors, or sell direct to either interested retailers or to the public by mail-order. According to Charlie Lourie, now manager of the reissue label Mosaic, "Outside of New York, Los Angeles, Chicago and a few other major urban centers, there isn't a place in this country where you can buy a non-mass-market jazz album. Try living in Cincinatti, for instance—there aren't any jazz record stores there." The situation is no better outside the large towns of Europe, either.

Perhaps Artists House, the model independent label, would have been the logical place to discover a significant stylistic breakthrough akin to Lester Young's 1936 debut and Ornette Coleman's in 1958. Maybe Artists House could have made a similar underground and long-term impact while free-funk was enjoying relative popularity. Failing an American source and given the internationalization of jazz, it is tempting to look for the "next big thing" in Japan or in Western European improvised music. The latter, by some definitions, is now as distinct from jazz as are blues and gospel. It is equally tempting to look to Russian free jazz, on which the reputation of the British-based Leo Records has been founded. It is tempting, but not ultimately convincing.

The truth of the matter is that jazz has changed too much since artists like Young and Coleman burst on the scene. If, as is frequently pointed out, Coleman and Coltrane were the last innovators to have an internationally influential sound and personal style, this is because such immense individual contributions are no longer possible. A student of mine astutely pointed out years ago that since all the stylistic barriers to an all-encompassing jazz language have been broken down one by one, the kind of strong leadership which breaks barriers is no longer needed.

In a sense, the condominium has now been built, and each new floor (however unsteady it first looked to some observers) has stood the test of time and has contributed to the appearance, and the acceptance, of the whole edifice. Some external and internal decoration is still feasible and even desirable; part of the work will be done to the highest international standard, and part of it will draw on the virtues of local craftsmen (Oliver Lake's reggae-jazz, Ken Hyder's Celtic folk-jazz, Akira Sakata's jazz-with-traditional-Japanese-drumming). Constant restoration will also be required, and not just in terms of better and better reproduction of old recordings. The "jazz repertory" movement will continue to gather strength, and to cover a wider and wider range of activities. Some restorers will attempt (and inevitably fail) to reproduce the original styles exactly down to the finest detail; others will want to modernize materials and have microchips with everything, while still ostensibly re-creating an earlier style. And there will continue to be the occasional "sports"—such as Henry Threadgill's trio Air imposing their interpretation on repertoire from the 1910s and 1920s, or France's Anachronic Jazz Band playing bebop tunes with a Dixieland approach. Certainly, when writer Richard Williams described the jazz of the 1980s as eclectic (and did so already in 1979), he could have been outlining its entire future.

Whether the major multinational corporations take an interest in that future seems both important and unimportant. Despite the fact that the majority of jazz documentation is now firmly in the hands of the small specialty labels, the corporations have the muscle power to sell jazz to people who don't already know all about it, and to give it a higher profile in the media. It may reasonably be argued that when the major labels show interest in jazz, as they have done in recent years, they are not so much leading public taste as responding to record-buyers' partial disaffection from the music of the pop charts. Nonetheless, the large corporations can make jazz "respectable" in a way that grass-roots interest alone seldom can.

Unfortunately, the large corporations are also more fickle than the average person, and more subject to financial nervousness. For them, the start of the 1980s, in the words of a younger and pop-oriented writer, saw "the record industry . . . undergoing its worst-ever economic slump." The managing director of CBS UK recently offered this assessment: "In the late 1960s and early 1970s, the creative mob [in pop production] totally swamped the admin people. That was the era of the gifted amateur. Then after the slump of 1979 the lawyers and accountants came charging back and completely annihilated the creative people." Of course, the extreme sensitivity to the profit motive is not exactly surprising, given that many huge and respectable organizations are indebted to the proceeds of organized crime. (The influence of the underworld is said to go back at least as far as the late 1940s, when the introduction of Top 40 sales charts was soon followed by the first attempts to fix the charts.) Another description of 1979–80 is that "mismanagement on the pop level caused people to react out of panic. The more aesthetic, less commercial things were out, and jazz was one of them."

Those were the words (in 1987) of Steve Backer, who now works for RCA. Before being taken over by the Bertelsmann Publishing Group in 1986, RCA had no jazz recording activity to cut out in the first place. On the other hand, the reissues of older material which the French RCA company had specialized in for 20 years (always with just one person in charge, originally an outside adviser, as with the 1950s "X" label) continued unaffected by the slump. Indeed, given the minimal expense of repackaging records that were done for a flat fee with no royalty agreement, the international sale of such reissues probably made a small but handy contribution to the company balance sheet.

Other corporations had less faith in their back catalogues —or perhaps never had anyone with enough knowledge of them. In the 1960s, MCA took over U.S. Decca, then absorbed both ABC and Chess in the 1970s. Even the intermittent reissue efforts of MCA's various European licensees had left the parent company cold until, in the 1980s, they first reprinted a French reissue series and, more recently, reactivated the Impulse label. Likewise, WEA had nothing to cut out during the slump, except for their reissues and a couple of mass-market crossover artists such as Herbie Mann.* Even the Blue Note series would have become completely extinct at this period were it not for the demand for reissues from their licensees, King Records in Japan and later EMI/Toshiba.

Backer's generalization that jazz was out is still too wide. At CBS, new jazz recording did continue, doubtless because it had advocates in a position of some power. Dr. George Butler, the black former president of Blue Note in the late 1970s, had joined CBS before the slump and before the departure of Bruce Lundvall. Though until recently uninterested in reissues, Butler has commissioned as executive producer a multitude of sessions, both mass-market and hard-core jazz. Some artists have even attempted both styles, like "Black" Arthur Blythe (as he once was known), whose first album for the label was produced by

---

* WEA let Mann go after 20 years in the same way that Blue Note (after EMI had been taken over) dispensed with Horace Silver after a mere 28 years, 24 of them under exclusive contract. Silver took the obvious course of founding his own label.

Bob Thiele. (He was then free-lancing after the demise of Flying Dutchman, and before setting up his 1980s company, Doctor Jazz.) On the other hand, ex-Jazz Messenger Wynton Marsalis, whose early albums were produced by Herbie Hancock, straddles the worlds of hard-core jazz and European classical music. Marsalis is one of the products of the collective performance/education organization of New Orleans; if the extension of earlier styles is a symptom of the eclectic 1980s, then Marsalis's work with the tenets of the 1960s "Blue Note School" is a powerful symbol of its possible benefits.

The widespread economic recession at the start of the 1980s also inspired the majors to think of much more long-term strategies, rather as they considered marketing the jukebox in the early 1930s. Especially as the oil-price crisis was expected to have eventual repercussions on the cost of vinyl, the leading electronics manufacturers Sony and Philips (with their respective interests in CBS and Polygram) were spurred to complete research into the compact disc, which was first marketed in Japan in 1982.

The compact disc is a wafer-thin piece of aluminum with a plastic coating. Its sounds are encoded digitally and, when decoded by laser beam, the CD yields such superior reproduction that familiar old analog recordings sound fresh and new. Since the CD can also add half as much playing time again to that of the average LP, jazz reissues have been thrown into a state of confusion. Many companies supplement classic performances with extra material for their CD reissues, while others eschew this policy but charge the same price for a remastered album which may play for only 30 or 33 minutes.

The combination of the CD's high sound quality with records which are no longer in copyright (i.e. anything cut over 50 years ago) has engendered another retrograde step in reissue trends. The thinking is clearly that the CD market will not yet bear the kind of comprehensive collections put out in the

1970s of a single artist's works arranged chronologically. So, even on single artist issues, there has been a sudden lurch into random compilation, with the result that some individual tracks of early Ellington or Armstrong are included on two or even three CDs while many, many more are not available on CD and presumably will not be for a long time to come.

At the same time, CD technology has provided a stimulus to new recording. As Michael Brecker has noted: "I seemed to be getting more offers from record companies than usual— I think it was because CD was coming in, and the companies had little extra budgets they were trying to dispose of." Because of the greater playing time of CDs, even new issues may include more material than on the equivalent LP, although the playing time of an LP is often liable to be greater than it would have been in the recent past. At first, record companies tried to limit the amount of artist royalties paid on CD sales because of the much higher retail prices upon which percentage calculations would have been based. But with the whole field having taken off so rapidly and production costs falling as a result, the labels are now more willing to pay the same rate as for LP royalties—at least to popular artists with lawyers and accountants at their side.

The same doubts about the future of vinyl doubtless stimulated the more aggressive marketing of portable cassette players like the Sony Walkman. Pre-recorded reel-to-reel tapes had been issued commercially ever since the mid-1950s, but had remained largely the province of high-fidelity fans rather than music fans. (The same thing is true of the quadraphonic craze of the late 1960s as well as the late-1970s rash of direct-cut discs, whereby for the sake of better reproduction, artists were expected to record a whole LP side in a single take.) But the pre-recorded cassette, though only now becoming a significant part of jazz release patterns, had in other areas of music been popular enough to rival the sales of the equivalent LP. Good as this was from the point of view of the industry, the prevalence of cassette recorders caused some largely justified concern about private copying of commercially-issued albums.

Home taping is something of a pin-prick for the industry compared to their enormous problem with counterfeiting. The "pirating" business is sufficiently well-organized around the world for multi-million-selling pop records to sell *as many* counterfeit copies as ones legitimately produced by the originating company. Record companies must also contend with the tangled web of copyright legislation in different countries. Until recently in Scandinavia, for instance, recording copyright only covered 25 years after publication, after which anyone was free to reissue the material. Copyright issues can clearly have an impact on an artist's earnings as well as the company's.

On the other hand, tape copying can have a much greater impact, and there are obvious flaws in the argument that anyone should be free to copy anything they like, especially in a small specialty field. In February 1987, Blue Note began enclosing a letter with each record they pressed, containing the facsimile signatures of 20 of their artists such as Dexter Gordon, Stanley Turrentine, Freddie Hubbard and McCoy Tyner. The letter read in part: "Jazz is not a mass-market phenomenon . . . The truth is that even big-time bootleggers ignore our product because they've learned even our biggest 'hits' add up to too-small numbers . . . Home-taping is now so common-place, so unrestrained, it has put a sizeable dent in our incomes, is jeopardizing our recording and 'live appearance' careers and is already causing record companies to limit the number of new artists and new albums they invest in and promote." One leading London jazz record store went so far as to post this letter on their door. And in the autumn of 1987, Blue Note dropped some of their contract artists.

In truth, jazz is not mass-market music. Although it grew from roots that have long since become widely accepted, and each of its stylistic renewals has had an influence on far more popular efforts, jazz began as a minority's music and is likely to remain music for the minority. For one thing, it is not background music because, as has already been shown, there is usually too much going on for it to be ignored. Also, far more than is usually recognized, most consumers use music as a background for some other activity, even if it's only daydreaming. A survey published in the U.S. in 1980 of "the type of music most often bought in pre-recorded form" gave jazz a handsome two percent of the market; in more recent years, it has been suggested that the figure has risen to four percent and, in territories such as Europe and Japan, it might even be as much as six percent.

Even these figures are, of course, based on the widest possible definition of jazz. Especially in the U.S. trade, the category "jazz" seems to include everything non-vocal which is not pop, middle-of-the-road or European classical. No reliable figures are available for the proportion of purchases that consist of reissued material, albums which—even before the arrival of CDs—were geared by major companies for the "replacement market," which is why the same old best-sellers keep getting endlessly repackaged. Luckily, with the greater readiness of the majors in the 1980s to lease out older material which they would find unprofitable to reissue themselves, specialty companies like Mosaic, Ace and Charly are reaching the new audiences who have helped to make reissues the backbone of the jazz market.

Obviously, the lifeblood of jazz itself, and thus eventually of the market, must be the young musicians. Some of them have been remarkably successful, not only on the bandstand but in the record marketplace. It is important, however, that especially the larger record companies should not have unwarranted expectations. Courtney Pine's combination of ability and charisma, and Island Records' contribution of good timing and good promotion, sold 70,000 copies of his first album in a year, nearly all in the UK (though, untypically for a British artist, the record was released in America and Pine has his supporters among American musicians). But if Island—or the British arms of EMI, Polygram and RCA/BMG who have followed Island's lead and signed several younger British bands— assume that all these artists will sell as many albums, the lawyers and accountants will soon tell them different.

It seems much more likely that new jazz recording, like reissues, will be largely left to the initiative of the still-multiplying small labels. After all, it is only thanks to them that even veteran musicians like Stephane Grappelli or Art Blakey have recorded so many albums in the last ten years. Many of these small labels have a hard time surviving or, at the very least, demand an awful lot of under-remunerated work from their dedicated proprietors. The financial constraints of these operations are such that even the disappearance of a specialty distributor owing them $2,000 is going to have a disastrous effect on their balance sheet for the year. But the positive side is the close relationships they develop with their regular artists, and which would be impossible in a larger organization—for example, the Ogun label's continuing work with (among others) London-based South African exiles, and the Edinburgh-based Hep Records' albums with Scots who have left the homeland.

Many of the small labels of the last decade are owned by musicians who play on virtually every one of their releases. The Loose Tubes band has an eponymous label; Stan Tracey owns Steam, an outfit which began life by purchasing one of his out-of-print earlier albums from a major company; Humphrey Lyttelton runs Calligraph. Despite the hassles, such labels find that each release pays for itself well enough to finance the next release.

In addition, all these new labels have a small but international market. As with reissues, more and more new recordings are no longer pressed separately in the U.S., Europe and Japan. Instead, they are printed in one country only, and imported by the specialty retailers all around the world. Many leading British-based players now do all their recording for foreign labels—John Surman and Kenny Wheeler for ECM; Tony Coe for the French company, nato; Gordon Beck, who appears either on JMS or Owl Records (both French), last made an album for a British label 20 years ago; and Mike Westbrook, who has been some-what better treated by (mostly small) British labels, now records for the prestigious Swiss company, Hat Hut Records.

Something which has occasionally facilitated the task of getting new music onto record is the availability of government or private subsidy. With the latter being so much more in favor in the West in the 1980s, it is encouraging to see that Hat Hut has in recent years received backing from the Swiss Bank Cor-poration. As long ago as 1971, the Arts Council of Great Britain extended its recording subsidies to cover the occasional jazz venture, a policy which continues to this day, while the Swedish Rikskonserter agency funds records, including jazz, on the Caprice label.

Such European initiatives influenced American activity for a while in the 1970s. For instance, a Roscoe Mitchell album on Nessa was made possible by the matching-grant system, and New World, a "non-profit record company dedicated to Amer-ica's music," issued new albums by such as Cecil Taylor and Ricky Ford as well as reissue compilations in their jazz program. Even where available, however, the process of applying for and obtaining such subsidy is terribly hit-and-miss. Dealing with the relevant bureaucrats can also be rather disheartening for personalities capable of creating this music in the first place.

One other, largely bureaucratic problem facing the cre-ator after his music has been released is the collection of pub-lishing royalties on an international basis. ASCAP and BMI long ago adopted a live-and-let-live policy, and do the necessary work for their members efficiently on American soil. But their cooperation with foreign equivalents like GEMA (West Germany), SACEM (France), STEMRA (Holland) and SIAE (Italy) apparently leaves much to be desired, with the result that American musicians making the bulk of their records in such countries need to become members of the local royalty collection agency. Even with royalties arising from American sales of such records or American radio use (more or less restricted to college radio stations)—royalties which ought to be passed on by the American agencies to the organization the composer is registered with—there seems to be a lack of reciprocity. In the past, this was no doubt influenced by the U.S. not being a signatory to the Berne Convention on copyright. Indeed, until 1978, the U.S. was ineligible because it had not enacted laws guaranteeing copyright for the requisite 50 years following an author's death. As we have seen, performers and especially producers of early jazz records hardly thought of the long-term viability of their creations. But since the most recent manifestations of jazz have also achieved greater and more lasting validity than even the musicians hoped for, the mechanisms for ensuring them and their immediate descendants a continuing income clearly need tightening up.

Certainly, as far as it lies within their power, we are seeing more and more performers taking charge of their own destinies, or at least their recording careers. In a decade which has also seen a great revival of interest in Latin-jazz, the Brazilian percussionist Airto Moreira is representative of the artist in control of his own product. Moreira self-produced an album which he recorded to fulfill a contractual agreement. The label had still not released it when Moreira pointed out that "it's in our contract that, if it's not issued after a certain time, it reverts to us." It perhaps follows from the ability to hold the reins— and where necessary, hold out for their rights—that musicians now have a more skeptical attitude toward the necessity of records. According to Airto, "Records are not that important to me in my career. It's just like you take a picture that shows how things were on a particular day, and then, like, seven months later you take another picture."

Reflecting a more positive but still pragmatic approach to the usefulness of a record was the comment of saxophonist Dave Liebman. "I spoke to a Danish record company that has distribution, like, from here to the door," he said. "'Record us; if you release it, give us a thousand [dollars] apiece, whatever. If not, I'll pay your expenses, you give me the tape and I'll try to get rid of it somewhere' . . . Even if only 500 people listen to an album, at least you have chronicled your work at a certain point. Then you can move on."

Even those who formerly considered recording an unsatisfactory activity are benefiting from being in charge. Steve Swallow, for example, used to find the studio "an intimidating adversary situation . . . The trick is to get the producer out of the booth. One way to do it is to *become* the producer, which I've done. Finally figured that one out." The guitarist John Scofield, whose albums Swallow produces as well as his own, has also seen the benefit of really using the studio as his ally: "You've got real microscopic sound, where you can really hear everything . . . I can't wait to do another live album but at the moment, because Gramavision has come up with the kind of budget so that I can really do a good studio project— it's not that you go in for one day and just do it as if it was a live date—I've been enjoying that lately."

The other advantage of controlling their own recording situation in the fullest sense is that jazz musicians, especially those of an earlier generation, often have a healthy disregard for the so-called benefits of modern recording technology. Sonny Rollins, who now produces his own albums, said of the 1950s and 1960s, "When we had to go in and record maybe in one day, somehow we seemed to get more of that feeling together than nowadays . . . Then came a period when you had all the options, and then the studio suddenly became very restrictive on an artist, at least on me and, I guess, on others also." One of the most telling anecdotes about studio technology *versus* jazz feeling comes from a recording session by the Count Basie Orchestra. Basie was gone, but the band still had its walking metronome, guitarist Freddie Green. A recording engineer asked, "Does the conductor want click?"—in other words, a click-track playing in his headphones to help him keep time. Naturally enough, the question was ignored and, naturally enough (for the 1980s, that is), the recording was done for compact disc release only and is available exclusively from Japan.

It still seems that the bigger the record label and the bigger the artist's name, the more friction there is likely to be. By 1985, Miles Davis had logged an unbroken 29 years with the same company, remaining under contract even through a five-year lay-off in the 1970s, enjoying the company's support during a success-filled return to performing in the 1980s. However, in 1985, CBS turned down the idea of releasing Miles's recording of a special big-band composition inspired by and dedicated to him called *Aura*; naturally enough (again, for the 1980s), this piece was written by a European musician, Danish trumpeter Palle Mikkelborg.

Miles being Miles, he was undaunted by what he considered the philistinism of CBS, and signed a new and lucrative contract with WEA. Davis made the absorbing and highly influential *Tutu* and *Amandla* for Warner Bros., but there was no sign of the label showing any more enthusiasm than CBS for issuing Miles's recording of Mikkelborg's composition. It seemed distinctly possible that *Aura* would become one of the great unknown works, except to people who had heard a private tape of its concert premiere. However, as they had already done during Davis's break in the 1970s, CBS was free after Miles's departure to repackage his earlier material and issue out-takes for the first time. It was not until late 1989 that CBS finally released, to considerable acclaim, their 1985 recording of *Aura*.

As we said at the outset, the history of jazz on record is not the same as the history of jazz. Even where a specific development or performance has been satisfactorily documented, its release may be delayed. The recording may be issued on a label with limited distribution, or on a major label that considers its sales potential so small that it is cut out before having a chance to sell. All these things have happened to items now considered classics of recorded jazz.

Looked at one way, the mere idea of recorded jazz can distort the priorities of a music which balances the needs of the audience against the instant collaboration of creative performers. Yet without the existence of records and the inspiration they gave to listeners and other musicians, jazz would have remained an obscure regional folk-style instead of influencing a worldwide musical revolution. For that, we must remain profoundly grateful to all those players and middlemen who continue to grapple with the music industry and who labor to bring us the jazz that has made its way onto records.

RECORD GUIDE

$\blacklozenge$

This is an attempted listing of all the artists and individual performances, roughly in the order they appear in the text. Some of these are only available second-hand, and catalogue numbers often (but not always) change when they are reissued, so it's best to consult a specialty retailer. CD numbers are shown after a / and, when marked +, they contain more material than the equivalent record.

◆ CHAPTER 1

Jim Europe (1881-1919) Five tracks on RCA PM 42402, seven on Saydisc SDL 221, both including "Down Home Rag"

Wilbur Sweatman (1882-1961) One item on soundtrack of *Tender Is the Night*, BBC REB 582

Freddie Keppard (1890-1933) Smithsonian R 020

Nick LaRocca (1889-1961) Victor recordings of the ODJB from 1917-20 and the 1936 comeback on RCA NL 90026; smaller selection on ASV AJA 5023; both include all tracks discussed (and "Margie," mentioned in Chapter 2). Only one of the very first Columbia sides has ever been on LP (Columbia C3L 30), though both were once on a 45 RPM EP (Philips BBE 12488)

195

Eubie Blake (1883–1983) Piano rolls reproduced on Biograph BLP 1011Q

Luckey Roberts (1887–1968) One item on Biograph BLP 1001Q (which also includes two piano rolls by James P. Johnson, one by Fats Waller, and the 1925 "Cow Cow Blues" by Cow Cow Davenport)

Willie The Lion Smith (1897–1973) 1938–39 tracks on Commodore 6.25491AG; and six 1958 tracks on Good Time Jazz S 10035, which also has six from the same session by Luckey Roberts

James P. Johnson (1894–1956) Piano rolls on Biograph BLP 1003Q and BLP 1009Q, the latter including the 1918 "Carolina Shout" and two versions of "Mama's Blues." One 1921 record on CBS 67257, which includes Eubie Blake's "Sounds Of Africa" and single tracks by 29 pianists ending with Bill Evans and Cecil Taylor

Mamie Smith (1883–1946) One item ("Crazy Blues") on Columbia C3L 33, which also includes one by Edith Wilson (both singers backed by Johnny Dunn) and the same items by James P. Johnson and Eubie Blake as the album above

Ma Rainey (1886–1939) VJM VLP 82

Bessie Smith (1895–1937) BBC REB 602/CD 602

Johnny Dunn (1897–1937) VJM VLP 11

Mutt Carey (1891–1948) 1922 tracks with Kid Ory on NoLa LP 12

King Oliver (1885–1938) VJM VLP 49 includes "Krooked Blues," "Weather Bird Rag," "Dipper Mouth Blues," and "Snake Rag" (Gennett version) and two takes of "Mabel's Dream" (from Paramount); EMI EG 260579 1 has the OKeh "Snake Rag" and "Mabel's Dream"; VJM VLP 35, four tracks including "Camp Meeting Blues" mentioned in Chapter 2; 1926 recordings including "Someday Sweetheart" on Classic Jazz Masters CJM 19

◆ **CHAPTER 2**

Clarence Williams (1898–1965) 16 tracks on Rhapsody RHAP 6031, 10 of them with Louis Armstrong and 14 with Sidney Bechet

Leon Roppolo (1902–43) New Orleans Rhythm Kings output on Classic Jazz Masters CJM 12 (including "Livery Stable Blues") and CJM 13 (including "Milenberg Joys" and other tracks with Jelly Roll Morton)

Paul Whiteman (1890–1967) RCA NL 89783

Fletcher Henderson (1897–1952) 1924–25 items featuring Louis Armstrong on VJM VLP 60; 1926–30 material on VJM VLP 42

Louis Armstrong (1901–71) The Hot 5 recordings such as "Cornet Chop Suey" and "Heebie Jeebies" on Columbia CJ 44049; Hot 7 sides including "Potato Head Blues" on EMI EG 260458 1; Savoy Ballroom 5 items such as "Muggles," "Tight Like That," "West End Blues" and "Weather Bird" on EMI SH 407; overlapping selections available on BBC REB 597/CD 597 and on Hermes CD HRM 6002. The words of Baby Dodds are from Folkways FJ 2290.

Lil Armstrong (1898–1971) Lil's Hot Shots with Louis Armstrong on Swaggie 818

Jabbo Smith (1908–   ) Affinity AFS 1029

Red Allen (1908–67) 1929 tracks on RCA FXML 7060

Bennie Moten (1894–1935) Retrieval FJ 120 (from OKeh); Halcyon HDL 108 (from RCA)

Charlie Creath (1890–1951) Ten tracks on Parlophone PMC 7159

Don Redman (1900–64) Tracks with McKinney's Cotton Pickers including "Milenberg Joys" on RCA NL 89766

Red Nichols (1905–65) Affinity AFS 1038

Miff Mole (1898–1961) EMI SH 503

Adrian Rollini (1904–56) The Goofus 5 featuring Rollini on Parlophone PMC 7183

Bix Beiderbecke (1903–31) The Wolverines on Fountain FJ 114; featured with Jean Goldkette, Paul Whiteman etc. on RCA NL 89572; with Frank Trumbauer including "Singin' The Blues" on EMI EG 260527 1; selection on BBC REB 601/CD 601

Joe Venuti (1903–78) and **Eddie Lang** (1902–33) BBC REB 644/CD 644

Earl Hines (1903–83) Piano solos on Milestone MLP 2012

Jimmie Noone (1895–1944) Affinity AFS 1023

Johnny Dodds (1892–1940) VJM VLP 48 and VLP 61; selection on BBC REB 603/CD 603

Jelly Roll Morton (1890–1941) 1923–24 solos on Fountain FJ 104; 1923–26 groups including duets with King Oliver on Rhapsody RHA 6021; 1926–27 Red Hot Peppers ("Black Bottom Stomp," "Dead Man Blues," "Grandpa's Spells" etc.) on RCA NL 89768; 1928–29 Peppers ("Deep Creek Blues," "Burnin' The Iceberg" etc.) on RCA NL 89769; selection on BBC REB 604/CD 604

Luis Russell (1902–63) 1926–30 tracks (including "Saratoga Shout") on VJM VLP 54; 1930–34 (including "Panama") on VJM VLP 57

Duke Ellington (1899–1974) "Black And Tan Fantasy," "East St. Louis Toodle-oo," "Mood Indigo," the Brunswick "Creole Rhapsody" (1926–31) on Affinity AFS 1034; "Creole Love Call," the Victor versions of "Black And Tan," "East St. Louis" (1927–29) on RCA NL 89749; "Mood Indigo," the Victor "Creole Rhapsody," "Stompy Jones" etc. (1930–34) on RCA NL 89672; overlapping selections on BBC REB 643/CD 643, Hermes CD HRM 6001 and ASV AJA 5024/CDAJA 5024R

♦ **CHAPTER 3**

Casa Loma Orchestra Hep HEP 1010

Horace Henderson (1904–88) His and others' records for the UK market produced by John Hammond on EMI SHB 42/Swing CDSW 8453-4

Teddy Wilson (1912–86) 1934–42 solo tracks in boxed set CBS 66370

Washboard Rhythm Kings RCA PM 42404

Louis Armstrong's 1932–33 sessions on RCA NL 89747

Sidney Bechet (1897–1959) 1932 New Orleans Feetwarmers and 1938 Tommy Ladnier session produced by Hugues Panassié (see Chapter 4) on RCA NL 89743

Cab Calloway (1907–   ) 1933–34 tracks on RCA NL 89560

Don Redman's 1931–32 band on Hep HEP 1001

Mills Blue Rhythm Band Hep HEP 1008

Tommy Dorsey (1905–56) and **Jimmy Dorsey** (1904–57) The Dorsey Brothers Orchestra on Hep HEP 1005

Earl Hines's 1932–33 Brunswick tracks on Hep HEP 1003; 1934 Deccas on MCA 1311; 1940 Bluebirds on RCA NL 89764 ("Boogie Woogie On St. Louis Blues") and NL 89605 ("Jelly Jelly")

Fletcher Henderson's tracks from 1934 on Hep HEP 1009

Chick Webb (1909–39) Affinity AFS 1002 including "A-Tisket A-Tasket" with Ella Fitzgerald

Jimmie Lunceford (1902–47) 1934–35 tracks (including "Sleepy Time Gal") on Hep HEP 1013; "Organ Grinder's Swing" and "Rhythm Is Our Business" on Affinity AFS 1003-1; "Lunceford Special" on CBS 66423

Benny Goodman (1909–86) "Stompin' At The Savoy" on RCA NL 89755; "Goody Goody" on Phontastic NOST 7659/CD 7659; "Sing, Sing, Sing" on RCA NL 89756; "Don't Be That Way" on RCA NL 89587 (last two titles both on CD RCA ND 85630). The Thesaurus transcriptions reissued on Sunbeam 101, 102 and 103.

Duke Ellington's entire 1936–40 output, including small groups mentioned in Chapter 4, on nine CBS albums (Complete Duke Ellington Vols. 7 to 15)

Django Reinhardt (1910–53) Hot Club of France Quintet's first records including "Dinah" and the originally rejected Odeons on Vogue VJD 6950

Benny Carter (1907–   ) Paris recordings (including Coleman Hawkins Jam Band) on Swing SW 8403/CDSW8403

Coleman Hawkins (1904–69) 1929 Mound City Blue Blowers session, 1939 "Body And Soul" etc. on RCA NL 89277/ND85717; 1935–37 tracks with the Ramblers on Jasmine JASM 2011; 1937–38 duos with Freddy Johnson on Xanadu 189

Nat Gonella (1908–   ) New York tracks included on EMI SH 369 (Leonard Feather's and Vic Lewis's American sessions, both featuring Bobby Hackett, are on MCA 1324 and Esquire ESQ 313 respectively)

Red Allen's 1934–35 tracks on Collector's Classics CC14 (Putney Dandridge's and Bob Howard's series both reissued on Rarities)

Fats Waller (1904–43) 1927–41 solos (including "Ain't Misbehavin'," "Keepin' Out Of Mischief Now" and the 1941 "Honeysuckle Rose") on RCA NL 89741; 1934–35 tracks with his Rhythm on JSP 1106 and 1108; 1935–36 (including "I'm Gonna Sit . . ." and "It's A Sin . . .") on RCA NL 89819; overlapping selections on BBC REB 598/CD 598, ASV AJA 5040/CDAJA 5040R, and RCA CD ND 86288

Louis Jordan (1908–75) Juke Box Lil JB 602

Harlem Hamfats "Oh Red" on Folklyric 9029

Billie Holiday (1915–59) "I Cried For You," "Easy To Love" etc. (with Teddy Wilson) on CBS 460060 1; "Summertime" on CBS 32733; "Way You Look Tonight" on CBS 66377; 1937 sessions with Wilson, Lester Young etc. on CBS 88223

Erskine Hawkins (1914–   ) RCA NL 89603 ("Tuxedo Junction"); NL 89482 ("After Hours")

Edgar Hayes (1904–79) One track ("In The Mood") on MCA MCM 5025

Mary Lou Williams (1910–81) 1930 solo on Stash ST 109

Andy Kirk (1898–   ) "Walkin' And Swingin" and "Until The Real Thing Comes Along" on Affinity AFS 1011

Count Basie (1904–84) Jones-Smith Inc. session on CBS 88667; "One O'Clock Jump" on Hep HEP 1025; "Swingin' The Blues," "Doggin' Around," "Jumpin' At The Woodside" on Affinity AFS 1010; All-American Rhythm Section tracks on MCA 0052.045; "Tickle Toe" (mentioned in Chapter 4) on CBS 88668. The first Jo Jones quotation is from Jazz Odyssey 008.

◆ **CHAPTER 4**

Artie Shaw (1910–   ) RCA NL 89820/ND86274; Gramercy Five and 1941–42 band with Lips Page on RCA NL 89774

Charlie Barnet (1913–   ) RCA NL 89743 (including "Cherokee"); Affinity AFS 1012 ("Skyliner")

Harry James (1916–83) Savoy WL 71409 (including "Flight Of The Bumble Bee")

Gene Krupa (1909–73) Band tracks on Roy Eldridge compilation Columbia C2 38033

Teddy Wilson's 1939–40 big band on Tax M 8018

Lionel Hampton (1908–) Small groups on RCA NL 89583/ ND86458; big band (including "Flying Home") on Affinity AFS 1000

Bunny Berigan (1908–42) RCA NL 89744

Jack Teagarden (1905–64) Two big band tracks on Teagarden compilation Affinity AFS 1015

Benny Goodman's 1938 Carnegie Hall concert on CBS 450983/1/2; 1940–41 big band (including "Benny Rides Again" and "Clarinet A La King") on CBS 65040; 1936–37 trio and quartet on RCA NL 89753/ND 85631; 1939–41 sextet on CBS 460612 1

John Kirby (1908–52) RCA NL 89484

Bob Crosby (1913–) MCA MCFM 2578 (including "Honky Tonk Train Blues")

Tommy Dorsey's big band (including "Boogie Woogie") and Clambake Seven on RCA NL 89163; "Deep River" last available on RCA DPM 2042

Meade Lux Lewis (1905–64) 1939–41 solos (plus 1935 "Honky Tonk Train") on Mosaic MR 3-103

Albert Ammons (1907–49) Solos and duets with Lewis on Mosaic MR 3-103

Spirituals To Swing Excerpts from concert featuring Ammons, Lewis, Count Basie, Sidney Bechet etc. on Vogue VJD 550

Eddie Condon (1905–73) 1938 tracks on Commodore 6.24054 AG/ 8.24054 ZP; 1939 Decca album of Chicago Jazz on Coral CP38

Billie Holiday's "Strange Fruit" etc on Commodore 6.24055 AG/ 8.24055 ZP

Chu Berry (1910–41) Commodore 6.24293 AG/8.24293 ZP (with Roy Eldridge and Lips Page)

Sidney Bechet's Blue Note sessions on Mosaic MR 6-110; Hot Record Society tracks (with Muggsy Spanier) on Swaggie S 1392; Bluebirds (including "12th Street Rag" mentioned in Chapter 5) on RCA NL 89759; 1949 UK recording (with Humphrey Lyttelton) on Savoy WL 70513

Decca's *Kansas City Jazz* on Coral CP 39; four Armstrong/Bechet tracks from *New Orleans* album on Affinity AFS 1024

Muggsy Spanier (1906-67) RCA 731061

Bud Freeman (1906-   ) Affinity AFS 1036

Jelly Roll Morton's Library of Congress interviews later issued on Classic Jazz Masters CJM 2-CJM 9; *New Orleans Memories* album on Commodore 6.24062 AG/8.24062 ZP; Bluebirds (some with Bechet) on RCA NL 89748

Kid Rena (1898-1949) Delta session on Esquire 331

Bunk Johnson (1889-1949) Jazz Man tracks on Good Time Jazz M 12048; Jazz Information session on Commodore 6.24547 AG; American Music material on Storyville SLP 202

Duke Ellington's 1940-41 band ("Harlem Air Shaft," "Ko Ko," "Take The A Train" etc.) and duets with Jimmy Blanton on RCA NL 89750; V-Disc tracks on Musidisc JA 5103 and JA 5165

Art Tatum (1910-56) V-Disc sessions on Black Lion BLP 30203

Roy Eldridge (1911-89) Metropolitan Opera House concert (with Coleman Hawkins) on Hot 'n Sweet CD FDC 25118; see also under Gene Krupa above

Coleman Hawkins's Commodore sessions on 6.24056 AG/8.24056 ZP; Signature tracks (including "Stumpy") on Doctor Jazz ASLP 1004/FDC 5008; 1946-47 sessions (*New 52nd Street Jazz* album etc.) on RCA NL 89277/ND 85717; unaccompanied solo (mentioned in Chapter 5) on Verve 230453

Lester Young (1909-59) 1938 Kansas City Six on Commodore 6.24057 AG; 1944 ditto on Commodore 6.24292 AG; Keynote sessions on Emarcy CD 8309322; . . . Savoy material on WL 70519/ZL 708191; "Jumpin' With Symphony Sid" (see Chapter 5) on Aladdin 801

Don Byas (1912-72) Savoy WL 70512

Ben Webster (1909-73) Signature tracks on RCA FXM3 7324/Doctor Jazz FDC 5008

Nat King Cole (1917-65) Herbie Haymer quintet with Charlie Shavers on Black Lion BLP 30104

Billy Eckstine (1914-   ) 1944 big band on Swingtime ST 1015; 1945-46 band on Savoy WL 70522/ZDS 4401

Dizzy Gillespie (1917-   ) With 1939-41 Cab Calloway band on CBS 62950. Four tracks with Byas and Trummy Young on Queen-Disc Q 039; Guild/Musicraft material ("Groovin" High," "Things To Come" etc.) on Atlantis ATS 11; "Night In Tunisia," "52nd Street Theme" (see Chapter 5) and 1947-49 big band on RCA NL 89763; Jerome Kern Memorial (see Chapter 5) on Phoenix LP 4; Dee Gee material ("The Champ") on Savoy WL 70517/ZD 70517

Charlie Parker (1920-55) With 1941-42 Jay McShann band on MCA 1338. With Tiny Grimes (Savoy WL 70520); "Koko" (WL 70527); "Donna Lee" (WL70548); "Another Hair-Do"; "Constellation" (WL 70813); and "Parker's Mood" (Chapter 5) (WL 70832); selection with these titles on CD Savoy ZD 70737; "Night InTunisia," "Lover Man" on Spotlite 101; "The Hymn" on Spotlite 104; "The Bird" and with strings (both Chapter 5) on Verve 817442 1

Sarah Vaughan (1924-90) Official 3003

◆ **CHAPTER 5**

Illinois Jacquet (1922-) Aladdin 803 ("Robbins' Nest"); with JATP on Verve 2610.030

Billie Holiday's 1944-49 tracks (some with strings) on MCA MCM 5011 and BHTV I

Dexter Gordon (1923-90) and Wardell Gray (1921-55) *Hollywood Jazz Concert* on Savoy SJL 2222

Howard McGhee (1918-87) and **Lucky Thompson** (1924-   ) *Junior Jazz at the Auditorium* on Spotlite SPJ 144

Benny Goodman's and **Charlie Barnet's** 1949 bands on Capitol M 11061; Artie Shaw's 1949-50 band on Coral CP 103

Stan Kenton (1912–79) Capitol SM 2327

Woody Herman (1913–87) 1939–43 tracks (including "At The Woodchoppers' Ball") on Affinity AFS 1008; 1945–54 tracks (including "Apple Honey") on Affinity AFS 1043, same plus "Caldonia" on CD CHARLY 100+

Serge Chaloff (1923–57) Affinity AFF 146

Fats Navarro (1923–50) and **Tadd Dameron** (1917–65) Blue Note BST 81532 (including two takes of "Jahbero")

Bud Powell (1924–66) With Cootie Williams (mentioned in Chapter 4) on Affinity AFS 1031; "Nice Work If You Can Get It" on Jazz Reactivation JR 112/Vogue 600101; "52nd Street Theme" and "Un Poco Loco" on Blue Note BST 81503 and on Mosaic MR 5-116

Thelonious Monk (1917–82) With Coleman Hawkins (see Chapter 4) on Harlequin HQ 2004; "Nice Work If You Can Get It" on Blue Note BST 81511, and "Round Midnight" on BST 81510, both included in Mosaic MR 4-101

Oscar Peterson (1925–   ) Studio recording of "Tenderly" on Verve MGV 2046; concert version on Verve MGV 8363

Erroll Garner (1921–77) 1945 recording of "Laura" on Savoy WL 70521/ZDS 4408; 1951 version on CBS 21062/CK 40863

Louis Armstrong's 1947 Town Hall concert on RCA NL 89746/ND 86378; originally issued version of *Plays W.C. Handy* on CBS 21128 (also reissued without overdubbing on CBS 450981 1/2)

Dizzy Gillespie and Charlie Parker's 1947 Carnegie Hall concert on Savoy SJL 1177; *Jazz at Massey Hall* on Debut OJC 044/JCD 707124

Duke Ellington's "Tattooed Bride" on CBS 63838; "(A Tone Parallel To) Harlem" on CBS 62686; *At Newport* on CBS 450986 1/2

Charlie Christian (1916–42) With Benny Goodman (plus "Blues In B" and "Waiting For Benny") CBS 460612 1; live recordings at Minton's on Esoteric ES 548/Vogue 600135

George Lewis (1900–68) and **Jim Robinson** (1890–1976) Atlantic SD 1411

Chris Barber (1930–   ) Jasmine JASM 2028

Humphrey Lyttelton (1921–   ) Dormouse DM 4 (includes 1952 tracks by Grant-Lyttelton Paseo Jazz Band); 1954 band reissued on Calligraph (see Chapter 8) CLGLP 0006

Art Tatum's 1953–56 small groups in boxed set Pablo 2625706, and solos in Pablo 2625703; some individual albums on CD

Vic Dickenson (1906–84) Vogue VJD 551

Buck Clayton (1911–   ) *Jam Session* on CBS 21112

Lennie Tristano (1919–78) 1949 tracks including "Intuition" on Capitol M 11060; 1951 Jazz single on East Wind EW 8040

Lee Konitz (1927–   ) 1949 session (released as by Tristano but reissued as by Konitz) on New Jazz OJC 186; 1976 *London Concert* by Konitz and Warne Marsh (mentioned in Chapter 7) on Wave LP 16

Miles Davis (1926–   ) *Birth of the Cool* on Capitol CAPS 1024; "Dig" and "Out Of The Blue" on Prestige OJC 005/CA98452; first versions of "Tune Up" and "Four" (PR 7822), "Oleo" (PR 7109/CA 98402) and "Vierd Blues" (OJC 071/CA 98406), re-made by 1956 quintet on, respectively, *Cookin'* (OJC 128/CA 98465), *Workin'* (OJC 296/CA 98404) and the last two titles on *Relaxin'* (OJC 190/CA 98428); "Dr. Jackle" on OJC 012, re-recorded on *Milestones* (CBS 85553); *Miles Ahead* on CBS 460606 1/2; *Sketches of Spain* CBS 460604 1/2; *Kind of Blue* CBS 460603 1/2

Shorty Rogers (1924–   ) RCA NL 70110 (including *The Wild One* and "Block Buster"); Atlantic 790042 1

Gerry Mulligan (1927–   ) "Bernie's Tune" and "Walkin' Shoes" on Mosaic MR 5-102; 1960 big band on Verve 2304410

Chet Baker (1929–88) Mosaic MR 4-122 including 1954 vocal tracks

Teo Macero (1925–   ) 1953 album on American Clave AMCL 1002

Lars Gullin (1928–76) Dragon DRLP 36

Dave Brubeck (1920–   ) "These Foolish Things" on Fantasy OJC 046/CA 98569

John Lewis (1920–   ) Modern Jazz Quartet including "Django" on Prestige OJC 057/OJCCD 057-2

Kenny Clarke (1914–85) *Opus De Jazz* on Savoy WL 70501

Milt Jackson (1923–   ) *Plenty, Plenty Soul* on Atlantic SD 8811 (NB: some earlier reissues accidentally omit Jackson's overdubbing on "Blues At Twilight")

Horace Silver (1928–   ) "Doodlin'" and "The Preacher" on Blue Note BST 81518/CDP 746140 2; "Ecaroh" and "Song For My Father" (both mentioned in Chapter 6) respectively on BST 81520 and BST 84185

Art Blakey (1919–90) *A Night at Birdland* on Blue Note BST 81521 and 81522/CDP 746519 2 and 746520 2 + (the CDs including additional material which is also on Mosaic MR 5-104); *At Club St. Germain* on RCA FXL3 7052

Max Roach (1924–   ) and **Clifford Brown** (1930–56) "Clifford's Axe" and "All God's Children" on Jazz Reactivation JR 118/ Vogue 600032; "Daahoud" and "Joy Spring" on Emarcy 6649575; "Junior's Arrival" on Emarcy 6649644

Sonny Rollins (1930–   ) *Way Out West* (with Shelly Manne) on Contemporary COP 006/CDCOP 006 + ; *Newk's Time* on Blue Note BST 84001; *A Night at the Village Vanguard* on Blue Note BST 81581/CDP 746517 2 and 746518 2 + ; *Our Man in Jazz* (see Chapter 6) on RCA 741092

Jackie McLean (1932–   ) Blue Note BST 84106/CDP 746527 2

J.J. Johnson (1924–   ) and Kai Winding (1922–83) Affinity AFF 161

Gil Evans (1912–88) With Claude Thornhill on Affinity AFSD 1040/CD CHARLY 82; Manhattan WP 2

◆ **CHAPTER 6**

Charlie Parker broadcasts originally issued by Le Jazz Cool now included on Savoy WL 70541, 70825, 70831 and CBS 88250; live recordings issued by Jazz Workshop on Debut OJC 041 and 114

Thelonious Monk's "Locomotive" and the original "Little Rootie Tootie" respectively on Prestige OJC 016 and 010; *Brilliant Corners* on Riverside RLP 226; *With John Coltrane* on Riverside OJC

039/OJCCD 039-2; *At Town Hall* (including big-band version of "Little Rootie Tootie") on Riverside OJC 135; Lincoln Center concert (see Chapter 7) on Columbia CS 8964

Charles Mingus (1922–79) *Pithecanthropus Erectus* on Atlantic SD 8809/781456 2; *East Coasting* on Affinity AFF 86/CD CHARLY 19+; "Jump Monk" on Debut OJC 045; "Reincarnation Of A Lovebird" on Atlantic 790142 1; "Dizzy Moods" on RCA PL 85635/ND 85644; *CM Presents CM* on Candid CS 9005/CD 9005; *Black Saint and the Sinner Lady* (see Chapter 7) on Impulse AS 35/MCAD 5649; Charles Mingus Enterprises albums on Debut OJC 042/CA 98425 and East Coasting 12001; trio with Duke Ellington and Max Roach on Blue Note BT 8 5129/CDP 746398 2+

Max Roach's *We Insist—Freedom Now* on Candid CS 9002/CD 9002

John Coltrane (1926–67) *Blue Train* on Blue Note BST 81577/ CDP746095 2; *Giant Steps* on Atlantic SD 1311/781337 2+; *Coltrane Jazz* on Atlantic SD 1354; *My Favorite Things* on Atlantic SD 1361/781346 2; *A Love Supreme* on Impulse AS 77/MCAD 5660; "Brasilia" on Impulse AS 85; *Ascension* with Archie Shepp, Marion Brown, Pharoah Sanders et al. on Impulse AS 95

Eric Dolphy (1928–64) Prestige OJC 133; *Last Date* [see Chapter 7] on Fontana 681008 ZL

Ornette Coleman (1930–   ) *Somethin' Else!!!!* on Contemporary COP 024; *The Shape of Jazz to Come* on Atlantic SD 1317/ 781339 2; *Change of the Century* on Atlantic SD 13271; *Free Jazz* on Atlantic SD 1364/781347 21; *Town Hall 1962* on Magic Music 10010/30010; one track with Yoko Ono (see chapter 7) on Apple SAPCOR 17

Bill Evans (1929–80) Riverside OJC 088

Zoot Sims (1925–85) Affinity AFF 87/CD CHARLY 59

Stan Getz (1927–   ) Verve 2367.204/831272 2 + ; Verve 2304271/ 810048 2

Wes Montgomery (1925–68) Riverside RSLP 310/CA 98974

Lou Donaldson (1926–   ) Blue Note BST 81593/CDP 746525 2

Cannonball Adderley (1928–75) Blue Note BST 81595/CDP 46338 2+; "Sack O' Woe" on Landmark LLP 1305/LCD 1305-2; "Country Preacher" on Capitol E-ST 404

Quincy Jones (1933–   ) Mercury 6430130/822469 2

Roland Kirk (1936–77) Mercury 826455 1/2

Herbie Hancock (1940–   ) "Watermelon Man" on Blue Note BST 84109/CDP 746506 2; VSOP quintet (see Chapter 7) on CBS C2 34976

Lee Morgan (1938–72) "Sidewinder" on Blue Note BST 84157/CDP746137 2

Cecil Taylor (1929–   ) Transition album on Blue Note BN-LA 458H-2; *Coltrane Time* [sic] on Boplicity BOP 1; Contemporary album on Boplicity COP 030; first Candid album on CS 9006/CD 9006; second (originally by Buell Neidlinger but eventually released as by Taylor) on Candid CS 9017 and CS 9013/CD 9013; *Into the Hot* on Impulse IMPL8016; Cafe Montmartre session on Freedom FLP 40124; *Unit Structures* and *Conquistador* on Blue Note BST 84237 and BST/84260CDP 746535 2; duo with Max Roach (mentioned in Chapter 8) on Soul Note SN 1100–01

Sun Ra (1914–   ) Delmark DS 411 (Transition album); Impulse AS 9242 (reissue from Saturn); Rounder 3035/CD 3035

McCoy Tyner (1938–   ) Blue Note BST 84264/CDP 746512 2

Albert Ayler (1936–70) *My Name Is Albert Ayler* on Fontana 688603 ZL; *Spiritual Unity* on BASE ESP 1002; *Vibrations* (with Don Cherry) on Freedom FLP 41000/FCD 41000; *New Grass* on Impulse IMPL 8022

Don Cherry (1936–   ) Blue Note BST 84226 (with Gato Barbieri); Caprice RIKSLP 44 (with Okay Temiz); Chiaroscuro CR 187 (with Abdullah Ibrahim and Johnny Dyani); JCOA 1006 (with Jazz Composers' Orchestra Association, mentioned in Chapter 7)

◆ **CHAPTER 7**

Gary Burton (1943–   ) RCA PL 43260; ECM 1329/831110 2

Charles Lloyd (1938–   ) Atlantic SD 1473

Keith Jarrett (1945–   ) Atlantic SD 8808; *Köln Concert* on ECM 1064-5/810067 2

Alice Coltrane (1937–   ) *Cosmic Music* on Impulse AS 9148; *Journey in Satchidananda* on Impulse AS 9203

Pharoah Sanders (1940–   ) *Karma* on Impulse AS 9181; Strata-East SES 19733

Gato Barbieri (1934–   ) Magic Music 10019/30019; Flying Dutchman FD 10117

Charlie Haden (1937–   ) *Liberation Music Orchestra* on Jasmine JAS 55; duet sessions (mentioned in Chapter 8) on Horizon AMLJ 727 and Artists House AH 4

Michael Mantler (1943–   ) JCOA 1001-2

Carla Bley (1938–   ) *Escalator Over the Hill* on JCOA EOTH LP 1003-5

Archie Shepp (1937–   ) *Four for Trane* on Jasmine JAS 31; *Cry of My People* on Impulse AS 9231; Freedom FLP 41016/FCD 41016

Joe Harriott (1928–73) 1954 recordings on Esquire ESQ 326; 1961–62 quintet on Columbia SX 1477; *Indo-Jazz Fusions* on Columbia SCX 6025

Albert Mangelsdorff (1928–   ) L + R LR 410071; *Live in Tokyo* (see Chapter 8) on Enja 2006

Stan Tracey (1926–   ) Steam SJ 114; Steam SJ 101 (reissue from EMI mentioned in Chapter 8)

Evan Parker (1944–   ) Duo with John Stevens on Ogun OG 120 and OG 420

Derek Bailey (1930–   ) ECM 1013; *London Concert* with Evan Parker on Incus 16

John Stevens (1940–   ) Spontaneous Music Ensemble on Island ILPS 9078; Polydor 2384009

John Surman (1944–   ) Deram SMLR 1045; ECM 1148 (see Chapter 8)

Michael Gibbs (1937–   ) Deram SML 1063

Mike Westbrook (1936–   ) Deram SML 1047-8; RCA PL 25229; Hat ART 2012 (see Chapter 8)

Chris McGregor (1936–90) Polydor 1841371; RCA Neon NE 2

Tony Oxley (1938–   ) CBS 64071

Howard Riley (1943–   ) CBS 52669

Keith Tippett (1947–   ) Vertigo 6360024

Ian Carr (1933–   ) Vertigo 6360119

Han Bennink (1942–   ) *New Acoustic Swing Duo* with Willem Breuker on ICP 001

Manfred Schoof (1936–   ) *European Echoes* on FMP 0010

Alex von Schlippenbach (1938–   ) *Globe Unity* on MPS 2120.630

Peter Brötzmann (1941–   ) FMP 0080

Don Pullen (1944–   ) Duo with Milford Graves on PG 2861; solo on Black Saint (see Chapter 8) BSR 0010

Gunter Hampel (1937–   ) Birth NJ 001 with Anthony Braxton

Charles Tolliver (1942–   ) and Stanley Cowell (1941–   ) Strata-East SES 1971

Betty Carter (1930–   ) Bet-Car MK 1000

Miles Davis's 1963 quintet *In Europe* on CBS 62390/CD CBS 62390; "Nefertiti" on CBS 85551 ; *In A Silent Way* on CBS 450981 1; *Bitches Brew* on CBS 460602 1/2; *Jack Johnson* on CBS 702161; "Go Ahead John" on CBS 88024; "Red China Blues" on CBS 88092; *Aura* (see Chapter 8) on CBS 463351 1/2; *Tutu* (see Chapter 8) on WEA 925490 1/2

Chick Corea (1941–   ) Atlantic ATL 50302; the group Circle (with Anthony Braxton) on ECM 1018-9; solo on ECM 1014 and 1020; the group Return To Forever on ECM 1022

Freddie Hubbard (1938–   ) Blue Note BST 84196/CDP 746545 2+; CTI 6013/EPC 450562 2

Wayne Shorter (1933–   ) *Odyssey of Iska* on Blue Note BST 84363

Joe Zawinul (1932–   ) *Zawinul* on Atlantic SD 1579; Weather Report's *Sweetnighter* on CBS 32110

Miroslav Vitous (1947–   ) *Mountain in the Clouds* on Atlantic SD 1622

Ron Carter (1937–   ) *Uptown Conversation* on Embryo ED 521

Herbie Mann (1930–   ) *Memphis Underground* on Atlantic SD 1522

Tony Williams (1945–   ) Polydor 2425019

Buddy Rich (1917–87) Big band on RCA CD ND 86459

John McLaughlin (1942–   ) *My Goal's Beyond* on Elektra Musician MUSK 52364/Rykodisc RCD 10051; the Mahavishnu Orchestra's *Birds of Fire* on CBS 31996/CDC 856532 1; the group Shakti on CBS 34162

Jean-Luc Ponty (1942–   ) *Enigmatic Ocean* on Atlantic 19110

Billy Cobham (1944–   ) "Flash Flood" from *Crosswinds* on Atlantic 7300

Randy Brecker (1945–   ) The Brecker Brothers's *Heavy Metal Bebop* on Arista 4085

Michael Brecker (1949–   ) MCA Impulse 5980

Dave Sanborn (1945–   ) *Taking Off* on Warner 2873

George Benson (1943–   ) *White Rabbit* on CTI 6015/EPC 4505552

Stanley Turrentine (1934–   ) CTI 6005/EPC 450573 2+

Grover Washington (1943–   ) Motown STML 6011/ZD 72366

Randy Weston (1926–   ) CTI 6016; Freedom FLP 1014/FCD 41014

Enrico Rava (1943–   ) ECM 1063

Pat Metheny (1954–   ) *Bright Size Life* on ECM 1073/827133 2; *First Circle* on ECM1278/823342 2

John Abercrombie (1944–   ) *Gateway* on ECM 1061/829192 2

Ralph Towner (1940–   ) The group Oregon on ECM 1258/ 8117112

Jan Garbarek (1947–   ) *Dansere* on ECM 1075/829193 2

Eberhard Weber (1940–   ) *Silent Feet* on ECM 1107

Jack DeJohnette (1942–   ) ECM 1152/827694 2

Lester Bowie (1941–   ) Nessa 1; ECM 1296/825902 2

Roscoe Mitchell (1940–   ) Nessa 2; with Art Ensemble of Chicago, *Fanfare for the Warriors* on Atlantic ATL 50304 and *Nice Guys* on ECM1126/827876 2

Anthony Braxton (1945–   ) *For Alto* on Delmark DS 420-1; Freedom AL 1902; "Maple Leaf Rag" on Arista AL 4101; *For Four Orchestras* on Arista A3L 89001; duo with Max Roach (mentioned in Chapter 8) on Black Saint BSR 0024/BSR 0024 CD

◆ CHAPTER 8

Sam Rivers (1930–   ) Impulse ASD 9316; one track on Vol. 1 of *Wildflowers Vols. 1–5* featuring 20 different groups on Douglas NBLP7045-9

David Murray (1955–   ) "Flowers For Albert" on India Navigation IN 1026; with the World Saxophone Quartet on Black Saint BSR0027

Steve Lacy (1934–   ) Prestige MPP 2505 (with Don Cherry); Black Saint BSR 0008 (with Roswell Rudd)

Chico Freeman (1949–   ) Black Saint BSR 0036/BSR 0036 CD

George Lewis (1952–   ) Black Saint BSR 0016

Henry Threadgill (1944–   ) The group Air on RCA CD ND 86578

Mal Waldron (1926–   ) Enja 2004

Terumasa Hino (1942–   ) Enja 2010

Dexter Gordon's 1976 *Homecoming* on CBS 88682; *Sophisticated Giant* on CBS 450316 1; Blue Note BT 85135

Art Pepper (1925–82) *Meets the Rhythm Section* on Contemporary COP004/CA 98636; Village Vanguard recording on Contemporary COP027/CA 98627

Bobby McFerrin (1950–   ) Blue Note BT 85110

Jimmy Smith (1925–   ) *Back at the Chicken Shack* on Blue Note BST 84117/CDP 746402 2+; Blue Note BT 85125/CDP 746297 2

James Blood Ulmer (1942–   ) CBS 25064

Steve Coleman (1956–   ) JMT 850001

Ornette Coleman's *Dancing in Your Head* on Horizon AMLJ 722 and further material on Artists House AH 1

Oliver Lake (1944–   ) Gramavision GR 8106/GRCD 8206

Ken Hyder (1946–   ) JAPO 60016

Anachronic Jazz Band Open OP 09

Horace Silver's 1980s recordings on Silveto SPR 101, 102 and 103

Arthur Blythe (1940–   ) CBS 63350

Wynton Marsalis (1961–   ) CBS 26686/CD 26686

Courtney Pine (1964–   ) Antilles AN 8725/ANCD 8725

Stephane Grappelli (1908–   ) Concord CJ 139/CDD 4139

Art Blakey's 1980s albums include Timeless SJP 165

Loose Tubes Loose Tubes LTLP 003

Kenny Wheeler (1930–   ) ECM 1102/829385 2

Tony Coe (1934–   ) nato 19

Gordon Beck (1938–   ) JMS 09

Ricky Ford (1954–   ) New World NW 204

Airto Moreira (1941–   ) *Identity* on Arista AL 4068

Dave Liebman (1946–   ) Owl 46

John Scofield (1951–   ) Gramavision GR 8405

Sonny Rollins's solo album on Milestone M 9137/CA 98172

Count Basie's posthumous band on Denon CD 33CY 1018

BIBLIOGRAPHY

◆

Each of the books listed here provided me with useful information, and taken together, they constitute a basic library. The reference books indicated by an asterisk were especially valuable. When there are two publishers named, the second one indicates a reprint or reissue.

Albertson, Chris. *Bessie* (Stein & Day, 1972)

Allen, Walter C. *Hendersonia* (Allen, 1973)

Basie, Count and Albert Murray. *Good Morning Blues* (Random House, 1986)

Berendt, Joachim. *The Jazz Book*, rev. ed. (Lawrence Hill, 1982)

Blesh, Rudi. *Shining Trumpets: A History of Jazz* (Knopf/Da Capo, 1946)

Brown, Scott E. and Robert Hilbert. *James P. Johnson* (Scarecrow Press, 1986)

Brunn, H.O. *The Story of the Original Dixieland Jazz Band* (Louisiana State University Press/Da Capo, 1960)

*Bruyninckx, Walter. *Jazz Discography* (Bruyninckx, 1985–   )

Carr, Ian. *Miles Davis* (William Morrow, 1982)

*Carr, Ian, Digby Fairweather and Brian Priestley. *Jazz: The Essential Companion* (Prentice Hall, 1988)

Charters, Samuel and Len Kunstadt. *Jazz: A History of the New York Scene* (Doubleday/Da Capo, 1962)

Chilton, John. *Billie's Blues: The Billie Holiday Story* (Quartet/Da Capo, 1975)

Chilton, John. *Sidney Bechet: The Wizard of Jazz* (Oxford University Press, 1988)

Collier, James Lincoln. *Louis Armstrong: An American Genius* (Oxford University Press/Da Capo, 1983)

Davis, Francis. *In The Moment: Jazz in the 1980's* (Oxford University Press, 1986)

Delaunay, Charles. *Django Reinhardt* (Cassell/Ashley Mark, 1961)

*Dixon, Robert and John Godrich. *Blues Records 1902-1943*, 3rd ed. (Storyville, 1982)

Evans, Philip R. and Richard Sudhalter. *Bix: Man and Legend* (Arlington House, 1974)

Feather, Leonard. *The Jazz Years: Earwitness to an Era* (Quartet/Da Capo, 1986)

Gammond, Peter. *Duke Ellington: His Life and Music* (Roy/Da Capo, 1958)

Gitler, Ira. *Swing to Bop: An Oral History of the Transition in Jazz in the '40s* (Oxford University Press, 1986)

Hammond, John with Irving Townsend. *John Hammond On Record* (Ridge Press/Penguin 1977)

Handy, W.C. *Father of the Blues: An Autobiography* (Macmillan/Da Capo, 1941)

*Jepsen, Jorgen Grunnet. *Jazz Records 1942-1969* (Knudsen, 1963-1970)

Jones, Max. *Talking Jazz* (Norton, 1988)

*Laing, Ralph and Chris Sheridan. *Jazz Records: The Specialist Labels* (Jazzmedia, 1981)

Lomax, Alan. *Mister Jelly Roll* (Duell, Sloan/Grove Press, 1950)

Luzzi, Mario. *Uomini e Avanguardie Jazz* (Gammalibri, 1980)

Priestley, Brian. *Charlie Parker* (Spellmount, 1984)

Priestley, Brian. *John Coltrane* (Apollo, 1987)

Priestley, Brian. *Mingus* (Quartet/Da Capo, 1982)

Ramsay, Frederick and Charles E. Smith. *Jazzmen* (Harcourt Brace/Limelight, 1939)

*Rust, Brian. *Jazz Records 1897-1942*, 4th ed. (Arlington House, 1978)

Spellman, A.B. *Four Lives in the Bebop Business* (Pantheon/Limelight, 1966)

Taylor, Art. *Notes and Tones* (Quartet/Perigee, 1982)

Ullmann, Michael. *Jazz Lives* (New Republic/Perigee, 1980)

Williams, Martin. *Jazz Masters of New Orleans* (Macmillan/Da Capo, 1967)

Wilmer, Valerie. *Serious As Your Life: The Story of the New Jazz* (Allison & Busby/Chicago Review, 1977)

INDEX

◆

216